THE POEM THAT CHANGED AMERICA

SAN FRANCISCO STATE POETRY CENTER, 1955

THE POEM THAT CHANGED AMERICA

"HOWL" FIFTY YEARS LATER

———

EDITED BY JASON SHINDER

FARRAR, STRAUS AND GIROUX

NEW YORK

Farrar, Straus and Giroux
19 Union Square West, New York 10003

Owing to limitations of space, all acknowledgments for permission to reprint
previously published and unpublished material can be found on pages 289–290.

Library of Congress Cataloging-in-Publication Data
The poem that changed America : "Howl" fifty years later / edited by Jason
Shinder— 1st ed.
    p.   cm.
    Summary: Reflections from America's prominent writers on the seminal
poem "Howl" by Allen Ginsberg, on the eve of its fiftieth anniversary.
    ISBN-13: 978-0-374-17343-2 (hardcover : alk. paper)
    ISBN-10: 0-374-17343-5 (hardcover : alk. paper)
    ISBN-13: 978-0-374-17344-9 (pbk. : alk. paper)
    ISBN-10: 0-374-17344-3 (pbk. : alk. paper)
    1. Ginsberg, Allen, 1926– Howl.   2. National characteristics, American, in
literature.   3. Social change—United States—History—20th century.
I. Shinder, Jason, 1955–

PS3513.I74H6356 2006
811'.54—dc22

                                                              2005024289

Designed by Jonathan D. Lippincott

www.fsgbooks.com

1   3   5   7   9   10   8   6   4   2

Frontispiece: Allen Ginsberg reading at the San Francisco State Poetry Center,
November 20, 1955, with the poet Helen Adam seated at right. "A small school-
sponsored affair, not one of our wilder nites," A.G. wrote on the back of this
photograph. (*Journals Mid-Fifties 1954–1958: Allen Ginsberg*, Gordon Ball, editor.
HarperCollins, 1995.)

For the *6 Poets at the 6 Gallery Reading*, San Francisco, 1955:
Philip Lamantia, Mike McClure, Allen Ginsberg, Gary Snyder,
Phil Walen, and Kenneth Rexroth,

and for "all the remarkable collection of angels reading
their own poetry" who followed

What living and buried speech is always vibrating here, what howls restrain'd by decorum . . .

—Walt Whitman

CONTENTS

CONTENTS

PREFACE

In April 1976, when I was twenty-one, I sent a handwritten note to Allen Ginsberg asking if I could study with him. On a postcard with a picture of himself and Bob Dylan sitting cross-legged at the graveside of Jack Kerouac, Allen Ginsberg quickly responded. "Come when you can," he scribbled. By that summer I was working with him at the Jack Kerouac School of Dis-embodied Poetics at Naropa Institute in Boulder, Colorado. Cofounded by Ginsberg and the poet Anne Waldman, it was the first liberal arts college in America inspired by Buddhist teaching.

Although I was a young poet, Allen gave me access to his work (allowing me to help assemble his poetry collection *Mind Breaths*) and, more important, to his community. Dressed in a white shirt with a skinny, colorful tie, he was often on his way to teach a workshop, read from his work, or meet with a student or colleague. I frequently wondered what it felt like to be so busy and accessible, and would ask him questions about the condi-tions of his life—questions that at times bordered on the overly personal—but he always answered them.

I have heard many stories such as mine, in which strangers quickly found themselves part of Allen's life. Yet the long list of people he suggested I meet no matter where I was traveling never ceased to surprise me. His ever-increasing network of comrades even included several shopkeepers he wanted me to visit upon walking around the block to purchase a cold drink.

The wellspring of Allen's generosity was, of course, catalyzed by the losses, visions, and passions he had felt deeply. The perpetual sorrow, confusion, and joy triggered by the experiences of his private (and very public) life were almost always met with a genuine acceptance. He was, quite simply, interested in everything and everyone.

On one occasion, while I was visiting him at his apartment on the Lower East Side of Manhattan, he received a call from a stranger living in Portland, Oregon. I expected him to show little interest and end the conversation with a polite dismissal. Yet there was something in him, always curious, sensitive, and humorous, that surfaced when he was in touch with another human being. The world seemed to be continually saying to him: Here now is something that forever can change the vision of one's life.

When he had been on the phone for more than forty-five minutes with the stranger from the West Coast, he leaned over to me and said, in an aside, "She had a dream, very disturbing, vivid." The most common human circumstance was always new and intriguing to him.

"What do you regret most?" I once asked him. "I regret not spending more time with my family," he said without hesitation. The shift away from his immediate world, however, to the variegated family of America had marked his life ever since he moved toward his candid and public self as evidenced in "Howl," and his endless interactions prevented more time with his own flesh and blood.

On several occasions, to my surprise, Allen showed me the exact locations in New York City where he had met, often for the first time, his friends, heroes, and "enemies"—including Kerouac, Trilling, and Auden—all of whom now were dead. To me it seemed as though these visitations had never ended, and would never end.

Walking by one of these infamous locales I once asked, "Isn't that Auden on the corner of Christopher Street?" "He has an eternal presence," Allen replied.

Like Auden's, Ginsberg's candidly mindful and courageous voice does indeed spring eternal. But even more so, Allen had a genius for attentiveness and generosity. These qualities, which I witnessed firsthand, are the very things that inspired me to gather a collection of some of our best writers' personal narratives on "Howl." Unlike the myriad of critical texts about it, this book stands as testimony to the poem's extraordinary ability to continue to change so many individuals' works and lives in such indelible and uncanny ways.

Jason Shinder

INTRODUCTION

In the spring of 1997, for several weeks before his death, Allen Ginsberg often asked strangers if they had read his poem "Howl." Just about everyone had. And if they hadn't read it, they'd heard about it. And many of them recalled its memorable first lines:

I saw the best minds of my generation destroyed by madness, starving
  hysterical naked,
dragging themselves through the negro streets at dawn looking for an
  angry fix.

Fifty years since its publication, these lines, which launched the celebrated poem, are deeply rooted in our collective consciousness. The poem itself has never been out of print, has been translated into more than two dozen languages, is anthologized in high school and college textbooks worldwide, and by most standards is considered a literary classic. "The literary classic will find its response," T. S. Eliot observed in his 1944 essay "What Is a Classic?," "among all classes and conditions of men," and this is certainly true of "Howl."

The poem's importance stretches well beyond the boundaries of a literary treasure, however, and even the Beat Generation it helped shape. "Allen Ginsberg is responsible for loosening the breath of American poetry," the critic Helen Vendler wrote in celebration of Ginsberg's sixtieth birthday in 1986. And in many ways, "Howl" is also responsible for "loosening the breath" of homosexuality, politics, drugs, tyranny, loneliness, music, madness, and death.

"In the long run," Vendler wrote, "death is certainly victor. And the despair that is the enemy of political hope has visited Ginsberg many times. Yet 'over and over thru the dull material world the call is made' (Walt Whitman)."

Whitman's call in the midst of the crowd is Ginsberg's mantra throughout the four distinct movements of "Howl." The first section, the longest, creates a nightmare world in which the "best minds of [his] generation are destroyed." The "best minds" (his and his friends') are "starving," "looking for an angry fix" with both hell and heaven in sight. "Who fell on their knees in hopeless cathedrals," he chants, "praying for each other's salvation and light and breasts, until the soul illuminated its hair for a second."

The mood of the poem changes in the second section and becomes an indictment of those elements that are destructive of the best qualities of human nature and of the best minds. "What sphinx of cement and aluminum," it begins, "bashed open their skulls and ate up their brains and imagination?" "Moloch! Solitude! Filth! Ugliness!" he answers, and thus begins a litany of the soulless, materialistic, sexless, mechanized elements of Moloch (named after the Canaanite fire god who was worshiped by the sacrifice of children) "whose blood is running money" and whose presence leads to war.

What does one do in the face of "loveless" Moloch? In Part III of "Howl," Ginsberg offers the possibility of some imperfect fulfillment in the search of friendship and love he can almost find. "Carl Solomon! I'm with you in Rockland," he writes, "where you're madder than I am." In a personal address to a friend who is in a madhouse, he presents a specific relationship representative of an "America in tears."

Yet in spite of (and because of) the loss and despair "Howl" has shown, the "Footnote to Howl" says life, all life, is essentially holy and should be so lived. "The world is holy! The soul is holy! The skin is holy! The nose is holy!," the "Footnote" includes. And it ends with the declaration "Holy the supernatural extra brilliant intelligent kindness of the soul!"

Our understanding of "Howl," and the actual writing of the poem, has been given much attention by its author and critics. Yet our reflection upon its remarkably wide and various influence has not. That we have so few accounts of the poem and its transformative impact on generations of writers (and readers) as well as its impact on almost every aspect of our culture, on this, the fiftieth anniversary of its publication (and what would have been the poet's eightieth birthday), is the critical reason for the publication of this book.

As for the writers represented here, all detail the context and content of how the poem changed their lives—as authors, as persons, as community members. Original essays from some of our country's most distinguished writers of various backgrounds and generations serve to show, again and again, just some of the ways in which "Howl" summoned them. As Andrei Codrescu writes in his essay, " 'Howl' in Transylvania," the poem "tests the limits of my mind and the far reaches of liberty."

Many essays comment directly not only on the writers' highly

charged and transformative private experience of the poem but
also on the poem's public influence. Was "Howl" the first to
speak of a gay man's crisis and celebration of identity and ac-
ceptance? Why is it still difficult for writers (other than Gins-
berg) to strike so intimately and personally at the very erotic
nature of same-sex relationships? Mark Doty, in his essay, "Hu-
man Seraphim: 'Howl,' Sex, and Holiness" addresses these ques-
tions. He discovers the vortex of ideas and perceptions that
claim our strange and seemingly friendly response to the most
intimate details of Ginsberg's erotic life.

The poem's life of long-line verse is catalyzed by super-
charged chanting with clustered telegraphing phrases (e.g., "the
starry dynamo in the machinery of night"). Because these lines
flash and rise to a musical pitch, "Howl" inspired many to their
own chanting. Rick Moody recalls in his essay, "On the Granite
Steps of the Madhouse with Shaven Heads," the motivation the
poem provided for him and his band, the Null Set, when he was
a student and musician. Moody explores how punk's radical ide-
ological stance in opposition to the status quo is a direct descen-
dant of "Howl" and how he was changed by both.

"Howl" has emerged into the mainstream of literature as an
agent of change within the musical community, bringing with it
a sound arising out of the poet's lament (and celebration) of the
passing of time and experience as a source for wailing and wis-
dom. Such wisdom is also at the center of Jewish culture, mys-
tery, and mysticism, and in "Howl" Ginsberg strikes at the heart
of Jewish identity.

"Ginsberg in 'Howl,'" the contributor Alicia Ostriker
writes in her essay, "The Poet as Jew: 'Howl' Revisited," "will
record, in veiled fashion, the humiliation and crippling of a
population of [Jewish] immigrants to shores that promised hope
and produced despair. He will gather the threads dropped by
revolutionary poetry of the thirties, left dangling in the winter

of McCarthyism. He will *spritz* shamelessly alongside Henny Youngman and Lenny Bruce . . . It is . . . a tribute to his Yiddish-speaking ancestors and the obscure longevity of their gift for juicy emotional tragicomedy."

We have in many texts (such as *Howl: Original Draft Facsimile, Transcript & Variant Versions Fully Annotated by Author*, edited by Barry Miles, 1986, and *American Scream* by John Raskin, 2004) a fairly full account of the making of the poem.

When *Howl and Other Poems* appeared in 1956, Lewis Hyde writes in his introduction to a 1984 collection of published writings about Allen Ginsberg, "it must have seemed to many to have sprung without background, the spontaneous utterance of an unlettered young Bohemian . . . But Allen Ginsberg," Hyde continues, "was thirty years old at the time; he had earned a bachelor's degree from Columbia University, had studied and fought with and troubled its dons (Lionel Trilling and Mark Van Doren), had sought out teachers of his own beyond the walls of the academy (most notably William Carlos Williams), and had read until he found a usable poet, a literary tradition to inform his sensibility (Smart, Melville, Blake, and others.)"

What has always been unique about Ginsberg's sensibility as a poet is the way in which he simultaneously incorporated and retreated from the poetics of his father, Louis Ginsberg, a recognized lyric poet and high school teacher in their hometown of Paterson, New Jersey. What has also always been remarkable about Ginsberg's early poetics is the way in which the mental illness of his mother, Naomi, particularly her years in a mental hospital and suicide attempts, became such a transformative part of his emotional life and calling as a poet. "'Howl' is really about my mother," Ginsberg confessed in his 1976 essay "More Explanations Twenty Years After."

As Hyde reminds us, Ginsberg had been seriously dedicated to his calling as a poet over a decade before *Howl and Other Poems* was published in October 1956 by City Lights, a small San Francisco paperback bookstore founded by the poet Lawrence Ferlinghetti. With its trademark black-and-white cover, it was the fourth volume in the City Lights's Pocket Poets Series, costing seventy-five cents. And by the time the book's signature poem, "Howl," was printed, it had gone through as many as eighteen recorded drafts, the first of which was entitled "Strophes" in recognition of the poem's opening series of refrains.

An unpublished early 1956 mimeographed version of the poem is included in this book, marking the first time it appears in print. Of this version, and of other early drafts of the poem, Ginsberg later explained that the "crucial revision" was the substitution in line 1 of "mystical" to "hysterical."

I saw the best minds of my generation destroyed by madness, starving,
mystical, *naked*

I saw the best minds of my generation destroyed by madness, starving,
hysterical, *naked*

The single change, he argued, changed and set "the tone of the poem" with its sense of "comic realism" and "humorous hyperbole," which runs throughout.

Ginsberg's poem was at first dismissed by a number of critics. Literary figures such as Lionel Trilling found "Howl" "just plain dull." With its candid references to sex, drugs, madness, and nightmares, the poem was considered obscene by many, including San Francisco's collector of customs, Chester MacPhee. In March 1957, he confiscated 520 copies of the book's second printing under section 305 of the Tariff Act of 1930.

Although the U.S. attorney for San Francisco refused to press charges, Captain William Hanrahan of the San Francisco Juvenile Department did, and condemnation proceedings against "Howl" and its publisher commenced. In his essay "Horn on 'Howl,'" Lawrence Ferlinghetti outlines the proceedings against his press, and the eventual victory against the state. "In considering material claimed to be obscene," the presiding Judge Horn stated, "it is well to remember the motto: Honi soit qui y pense (Evil to him who thinks evil)."

Brief excerpts from responses of writers at the trial, and the responses of many other writers and readers, to "Howl" since its publication are interspersed through this book. These remarks are included for their various insights into the poem and the commentators, as well as for the flavor of the passing of time and cultural shifts at the time of, and since, the poem's publication. As with our responses to events that have changed ourselves and the nation, many, many people have something urgent to say about the poem, even if they do not recall exactly where they were when they first read "Howl."

None of the comments, none of the news, about the making of and reaction to "Howl" fully account, however, for the poet and his poem. Poetry that captures the imagination of a nation often emerges from points of stress in our culture. "When the time was right," Vivian Gornick writes in her essay, "Wild at Heart," the raw material of Ginsberg's life and poetic resources "would convert into a poetic vision of mythic proportion that merged brilliantly with its moment: the complicated aftermath of the Second World War characterized by atomic bomb anxiety, a manipulated terror of godless Communism, the strange pathos of the Man in the Gray Flannel Suit, and the subterranean currents of romanticized lawlessness into which the men and women ultimately known as the Beats would fun-

nel an old American devotion to the idea of revolutionary in-
dividualism."

Allen Ginsberg tapped into the one essential element of this
"old American devotion to the idea of revolutionary individual-
ism," that of being an outsider. He knew how it felt to be an
outsider (as student, as homosexual, as Jew, as poet), and he used
that knowledge and experience in "Howl" to connect emotion-
ally and intellectually with others who felt the same way. The
poem empathizes most strongly with those who are victims of
large and seemingly impersonal forces—politics, economics, the
dictates of culture. By often speaking through hyperbole, Gins-
berg attempts to direct our gaze upon those persons we might
not ordinarily have much concern for.

This ability to stand outside the community appears in almost
every essay in this book. It accounts in part for the continuing
interest in and influence of the poem, as well as its steady stream
of new readers in each generation. Because many (all? especially
the young and even those well positioned in the mainstream)
experience life as outsiders, "Howl" instinctively continues even
after five decades to connect with its readers.

The fact that "Howl" is perhaps the critical "outsider poem"
of the modern era does not mean that those who do not grasp its
meaning at every level, or do not follow along the renegade paths
it details, are necessarily "insiders," regular folk. Phillip Lopate
struggles with this issue in his essay, "'Howl' and Me." "What
about all those working stiffs," he writes, "who would not end
up raving lunatics, who could not afford to drop out of the acad-
emy but would guard our scholarship money, keep our heads,
and grind away; are we automatically to be judged mediocre and
condemned to a lower status than 'the best minds'?"

INTRODUCTION

Whether "Howl" exerted doubt or confidence with the contributors in this book, it did so by declaring and creating an alternative literary and cultural community. Several authors testify to the critical importance the poem had (and continues to have) in offering their generations what Amiri Baraka calls in his essay, "'Howl' and Hail," "the language. The stance. The sense of someone being in the same world, the defiance."

The central response of the outsider in "Howl" is illuminated in part by the poet's need to develop a community of his own. And the characters spoken of in the poem were linked by their knowledge of one another as a group that tried to cut across gender, race, and even circumstance, language, and time:

who threw their watches off the roof to cast their ballot for Eternity
*   outside of Time . . .*
who dreamt and made incarnate gaps in Time & Space through images
*   juxtaposed, and trapped the archangel of the soul between 2 visual*
*   images.*

The identification with the outsider and the need for a new community were an identification with a new language and a new America that inspired innumerable poets and artists. In his essay, "Holy the Fifth International," Robert Polito explores the critical impact of "Howl" on the careers of Robert Lowell, Bob Dylan, and Frank Bidart. "'Howl' aims to create a community, a society, a new nation," he writes. "This community stretches, of course, beyond Ginsberg's little Beat cabal."

Nothing can make the contributing writers more at home in the world, however, than the excitement they felt when first reading the poem's "visual images." "What thrilled me," Robert

Pinsky, in his essay, "No Picnic," writes, "was the leash-breaking manner, the deliberate unthrottled throwing around of parts of speech and images and phrases, a musical parade of words celebrating their berserk Mardi Gras of freedom."

The poem's irrational juxtapositions were made with the purpose of altering consciousness itself. It is something Ginsberg called an "electro-chemical reaction." He aimed to create a poetry that stimulated in the reader an actual change in perception—at a physiological level. "It was . . . the power of the phrase, overturning the memory," the contributor Sven Birkerts writes in his essay, "Not Then, Not Now," "and the received idea of the phrase-back-to-square-one . . . I found I was reading in bursts, as if it were something growing up spasmodically in a grate . . . I couldn't take it as a poem. Not then, not now."

Perhaps the physical experience in reading the poem explains John Cage's shifting poetic-essay response to "Howl." Published in 1986 in an edition of 250 copies, his piece, *Writing Through Howl,* is included in this book as a testimony to the poem's ability to trigger new states of awareness and of the imagination.

Marjorie Perloff, in her essay, " 'A Lost Battalion of Platonic Conversationalists': 'Howl' and the Language of Modernism," writes that the poem's capacity to render a new language and consciousness honored the principles of modernism. "Ginsberg's great hyperbolic-comic-fantastic-documentary poem thus memorializes that brief postwar moment when the creation of poems was still informed by the Modernist trust in the power of words to make a difference."

The shift away from this trust in language may explain, in part, why there hasn't been another poem since "Howl" that has presented such a convincing spectrum. Which raises the critical question regarding this book: Why is it that the poem continues to fascinate us? For one thing, of course, there is the undeniable epic—and legendary—arc (chronicled and nurtured, to some extent, by the author himself) in both the poem's history and in the Beat Generation it helped to foster. Certainly, too, as these anthologized writers indicate, the poem demonstrated (in a seismic way) that literary and social change could emanate from the shared spirit of a highly charged language. The "howl" Ginsberg brought forth was also unruly, powerful enough to upset traditions and values and incite action on its behalf. People changed their professions, moved, or created alternative lifestyles as a direct impact of having read the poem. How many poems stir such literary and social tumult? It helped shake up the order of things, and that always appeals to the rebel in us.

Allen Ginsberg could hardly have imagined that the poem written to himself in secret would play such a monumental role of liberation and would influence generations of writers and readers. Like many of the contributors in this book, however, he welcomed the influence of "Howl" wholeheartedly and intimately. His many public writings and comments about the poem are reflected in this book by the inclusion of one critical piece he wrote on the thirtieth anniversary of the publication of the poem, in 1986. "The appeal in 'Howl,'" Ginsberg wrote, "is to the secret or hermetic tradition of art 'justifying' or 'making up for' defeat in worldly life." He moved effectively back and forth from the private to the public in speaking of "Howl." In the same essay, he writes, "I was curious to leave behind after my generation an emotional time bomb that would continue exploding in U.S. consciousness in case our military-industrial-nationalist complex solidified into a repressive police bureaucracy."

Commenting on how his views had changed since the writing of "Howl," he wrote in 1976 (on the twentieth anniversary of the publication of the poem), in a letter to the poet Richard

Eberhart, "at the time [of 'Howl'] I believed in some sort of God and thus angels and religiousness—now as Buddhist I see an Awakened emptiness . . . No God, no Self, not even great Whitman's universal Self."

Few poets enjoy the opportunity to expand upon, and appreciate, one of their celebrated texts the way Ginsberg did. He took full advantage of this opportunity to honor the poem as what he called "a social and poetical landmark, notorious at worst, illuminative at best."

The context out of which Ginsberg spoke about "Howl" was contradictory at times. It reflected, of course, his various and changing poetic, political, and personal adventures. A chronology of his unusually many-faceted and productive life is included at the end of this book to provide readers with the settings out of which his lifelong views on "Howl" were made. It also offers evidence of his extraordinary calling as a poet before and after the publication of "Howl."

Perhaps one of the most prescient remarks about "Howl" (and also one that reflects one of the constant themes of the contributors in this book) and its remarkable impact on our lives is to be found in the poem itself:

the madman bum and angel beat in Time, unknown, yet putting down here what might be left to say in time come after death.

"HOWL" BY ALLEN GINSBERG:
1956 MIMEOGRAPHED COPY

Published on May 16, 1956, in San Francisco in an impression of twenty-five mimeographed copies by Allen Ginsberg, which he distributed free to his friends, the following is the first known publication of "Howl." This is the first time it appears in print.

"This copy one of twenty five paid for by me with pure human blood costed [*sic*] $10.00 typed by poet Robert Creely [*sic*] dittoed by Martha Rexroth transported by me to the hands of Robert Lavigne [*sic*] in exchange for several drawings—self portraits on the bed and the incredible plans with Circle for water and floers [*sic*] May 16, 1956 S.F. adios Robert till N.Y. fame fortune history and big private black cockly sad woes shared and grave to come. Love, Allen." (Autographed inscription by Allen Ginsberg on a rare copy of the mimeo from the library of Robert LaVigne)

H O W L

for

Carl Solomon

by

Allen Ginsberg

"Unscrew the locks from the doors!
Unscrew the doors themselves from their jambs!"

Dedicatory Page

To

Jack Kerouac newBuddha of American prose who spit forth intelli-
gence into eleven books written in half the number of years (1951-1956)
---ON THE ROAD, VISIONS OF NEAL, DR. SAX, SPRINGTIME MARY, THE SUBTER-
RANEANS, SAN FRANCISCO BLUES, SOME OF THE DHARMA, BOOK OF DREAMS, WAKE
UP, MEXICO CITY BLUES, & VISIONS OF GERARD---creating a spontaneous bop
prosody and original classic literature. Several phrases and the title
of Howl are taken from Him.

    William Seward Burroughs, author of NAKED LUNCH, an endless novel
which will drive everybody mad.

    Neal Cassady, author of THE FIRST THIRD, an autobiography 1949,
which enlightened Buddha. All these books are published in Heaven.

    Lucien Carr, recently promoted to Night Bureau Manager of New York
United Press.

H O W L

for Carl Solomon

I

I saw the best minds of my generation destroyed by
        madness, starving hysterical naked,
dragging themselves through the negro streets at dawn
        looking for an angry fix,
angelheaded hipsters burning for the ancient heavenly
        connection to the starry dynamo in the machin-
        ery of night,
who poverty and tatters and hollow-eyed and high
        sat up smoking in the supernatural darkness
        of cold-water flats floating across the tops
        of cities contemplating jazz,
who bared their brains to Heaven under the El and saw
        Mohammedan angels staggering on tenement roofs
        illuminated,
who passed through universities with radiant cool eyes
        hallucinating Arkansas and Blake-light tragedy,
        among the scholars of war,
who were expelled from the academies for crazy &
        publishing obscene odes on the windows of
        the skull,
who cowered in unshaven rooms in underwear, burning
        their money in wastebaskets amd listening to
        the Terror through the wall,
who got busted in their pubic beards returning through
        Laredo with a belt of marijuana for New York,
who ate fire in paint hotels or drank turpentine in
        Paradise Alley, death, or purgatoried their
        torsos night after night
with dreams, with drugs, with waking nightmares,
        alcohol and cock and endless balls,
incomparable blind streets of shuddering cloud and
        lightning in the mind leaping toward poles
        of Canada & Paterson, illuminating all the
        motionless world of Time between,
Peyote solidities of halls, backyard green tree ceme-
        tary dawns, wine-drunkeness over the rooftops,
        storefront boroughs of teahead joyride neon
        blinking traffic light, sun and moon and tree
        vibrations in the roaring winter dusks of
        Brooklyn, ashcan rantings and kind king light
        of mind,
who chained themselves to subways for the endless ride
        from Battery to holy Bronx on benzedrine until

the noise of wheels and children brought them
        down shuddering mouth-wracked and battered bleak
        of brain all drained of brilliance in the drear light
        of Zoo,
who sank all night in submarine light of Bickford's
        floated out and sat through the stale beer
        afternoon in desolate Fugazzi's, listening
        to the crack of doom on the hydrogen jukebox,
who talked continuously seventy hours from park to
        pad to bar to Bellevue to museum to the
        Brooklyn Bridge,
a lost batallion of platonic conversationalists jump-
        ing down the steeps off fire escapes off window-
        sills off Empire State out of the moon,
yacketayakking screaming vomiting whispering facts
        and memories and anecdotes and eyeball kicks
        and shocks of hospitals and jails and wars,
whole intellects disgorged in total recall for seven
        days and nights with brilliant eyes, meat for
        the Synagogue cast on the pavements,
who vanished into nowhere Zen New Jersey leaving a
        trail of ambiguous picture postcards of
        Atlantic City Hall,
suffering Eastern sweats and Tangerian bone-grindings
        and migraines of China under junk-withdrawal in
        Newark's bleak furnished room,
who wandered around and around at midnight in the
        railroad yard wondering where to go, and went,
        leaving no broken hearts,
who lit cigarettes in boxcars boxcars boxcars racketing
        through snow toward lonesome farms in grand-
        father night,
who studied Plotinus St. John of the Cross telepathy
        and bop kaballa because the cosmos instinctively
        vibrated at their feet in Kansas,
who loned it through the streets of Idaho seeking
        visionary indian angels who were visionary
        indian angels,
who thought they were only mad when Baltimore gleamed
        in supernatural ecstasy,
who jumped in limousines with the Chinaman of Okla-
        homa on the impulse of winter midnight streetlight
        smalltown rain,
who lounged hungry and lonesome through Houston seeking
        jazz or sex or soup, and followed the brilliant
        Spaniard to converse about America and Eternity,
        a hopeless task, and so took ship to Africa,
who disappeared into the volcanoes of Mexico leaving
        behind nothing but the shadow of dungarees
        and the lava and ash of poetry scattered in

fireplace Chicago,

who reappeared on the West Coast investigating the
F.B.I. in beards and shorts with big pacifist
eyes sexy in their dark skin passing out
incomprehensible leaflets,

who burned cigarette holes in their arms protesting
the narcotic tobacco haze of Capitalism,

who distributed Supercommunist pamphlets in Union
Square weeping and undressing while the sirens
of Los Alamos wailed them down, and wailed
down Wall, and the Staten Island ferry also
wailed,

who broke down crying in white gymnasiums naked and
trembling before the machinery of other skel-
etons,

who bit detectives in the neck and shrieked with
delight in policecars for committing no crime
but their own wild cooking pederasty and
intoxication,

who howled on their knees in the subway and were dragged
off the roof waving genitals and manuscripts,

who let themselves be fucked in the ass by saintly
motorcyclists, and screamed with joy,

who blew and were blown by those human seraphim, the
sailors, caresses of Atlantic and Carribean
love,

who balled in the morning in the evening in rosegardens
and the grass of public parks and cemetaries
scattering their semen freely to whomever come
who may,

who hiccupped endlessly trying to giggle but wound up
with a sob behind a partition in a Turkish Bath
when the blonde & naked angel came to pierce
them with a sword,

who lost their loveboys to the three old shrews of fate
the one eyed shrew of the heterosexual dollar
the one eyed shrew that winks out of the womb
and the one eyed shrew that does nothing but
sit on her ass and snip the intellectual golden
threads of the craftsman's loom,

who copulated ecstatic and insatiate with a bottle of
beer a sweetheart a package of cigarettes a
candle and fell off the bed, and continued
along the floor and down the hall and ended
fainting on the wall with a vision of ultimate
cunt and come eluding the last gyzm of con-
sciousness,

who sweetened the snatches of a million girls trembling
in the sunset, and were red eyed in the morning

but prepared to sweeten the snatch of the
sunrise, flashing buttocks under barns and
naked in the lake,
who went out whoring through Colorado in myriad stolen
night-cars, N.C., secret hero of these poems,
cocksman and Adonis of Denver-- joy to the memory
of his innumerable lays of girls in empty lots
& diner backyards, moviehouses' rickety rows
on mountaintops in caves or with gaunt waittresses
in familiar roadside lonely petticoat upliftings
& especially secret gas-station solipsisms of
johns, & hometown alleys too,
who faded out in vast sordid movies, were shifted in
dreams, woke on a sudden Manhattan, and
picked themselves up out of basements hungover
with heartless Tokay and horrors of Third
Avenue iron dreams & stumbled to unemployment
offices,
who walked all night with their shoes full of blood
on the snowbank decks waiting for a door in
the East River to open to a room full of
steamheat and opium,
who created great suicidal dramas on the apartment
cliff-banks of the Hudson under the wartime
blue floodlight of the moon & their heads
shall be crowned with laurel in oblivion,
who ate the lamb stew of the imagination or digested
the crab at the muddy bottom of the rivers of
Bowery,
who wept at the romance of the streets with their push-
carts full of onions and bad music,
who sat in boxes breathing in the darkness under the
bridge, and rose up to build harpsichords in
their lofts,
who coughed on the sixth floor of Harlem under the
tubercular sky surrounded by orange crates of
theology,
who scribbled all night rocking and rolling over lofty
incantations which in the yellow morning were
stanzas of gibberish,
who cooked rotten animals lung heart feet tail borsht
& tortillas dreaming of the pure vegetable
kingdom,
who plunged themselves under meat trucks looking for
an egg,
who threw their watches off the roof to cast their
ballot for Eternity outside of Time, & alarm
clocks fell on their heads every day for the next
decade,

who cut their wrists three times sucessively unsuccess-
        fully, gave up and were forced to open antique
        stores where they thought they were growing old
        and cried,
who were burned alive in their innocent flannel suits
        on Madison Avenue amid blasts of leaden verse
        & the tanked-up clatter of the iron regiments
        of fashion & the nitroglycerine shrieks of the
        fairies of advertising & the mustard gas of sin-
        ister intelligent editors, or were run down by
        the drunken taxicabs of Absolute Reality,
who jumped off the Brooklyn Bridge this actually happened
        and walked away unknown and forgotten into the
        ghostly daze of Chinatown soup alleyways &
        firetrucks, not even one free beer,
who sang out of their windows in despair, fell out
        of the subway window, jumped in the filthy
        Passaic, leaped on negroes, cried all over
        the street, danced on broken wineglasses bare-
        foot smashed phonograph records of nostalgic
        European 1930's German jazz finished the
        whiskey and threw up groaning into the
        bloody toilet, moans in their ears and the blast
        of colossal steamwhistles,
who barreled down the highways of the past journeying
        to each others' hotrod-Golgotha jail-solitude
        watch or Birmingham jazz incarnation,
who drove crosscountry seventytwo hours to find out if
        I had a vision or you had a vision or he had
        a vision to find out Eternity,
who journeyed to Denver, who died in Denver, who came
        back to Denver & waited in vain, who watched
        over Denver & brooded & loned in Denver and
        finally went away to find out the Time, & now
        Denver is lonesome for her heroes,
who fell on their knees in hopeless cathedrals praying
        for each others' salvation and light and breasts,
        until the soul illuminated its hair for a second,
who crashed through their minds in jail waiting for
        impossible criminals with golden heads and the
        charm of reality in their hearts who sang sweet
        blues to Alcatraz,
who retired to Mexico to cultivate a habit, or Rocky
        Mount to tender Buddha or Tangiers to boys or
        Southern Pacific to the black locomotive or
        Harvard to Narcissus to Woodlawn to the daiseychain
        or grave,

who demanded sanity trials accusing the radio of hyno-
          tism & were left with their insanity & their
          hands & an hung jury,
who threw potato salad at CCNY lecturers on Dadaism
          and subsequently presented themselves on the
          granite steps of the madhouse with shaven heads
          and harlequin speech of suicide, demanding
          instantaneous lobotomy,
and who were given instead the concrete void of insulin
          metrasol electricity hydrotherapy psychotherapy
          occupational therapy pingpong & amnesia,
who in humorless protest overturned only one symbolic
          pingpong table, resting briefly in catatonia,
returning years later truly bald except for a wig of
          blood, & tears and fingers, to the visible
          madman doom of the wards of the madtowns of
          the East,
Pilgrim State's Rockland's and Greystone's foetid
          halls, bickering with the echoes of the soul,
          rocking and rolling in the midnight solitude-
          bench dolmen-realms of love, dream of life a
          nightmare, bodies turned to stone as heavy
          as the moon, ·
with mother finally ******, and the last fantastic book
          flung out of the tenement window, and the last
          door closed at 4 AM and the last telephone
          slammed at the wall in reply and the last
          furnished room emptied down to the last piece
          of mental furniture, a yellow paper rose
          twisted on a wire hanger in the closet, and
          even that imaginary, nothing but a hopeful
          little bit of hallucination---
ah, Carl, while you are not safe I am not safe, and now
          you're really in the total animal soup of time---
and who therefore ran through the icy streets obsessed
          with a sudden flash of the alchemy of the use
          of the ellipse the catalogue the meter & the
          vibrating plane,
who dreamt and made incarnate gaps in Time & Space
          through images juxtaposed, and trapped the
          archangel of the soul between 2 visual images
          and joined the elemental verbs and set the noun
          and dash of consciousness together jumping
          with sensation of Pater Omnipotens Aeterna Deus
to recreate the syntax and measure of poor human prose
          and stand before you speechless and intelligent
          and shaking with shame, rejected yet confessing
          out the soul to conform to the rhythm of thought
          in his naked and endless head,

the madman bum and angel beat in Time, unknown, yet
        putting down here what might be left to say
        in time come after death,
and rose reincarnate in the ghostly clothes of jazz
        in the goldhorn shadow of the band and blew
        the suffering of America's naked mind for love
        into an eli eli lamma lamma sabacthani sax-
        aphone cry that shivered the cities down to
        the last radio
with the absolute heart of the poem of life butchered
        out of their own bodies good to eat a thousand
        years.

II

What sphinx of cement and aluminum bashed open their
        skulls and ate up their brains and imagination?
Moloch! Solitude! Filth! Ugliness! Ashcans and unob-
        tainable dollars! Children screaming under the stair-
        ways! Boys sobbing in armies! Old men weeping
        in the parks!
Moloch! Moloch! Nightmare of Moloch! Moloch the love-
        less! Mental Moloch! Molech the heavy judger
        of men!
Moloch the incomprehensible prison! Moloch the cross-
        bone soulless jailhouse and Congress of sorrows!
        Moloch whose buildings are judgement! Moloch
        the vast stone of war! Moloch the stunned
        governments!
Moloch whose mind is pure machinery! Moloch whose
        blood is running money! Moloch whose fingers
        are ten armies! Moloch whose breast is a
        cannibal dynamo! Moloch whose ear is a smoking
        tomb!
Moloch whose eyes are a thousand blind windows! Moloch
        whose skyscrapers stand in the long streets
        like endless Jehovahs! Moloch whose factories
        dream and creak in the fog! Moloch whose
        smokestacks and antennae crown the cities!
Moloch whose love is endless oil and stone! Moloch
        whose soul is electricity and banks! Moloch
        whose poverty is the spectre of genius!
        Moloch whose fate is a cloud of sexless hydro-
        gen! Moloch whose name is the Mind!
Moloch in whom I sit lonely! Moloch in whom I dream
        Angels! Crazy in Moloch! Cocksucker in Moloch!
        Lacklove and manless in Moloch!

Moloch who entered my soul early! Moloch in whom I
        am a consciousness without a body! Moloch
        who frightened me out of my natural ecstasy!
        Moloch whom I abandon! Wake up in Moloch!
        Light streaming out of the sky!
Moloch! Moloch! Robot apartments! invisible suburbs!
        skeleton treasuries! blind capitals! demonic
        industries! spectral nations! invincible
        madhouses! granite cocks! monsterous bombs!
They broke their backs lifting Moloch to Heaven! Pave-
        ments, trees, radios, tons! lifting the city to
        Heaven which exists and is everywhere about us!
Visions! omens! hallucinations! miracles! ecstasies!
        gone down the American river!
Dreams! adorations! illuminations! religions! the whole
        boatload of sensitive bullshit!
Breakthroughs! over the river! flips and crucifixions!
        gone down the flood! Highs! Epiphanies! Despairs!
        Ten years' animal screams and suicides! Minds!
        New loves! Mad generations! down on the rocks
        of Time!
Real holy laughter in the river! They saw it all!
        the wild eyes! the holy yells! They bade
        farewell! They jumped off the roof! to solitude!
        waving! carrying flowers! Down to the river!
        into the street!

                        III

Carl Solomon! I'm with you in Rockland
        where you're madder than I am
I'm with you in Rockland
        where you must feel very strange
I'm with you in Rockland
        where you imitate the shade of my mother
I'm with you in Rockland
        where you murdered your twelve secretaries
I'm with you in Rockland
        where you laugh at this invisible humor
I'm with you in Rockland
        where we are great writers on the same dreadful
        typewriter
I'm with you in Rockland
        where your condition has become serious and is
        reported on the radio
I'm with you in Rockland
        where the faculties of the skull no longer admit
        the worms of the senses

I'm with you in Rockland
> where you drink the tea of the breasts of the
> spinsters of Utica
I'm with you in Rockland
> where you pun on the bodies of your nurses the
> harpies of the Bronx
I'm with you in Rockland
> where you scream in a straightjacket that you're
> losing the game of the actual pingpong of the
> abyss
I'm with you in Rockland
> where you bang on the catatonic piano the soul
> is innocent and immortal it should never die
> ungodly in an armed madhouse
I'm with you in Rockland
> where fifty more shocks will never return your
> soul to its body again from its pilgrimage
> to a cross in the void
I'm with you in Rockland
> where you accuse your doctors of insanity and
> plot the Hebrew socialist revolution against
> the fascist national Golgotha
I'm with you in Rockland
> where you will split the heavens of Long Island
> and resurrect your living human Jesus from the
> superhuman tomb
I'm with you in Rockland
> where there are twentyfive-thousand mad comrades
> all together singing the final stanzas of the
> Internationale
I'm with you in Rockland
> where we hug and kiss the United States under
> our bedsheets the United States that coughs
> all night and won't let us sleep
I'm with you in Rockland
> where we wake up electrified out of the coma
> our own souls' airplanes are roaring over the
> roof they've come to drop angelic bombs the
> hospital illuminates itself imaginary walls
> collapse O skinny legions run outside O
> starry spangled shock of mercy the eternal
> war is here O victory forget your underwear
> we're free
I'm with you in Rockland
> in my dreams you walk dripping from a sea-
> journey on the highway across America in tears
> to the door of my cottage in the Western night

San Francisco 1955-56

THE POEM THAT
CHANGED AMERICA

VIVIAN GORNICK

WILD AT HEART

———

In 1947 Saul Bellow published a novel called *The Victim*, in which a derelict character named Kirby Allbee haunts another named Asa Leventhal, claiming that Leventhal is responsible for his downfall. Kirby, one of Bellow's fabled fast talkers—all feverish self-abasement and joking insult—repeatedly baits Leventhal, and at one point, when Leventhal murmurs something about Walt Whitman, says to him, "Whitman? You people like Whitman? What does Whitman mean to you people?" Who could ever have dreamed that less than a decade after the publication of *The Victim* not only would "you people" be announcing out loud that they liked Whitman but it would appear that they themselves had reincarnated him. The day after Allen Ginsberg's celebrated 1955 reading of "Howl" in San Francisco, Lawrence Ferlinghetti sent Ginsberg a telegram that read, "I greet you at the beginning of a great career"—the sentence Emerson had used writing to Whitman upon the publication, exactly a hundred years earlier, of *Leaves of Grass*.

Fifty years later, I think it can safely be agreed that Allen Ginsberg *is* the poet who, within living memory, most legitimately resembles Whitman. He, like Whitman, wrote an emblematic

American poem that became world famous; was experienced preeminently as a poet of the people, at home among the democratic masses; developed a public persona to match the one in his writing—hugely free-spirited and self-promoting, an openhearted exhibitionist. And he, again like Whitman, is remembered as a man in possession of an extraordinary sweetness that, throughout his life, welled up repeatedly to astonish the hearts of all who encountered him.

I met Ginsberg only twice, the first time at Jack Kerouac's funeral in 1969. I was there for *The Village Voice*. It was my very first assignment as a working journalist. Here is the scene as I remember it:

At the head of the viewing room stood the casket with Kerouac, hideously made up, lying in it. In the mourners' seats sat Kerouac's middle-class French-Canadian relatives—eyes narrowed, faces florid, arms crossed on their disapproving breasts. Around the casket—dipping, weaving, chanting *Om*—were Allen Ginsberg, Peter Orlovsky, and Gregory Corso. Then there was Kerouac's final, caretaker wife, a woman old enough to be his mother, weeping bitterly and looking strangely isolated. I sat mesmerized, staring in all directions. Suddenly Ginsberg was sitting beside me. "And who are you?" he asked quietly. I told him who I was. He nodded and wondered if I was talking to people. Especially the wife. I must be sure to talk to her. "Oh, no," I said quickly. "I couldn't do *that*." Ginsberg nodded into space for a moment. "You must," he murmured. Then he looked directly into my eyes. "It's your job," he said softly. "You must do your job."

The second time we met, nearly twenty years later, was at an infamous meeting of the PEN board called to debate a letter (drafted by Ginsberg) that the Freedom-to-Write Committee had sent to Israel's premier, taking his government to task for censoring Palestinian and Israeli journalists. I sat in my seat, listening to Ginsberg read his letter aloud to a packed room. He was now in his sixties, his head bald, his beard trim, wearing an ill-fitting black suit, the voice as gentle as I remembered it and twice as dignified. Although the letter had been signed by Susan Sontag, William Styron, and Grace Paley among others, it was Ginsberg himself who drew fire from the opposition. In a communiqué that had been sent earlier to the committee, Cynthia Ozick had practically accused him of being an agent for the PLO; and now, the essence of the charge coming from the floor seemed to be "It's people like you who are destroying Israel." I remember Ginsberg standing there, his glasses shining, nodding in all directions, urging people toward compassionate reason. He never raised his voice, never spoke with heat or animosity, never stopped sounding thoughtful and judicious while all about him were losing their heads. When he stepped from the microphone and was making his way through the crowd, I pressed his hand as he passed me and thanked him for the excellence of the letter's prose. He stopped, closed his other hand over mine, and looking directly into my eyes, said softly, "I know you. Don't I know you? I *know* you."

Allen Ginsberg was born in Newark, New Jersey, in 1926 to Louis and Naomi Ginsberg; the father was a published poet, a high school teacher, and a socialist; the mother, an enchanting free spirit, a passionate communist, and a woman who lost her mental stability in her thirties (ultimately, she was placed in an institution and lobotomized). Allen and his brother grew up inside a chaotic mixture of striving respectability, left-wing bohemianism, and certifiable madness in the living room. It all felt *large* to the complicated, oversensitive boy who, discovering that he lusted after boys, began to feel mad himself and, like his paranoid parents, threatened by, yet defiant of, the America beyond the front door.

None of this accounts for Allen Ginsberg; it only describes the raw material that, when the time was right, would convert into a poetic vision of mythic proportion that merged brilliantly with its moment: the complicated aftermath of the Second World War, characterized by anxiety about the atomic bomb, a manipulated terror of godless Communism, the strange pathos of the Man in the Gray Flannel Suit, and the subterranean currents of romanticized lawlessness into which the men and women ultimately known as the Beats would funnel an old American devotion to the idea of revolutionary individualism.

When Ginsberg entered Columbia University in 1942, he was already possessed of a presentation of self, shall we say, that would make it impossible for him to gain the love of the teachers he most admired, namely, Lionel Trilling and Mark Van Doren. (Trilling memorialized Ginsberg in his short story "Of This Time, of That Place" as the brilliant student whom the narrating academic can experience only as mad). Emulating these men would mean going into a kind of internal exile that Allen, even then, knew he could not sustain. His dilemma seemed profound. Then he met Jack Kerouac, also a student at Columbia. Through Kerouac he met William Burroughs; together they picked up a Times Square junkie poet named Herbert Huncke; and after that Neal Cassady, the wild man of all their dreams: a handsome, grown-up delinquent who drank, stole, read Nietzsche, fucked like a machine, and drove great distances at great speeds for the sake of movement itself. As Burroughs put it, "Wife and child may starve, friends exist only to exploit for gas money . . . Neal must move." (Cassady became Dean Moriarty in *On the Road* and the Adonis of Denver in "Howl.")

For Ginsberg, these friends came to constitute a sacred company of inspired madmen destined to convert the poisoned atmosphere of America's Cold War politics into one of restored beauty—through their writing. The conviction among them of literary destiny was powerful. And why not? People like Ginsberg, Kerouac, and Cassady are born every hour on the hour: how often do their lives intersect with a political moment that endows their timeless hungers with the echoing response of millions, thereby persuading them that they are, indeed, emissaries of social salvation? What is remarkable among this bunch—considering how much they drank, got stoned, and flung themselves across the country in search of heavenly despair—is how well they sustained one another throughout their faltering twenties, when life was all worldly rejection and self-dramatizing desperation.

In 1949, now twenty-three years old, depressed, and at loose ends, Ginsberg let Herbert Huncke—a true criminal—crash at his apartment, where Huncke proceeded to stash an ever-increasing amount of stolen goods. Inevitably, the police appeared at the door, and everyone was arrested. Rescued from a prison sentence by friends, family, and his Columbia teachers, Ginsberg was sent to the New York State Psychiatric Institute, where he spent eight months that did, indeed, change his life. Here he met the man to whom he would dedicate "Howl."

Carl Solomon was Allen's double—a Bronx-born bisexual self-dramatizing left-wing intellectual. They saw themselves in each other almost immediately. Solomon held out his hand and said, "I'm Kirilov" (a character in Dostoevsky's *The Possessed*). Allen responded, "I'm Myshkin" (Dostoevsky's fabled idiot). There was, however, one important difference between them. Solomon had lived in Paris, was soaked in existentialist politics and literature; and here, at New York State Psychiatric, he introduced Allen to the work of Genet, Artaud, and Céline, the mad writers with whom he instantly felt at one. Ginsberg marveled at Solomon's melancholy brilliance and proceeded to mythicize it. If Carl was mad, it could only be that Amerika had driven him mad. When Ginsberg emerged from the institution, he had his metaphor in place:

I saw the best minds of my generation destroyed by madness, starving
   hysterical naked,
dragging themselves through the negro streets at dawn looking for an
   angry fix.

For the next few years he wandered, all over the country and halfway around the world, becoming a practicing Buddhist along the way. Arrived at last in San Francisco in 1954 (with Kerouac, Cassady, and Corso dancing about him), here and now, in the American city experienced as most open (that is, farthest from the seats of eastern power), he wrote his great poem, read it aloud one night in October 1955—and awoke to find himself famous.

While thousands of young people responded to "Howl" as though they'd been waiting *years* to hear this voice speaking these words, the literary establishment promptly vilified it. Lionel Trilling hated the poem, John Hollander hated it, James Dickey hated it, and Norman Podhoretz hated it. Podhoretz hated it so much that he wrote about it twice, once in *The New Republic* and then again in *Partisan Review*. By the time these pieces were being written, *On the Road* had been published, as well as *Naked Lunch*, and for Podhoretz the American sky was falling. The Beats, he said, were the barbarians at the gate, rabble-rousers who "embraced homosexuality, jazz, dope-addiction and vagrancy" (he got that part right), at one with "the young savages in leather jackets who have been running amuck in the last few years with their switch-blades and zip guns." Jack Kerouac was cut to the quick and wrote to complain that the Beats were about *beatitude*, not criminalism; they were here to *rescue* America (from corporate death and atomic bomb politics), not destroy her.

In the summer of 1957, "Howl" was brought to trial in San Francisco on charges of obscenity, with a wealth of writers testifying on behalf of the poem's literary value. In retrospect, the trial can be seen as an opening shot in a culture war destined to throw long shadows across American life. And indeed, throughout the sixties, both the poem and its author were celebrated, the former as a manifesto of the counterculture, the latter as one of its emblematic figures.

Today, nearly fifty years after it was written, "Howl" is never out of print, is read all over the world (it's been translated into more than two dozen languages), and by most standards is considered a literary classic. Like *Leaves of Grass*, it is an ingenious experiment with the American language that did what Ezra Pound said a great poem should do: make the language new. Its staccato phrasing, its mad juxtapositions and compacted images, its remarkable combining of the vernacular with the formal— obscene, slangy, religious, transcendent, speaking now in the voice of the poet, now in that of the hipster—is simply an astonishment. The effect of all this on the reader? "Even today," as Jonah Raskin, one of Ginsberg's biographers, says, "reading the poem yields a feeling of intoxication. The words produce an electrical charge that is exhilarating."

That charge is actually the *dis*charge of a man and a time well met. There is a feverish hunger for poetry and glory in Ginsberg as he moves through the late forties that is absolutely at one with his political and cultural moment. Prowling the streets of New York as if it were Dostoevsky's Petersburg; rising in an English class at Columbia to terrify students and teachers alike with some brilliant, unpunctuated rant; looking for sex in Times Square; seeing Blake in a vision in his own kitchen; nodding wordlessly when the cops ask him if he is a homosexual— we have a vivid figure standing squarely in the foreground of significant disconnect.

Yet, we can also see why Ginsberg could survive his own youth to become an emblematic figure of growth and change while Kerouac and Cassady could not. Neal Cassady was a drifter through and through. To read his letters—although the ones to his writer friends are richly literate—is to see a man perpetually on the run from himself. It was all drugs, drink, women, and motion without a stop. He is forever in the car hurtling toward New York, Denver, or California. If he stops, it's to get one woman pregnant, marry a second, start an affair with a third, all in what feels like the space of a month; then it's back in the car, writing to each one, "I'll be home in a week, babe, ten days at the latest." Kerouac, except for the books, was not so very different. Neither of these men could inhabit the space he actually occupied at any given moment. Each had a leak somewhere in the middle of himself that made experience drain exhaustingly away (both were dead in their forties).

Ginsberg, by contrast, was remarkably heart-whole: it made all the difference. His experience nourished him, gave him the strength to complete the self-transformation he had been bent on from the beginning. I don't think it an exaggeration to say that when he died at seventy his life had given new meaning to the word "self-created." For the formal poets and critics of his own generation, Ginsberg would remain only an original: the gifted, problematic amateur (in 1963 Robert Lowell wrote to Elizabeth Bishop "the beats have blown away, the professionals have returned"). For the American culture, however, Ginsberg (indeed, like Walt Whitman) had become an inspirited incarnation: the authentic made-in-America holy fool.

MARK DOTY

HUMAN SERAPHIM: "HOWL," SEX, AND HOLINESS

The university in my town was a place of cultural and political foment, and three thousand people packed the auditorium—the biggest one at the University of Arizona—to hear chants and rants and ecstatic outpourings. I was still in high school; everyone I knew who wrote poetry or was passionate about social change—that is, everyone cool from Rincon High—was there, and we weren't disappointed. The small figure on the huge stage seemed to loom larger, not in a threatening or puffed-up way but in an intimate one, as if he were a grand, available personality becoming more available as he squeezed the harmonium and sang Blake, and hopped a little, and spoke rhythmically and passionately into the mic. I don't know that I've heard a more responsive audience at a poetry reading since; people clapped and laughed and shouted approval. When Allen Ginsberg mentioned "one sugarcube of lysergic acid diethylamide smuggled" across some border, the crowd sent up a wave of cheers; when he read the line "It'll be a relief when the Red Chinese take over Texas," there was a huge outcry of delight. The next day, at a bookstore called The Hungry Eye, I went to hear him again—this time Allen and Peter chanting together, making the narrow room of bodies reverberate. It was 1969, and a sort of heaven.

I didn't hear Ginsberg again for a decade. In Indianola, Iowa, at Simpson College, his reading was sponsored, who knows why, by one of the school's fraternities. It couldn't have been a more different scene: the audience was tastefully respectful; the poet read some of the short, sonorous, sorrowful lyrics about his father's illness, and afterward there was a party at the fraternity house. I was both looking forward to and feeling a bit shy about meeting this legendary presence, but I needn't have worried. A good twenty minutes into the party, Allen disappeared upstairs with a young fraternity member who wanted to show him some poems, and he never came back the rest of the evening.

Flash-forward twenty years, to the Geraldine R. Dodge Poetry Festival in Waterloo Village, New Jersey, a pastoral extravaganza of verse and good spirits. The second day of the festival is largely given over to teachers, and there are thousands of New Jersey high school teachers in attendance when Allen arrives on the stage of the big tent, his voice carried out to the back rows by a splendid audio system. It's maybe six months before his death, but Allen's in fine and sweetly energetic form, reading/chanting his late, playful chants—"don't smoke don't smoke, suck cock, suck cock"—and everyone just loves him. Then he starts in on his ode to his sphincter muscle, a quirky little paean of praise. This seems to me the most unlikely poem in the world to find a congenial welcome on the ears of the assembled secondary school teachers, so I can't help looking around the ranked seats to check it out. Sure enough, they are loving it, they are laughing and clapping, absorbed in delight. And I find myself thinking, Now what if I decided to write a poem in praise of my asshole? Wouldn't they be unsettled, maybe offended, certainly questioning my taste?

But Ginsberg entirely transcended the question of polite behavior, of queerness, of the appropriate. He somehow skipped right around our American obsession with a binary scheme of human sexuality, as though people were issued in two basic models, and "gay" and "straight" were permanent and coherent markers stamped on their genes or characters. Allen created some zone of permission and distinction for himself that seemed to make all things possible, and he seemed to occupy a category all his own.

The first time I read "Howl," fourteen years after it was published, I was the sort of digging-for-possibilities-for-myself kid who searched the library for evidence, looking for writers or at least characters in books who might share my own secret life of desire. I wanted books to teach me something about how to live, and sexuality was the most mysterious and charged part of that quest. Was it possible to have a life as an adult who loved people of the same sex? No evidence to be had in school—as if!—or on television or in the newspaper or in magazines—not till 1970 anyway, when a squib appeared in *Time* about the new gay liberation front in San Francisco, with a picture of a handsome, mustached man with a bandanna tied around his head and an open face that seemed to signal a world of possibility. I pored over Truman Capote and Tennessee Williams, and tried to read James Baldwin, and therefore you'd think that, when I came to "Howl," the poem would have been a revelation. But in truth it wasn't, not that way. Of course there's plenty of sex in the poem, enough to have earned its famous obscenity trial. I remember being fascinated by this:

who let themselves be fucked in the ass by saintly motorcyclists, and
*   screamed with joy,*

who blew and were blown by those human seraphim, the sailors, caresses
  of Atlantic and Caribbean love,
who balled in the morning in the evenings in rosegardens and the grass of
  public parks and cemeteries scattering their semen freely to whomever
  come who may,
who hiccuped endlessly trying to giggle but wound up with a sob behind
  a partition in a Turkish Bath when the blond & naked angel came
  to pierce them with a sword.

It's startling to think about that passage being published in 1956. It seems as if America's willful denial of queer sexuality might simply have crumbled in the face of it, and that a generation of gay men might have taken it as a clarion call to freedom, but neither of those things happened. Of course, this may simply have been because it was a poem, a form that tends to be a far advance scout of culture rather than an actual agent of change. Or it might be its oddly camp tone—the saintly bikers, seraphic sailors, and penetrating angel do feel a bit arch, don't they? And that giggling case of the hiccups is decidedly at odds with earnest sexual enjoyment; these elements make the passage less a cry of liberation or a celebration of eros than something more complex than either of those things.

"Howl," considered in 2005, seems, more than anything else, a poem of visionary friendship, of the longing to be part of a questing (albeit erratic) company. It's a chronicle of friends seeking—take your pick, satori, godhead, enlightenment, transcendence, the permanent ecstatic—through whatever means they find at hand: Buddhist teaching, drugs, sex, and a sort of self-abuse, to use a rough term for it, involving staying up all night, travel, drinking, and cigarettes, scraping the self raw, as it were, to open every pore.

Such longing, and such hammering of the individual in quest of the whole, takes place against a particularly unyielding background: the conservative, pragmatic, industrial, down-to-earth America of the late forties and early fifties, a culture that wants none of its sons' quest for the transcendent (and they *are* sons—this is a guys' vision of a juggernaut for holiness). America actively seeks to resist, tame, jail, medicate, or hospitalize them. What is not of the mainstream seems illicit or sick, as if their longing for firsthand experience of the divine is itself criminal, a subversive deviance.

This pose—transcendent wild boys versus spirit-crushing monolithic Moloch—is an affecting one, in small doses, though it might be a bit hard to take were "Howl" not so exuberantly funny. That's the part I'd forgotten, or perhaps never really seen. Was Ginsberg's humor harder to get, back when his transgressions seemed more incendiary? I can't quite imagine the contemporary equivalent of a William Carlos Williams telling us to protect our hems from the infernal poem we're about to enter today, not when that inferno is so self-mockingly playful. This queer visionary company has a bit of a Keystone Kops quality. For instance:

> who threw their watches off the roof to cast their ballot for Eternity outside of Time, & alarm clocks fell on their heads every day for the next decade,
> who cut their wrists three times successively unsuccessfully, gave up and were forced to open antique stores.

You can even hear Ginsberg's chuckle in the sonics; that "successively unsuccessfully" is meant to make us grin.

Which isn't to say there isn't real horror in "Howl," and genuinely vulnerability. I can't read this line without a shiver:

who broke down crying in white gymnasiums naked and trembling be-
    fore the machinery of other skeletons.

That's a strophe in which sexuality, shame, and mortality inter-
sect with grim power. And the threat of the ferocious "normal-
izing" force of the mental hospital looms everywhere, with its
policing of consciousness, its brutal medical intervention in un-
acceptable states of mind.

But look what happens even there:

who threw potato salad at CCNY lecturers on Dadaism and subse-
    quently presented themselves on the granite steps of the madhouse
    with shaven heads and harlequin speech of suicide, demanding in-
    stantaneous lobotomy,
and who were given instead the concrete void of insulin Metrazol electric-
    ity hydrotherapy psychotherapy occupational therapy pingpong &
    amnesia.

Just when the passage has turned from the nihilistic protest—*real*
Dada, instead of the academically presented sort—to the grave
list of treatments administered to those who won't or can't accept
the official version of reality, Ginsberg throws in that "ping-
pong." It's a signature gesture; any time he might start taking
himself too seriously, there's that laughter that keeps perspective,
keeps—despite the rants and big claims the poem makes all
along the way—one foot planted firmly in a sense of the absurd.

Sex, in "Howl," seems simply one more in the chain of experi-
ences pursued for their potential in revealing the divine, but it's
just as capable of offering the ridiculous as it is the transcendent.
This is decidedly not a middle-class position toward the ecstatic.
It isn't, I think, a stance that could easily be incorporated into a

broader culture, or a political platform. Can you imagine gay liberation as a religious juggernaut, exactly? Probably not. Whitman might be said to have attempted something of the sort, proclaiming the love of comrades as the foundation of a social order, but his interest is in a divinity apprehended entirely through its human embodiments, and he's completely earnest about the project.

Try to add a sense of humor to that religious impulse, it becomes unthinkable as a social movement. After Stonewall, gay activists would earnestly seek liberty and equality for their own sake; Ginsberg's platform calls for liberty in the service of the transcendent. And—in contrast to the earnest stance of gay liberation—he never loses sight of himself as a potentially comic figure. Does this make him a quintessentially Jewish Buddhist?

In a strange way, obscene and scandalous as "Howl" may have been, Ginsberg's complex position makes its sexual frankness acceptable. We have a tradition of sacred erotic literature. Admittedly, it's a ways from the poems of St. John of the Cross to that sword-bearing naked blond in the baths, but if you remember the poem where Christ wounds his earthly beloved's throat—well, there *is* a precedent. Eros has been spiritualized in the West ever since the Song of Songs. And if you can even go on to *laugh* at that celestial messenger who's about to spear you—well, you're immediately in a far less confrontational position with the reader.

This particular position—lusty spiritual comedian, let's call it—is why, ultimately, gay writers of the generations beyond Allen would think of him as a forefather but not exactly an influence. He feels like a cultural totem less of gay American history and culture than of "alternative" American life, a pioneer of psychic frontiers whose work probably has less to do with how I experience the world than does that of his East Coast contemporary Frank O'Hara. It's an interesting comparison. The O'Hara poem with the most direct engagement with the transcendent, "A True Account of Talking to the Sun at Fire Island," is also very funny, though inflected with a camp sensibility of a very different sort. The pratfalls and swooning exclamations in "Howl" serve to resist the heightened quality of the holy quest at their core. O'Hara doesn't believe in sacred quests, probably wouldn't even entertain such a notion, yet he seems visited one day by something broaching upon mystery anyway, a talking heavenly body with allegiances beyond the plane of earth. He brings the same sensibility, the same open-eyed gaze to an encounter with a heavenly body that he'd bring to anything else. Of course he jokes, but there's a different tenor to his humor, and the irony in his voice gives way, at last, to—or at least coexists with—an unmistakably genuine sense of awe.

I think Allen could sing to those assembled teachers about his usually-not-discussed-in-company body parts with such élan, and be accepted so freely, because everybody understood that on some level it wasn't really his ass he was talking about anyway. It was an attitude toward the world and toward the body, a sweet-natured, laughing acceptance of earthliness that existed, for Ginsberg, as a means to get off the earth plane. As bodily as his work may be, it usually tends upward and outward, away from gravity, moving through the fact of flesh toward other arenas. Amazingly, his most famous poem invented a new cultural category—neither homo nor straight, quite, but the "angel-headed hipster," the beat whose transcendent sexuality lifts him out of the familiar categories, knocking the binary off its high horse, setting himself loose to sing.

AMIRI BARAKA

"HOWL" AND HAIL

———

owl" reached Puerto Rico, late '55, whenever the early *Village Voice* did. I was there disguised as a colored Airman second-class, lower left gunner and weatherman on a B36. Reading at nights and 12 hrs every day under the Latino sun, while guarding somebody else's airplanes, and scoffing every stationary word in English Literature, all the best-sellers in *The NY Times* and with 7 or so comrades in an underground airman professional killer salon learning the history of western music and literature as night librarian at Ramey Air Force Base, Strategic Air Command, Aguadilla, Puerto Rico. At least two of these guys, both photographers, lurk somewhere even now in NYC, to tell the tale. James Lucas and Phil Perkis!

We read and kicked Hardy, Proust, Kafka, Hey, What's a Kafka, we yelled? I dunno . . . Hey Roi order it. And the night librarian did, plus a fifth of Rum. Motets, Gregorian Chants, Bach, Ulysses, Tess Durberville. I mean some under the earth dull as shit, but Ulysses, Rimbaud, Baudelaire, Satie. We were getting our under over graduate readiness preparation to return to Civilization, we thought, after roaming the sky scaring the world with nuclear frustration, American ignorance, and young arrogance, wandering what the big world wd be.

For me, the Voice was just more confirmation that like my High School hero Allen Polite, who I first was turned on to The Writer, him still a great unpublished poet. HE said, we thought, the VILLAGE, YEH, that's where everything was at! OH yeh. That's where the world-class intellectuals and knowers wd reside. Oh Yeh.

And finally, 1957, they booted me out of the service as undesirable, you bet, I had already got booted out of College as likewise, but now as a fucking commie Buddhist colored guy, busted for books and an alarming hostility to dumbness. You ever dig Curtis LeMay on his stomach on a go-cart speeding across the flight line Saturday mornings. Wd instruct the hell out of you. With both stripes now ripped off along with secret clearance, Gone, Gone, and so we shot off in ecstasy to the City, the Apple, New York, Bohemia, The Village, to try out our vicious learning on those we were sure wd dig how heavy we had got.

And it was Howl again. Plus Allen Polite and his cohorts, Cunningham, Cage, Charlip, Czernovitch, RhBlythe, Suzuki, Zen, gals in black stockings, Yeats, Poetry Poetry Poetry, that brought us panting into the Village. 1st crib 104 E. 3rd St, $28 a month 3 rms no heat, my mother wept. But hey wasn't this the joint?

But Alas! And Alas and Alack. IT was not that what that was in my head. Not the GV of PR. The west village was full of poseurs and empty bags of old pretense, where was Poetry? Where was heavy intellectual outness after all? But Howl was emerging full then. Being talked about Given Ink emerging full and clear. What struck me (and does still) . . . an Audaciousness I needed . . . in that McCarthy Eisenhower 7 Types of Ambiguity 50s. That oatmeal lying world. In Puerto Rico I'd sent my stuff to *Kenyon*, *Sewanee*, *Hudson*, *Partisan*, and all the cemeteries, and it came back almost before being mailed, *The New Yorker*'s poetry actually made we weep, at the deep nothingness they touted as feeling, yeh, but only of deep disgust.

So HOWL—the language. The stance. The sense of someone being in the same world, the defiance. Yeh—to the dead and to somebody else's version of Bohemian Intelligentsia there was here this HOWL. So I wrote Allen on a piece of toilet paper to Git Le Coeur asking was he for real. He answered on French toilet paper, which is better for writing, that he was tired of being Allen Ginsberg. And sent a broad registration of poetry for the new magazine *YUGEN*. And that began some forty years of hookup.

Allen was finally what I thought was everywhere in the Village, a genuine book-stuffed intellectual and, as well, a publicist, perhaps the best we knew of poetry itself. There were so many bullshitters and tasters and energetic imitating Marlon Brandos. Except Jack Micheline wasn't imitating, in those jazz sessions he was who Marlon Brando was imitating.

And we remained friends, Allen and I, for 40 years. His takes on Williams, and the variable foot, American speech, the breath phrase, the existence of an American language and literature, which the colleges still deny, was what was most important to me. The anti-Moloch heavy anti-imperialist line that wove through HOWL, "AMERICA Go FUCK YR SELF WITH YR ATOM BOMB!" Now that was poetry! Plus talking to Allen about Western poetry was always part of a course. On Blake, Smart, Rimbaud, the troubadours, we visited Pound and he apologized for being anti-Semitic, at least Allen heard that, that crazy motherfucker. William Carlos Wms funeral, we trooped over for, and before that to Weequahic high school to do a reading, in Newark, where we were both borned. Howard U, that historic trek, reading on the campus, refused from all buildings.

Allen was a font of ideas, and publicity for the new word, a new generation, on prosody, America and intros to the whole united front against dead people "they don't like the way we live" was the way AG summed it up. And for this, that we cd bring the San Francisco School, the Beats, Black Mountain, O'Hara and the New Yorkers together to do battle against the zombies of Euroformalism, neo colonial death verse was where our deepest comradeship was formed.

Allen and I argued relentlessly, soon as he and me, we went our separate ideological practical day to day paths. Malcolm's murder shot me out of the village for good, and our greetings and meeting became measure less frequent. The gap between Black nationalism and Tibetan Buddhism. I wanted to make War, Allen to make peace. For all our endless contention, often loud and accompanied by contrasting histrionics, we remained, in many ways, comrades in and of the word, partisans of consciousness!

The day before he split Allen called and sd he had to see me. Very important he sd. Can you come. Yeh, what's up . . . Well . . . he paused, then as usual, matter of fact—I'm gonna die . . . OH bullshit. Allen Why're you saying that? No—It's true. I just got out of the hospital. Maybe a couple of months . . . not long. Hey don't say dumb shit like that. No. No. it's true . . . Anyway you need any money? Money? Naw Naw I don't need no money . . . and you aint gonna die. Well, you still gonna come Monday. it's important. Yeah, I'll be there . . . but nix on that death shit. OK, see you . . . we exchanged our outs . . . the phone hit. Then the next day, the newspapers carried their stuff. A big drag . . . Man, a big big drag you know. Because the fundamental struggle for American poetry. For our speech and consciousness as part of the energy and power of the United States against the dead and their Ghosts. The anti-imperialist revolutionary democratic struggle itself is still running, and we must raise it again to more intense levels. Allen was part of that!

But then a last word for Allen, gone now, turned completely into spirit on us. What we uphold is the defiance and resistance to "Moloch," in the collective tongue of the multinational multi cultural American tongue and voice. What it was I first dug in *Howl*. And the great line from *America*. "America go fuck yrself with yr atom Bomb." Now that's poetry! That still rings and will ring true. And for this sentiment, and stance, and revolutionary democratic practice, part of revolutionary art for cultural revolution, we say Hail and Farewell my man, Hail and Farewell.

MARJORIE PERLOFF

"A LOST BATTALION OF PLATONIC CONVERSATIONALISTS": "HOWL" AND THE LANGUAGE OF MODERNISM

———

In 1957, just a year after the publication of the City Lights edition of *Howl*, Louis Simpson wrote a poem called "To the Western World":

A siren sang, and Europe turned away
From the high castle and the shepherd's crook.
Three caravels went sailing to Cathay
On the strange ocean, and the captains shook
Their banners out across the Mexique Bay.

And in our early days we did the same.
Remembering our fathers in their wreck
We crossed the sea from Palos where they came
And saw, enormous to the little deck,
A shore in silence waiting for a name.

The treasures of Cathay were never found.
In this America, this wilderness
Where the axe echoes with a lonely sound,

The generations labour to possess
And grave by grave we civilize the ground.★

Simpson had been a classmate of Ginsberg's at Columbia University in the late forties. He was older and "wiser"—a World War II veteran who had served in the 101st Airborne Division in Europe. When the newly celebrated author of "Howl" returned to Manhattan in 1956, he sought out Simpson, who was then editing, with Donald Hall and Robert Pack, *New Poets of England and America*, which was to become the standard anthology used in undergraduate classrooms. Ginsberg recalls giving Simpson "this *great* load of manuscripts of [Robert] Duncan's, [Robert] Creeley's, [Denise] Levertov's, mine, [Philip] Lamantia's, [John] Wieners's, [Gary] Snyder's, [Philip] Whalen's, [Jack] Kerouac's, even [Frank] O'Hara's—everything. And he didn't use any of it."†

Two decades later, when Simpson reviewed Ginsberg's *Journals: Early Fifties Early Sixties* for *The New York Times Book Review*, he admitted he had been wrong—"not merely wrong, obtuse," to have ignored Ginsberg's poetry in the fifties.‡ Indeed, anti-

---

★Louis Simpson, "To the Western World," in *Collected Poems* (New York: Paragon House, 1988), p. 90. The poem is included in Donald Hall, ed., *Contemporary American Poetry*, revised and enlarged edition (Baltimore: Penguin, 1972), p. 117.

†See Allen Ginsberg, *Journals Mid-Fifties 1954–1958,* edited by Gordon Ball (New York: HarperCollins, 1995), p. 176.

‡See Barry Miles, *Ginsberg* (London: Virgin, 2000), p. 470. In his memoir *North of Jamaica* (New York: Harper & Row, 1972), Simpson recalls the furor triggered by *New Poets* and explains, "we had not intended to imply that these were the only poets in England and America. We were trying to make a representative selection." As for "Howl," Simpson notes that Ginsberg's poem had not yet been published when the Hall-Pack-Simpson anthology was being put together (pp. 176–77). Later, in *A Revolution in Taste: Studies of Dylan Thomas, Allen Ginsberg, Sylvia Plath, and Robert Lowell* (New York: Macmillan, 1978), Simpson writes sympathetically of early poems such as "Paterson" and of "Kaddish."

thetical as the two poets were—the G.I. Bill graduate student who already had ties with the Establishment versus the Beat poet, one of those "who were expelled from the academies for crazy & publishing obscene odes on the windows of the skull"— Simpson, according to Ginsberg himself, makes a cameo appearance in "Howl" in strophe 55:

who threw their watches off the roof to cast their ballot
   for Eternity outside of Time, & alarm clocks
   fell on their heads every day for the next decade, . . .★

In Ginsberg's note for this passage we read:

> As author remembers anecdote, friend Walter Adams visited poet Louis Simpson's high-floored apartment near Columbia in 1946:
> L.S.: Do you have a watch?
> W.A.: Yes.
> L.S.: Can I have it?
> W.A.: Here.
> L.S. (throwing watch out of window): We don't need time, we're already in eternity.

In letter November 21, 1985, kindly responding to query from author, Louis Simpson writes:

★Allen Ginsberg, *Howl and Other Poems* (San Francisco: City Lights, 1956), 16. I use the City Lights text, subsequently cited as H, so as to reproduce the original typography of "Howl," but for documentation, line numbers, and notes, see *Howl: Original Draft Facsimile, Transcript & Variant Versions . . .* , edited by Barry Miles (New York: Harper & Row, 1986), subsequently cited as HH. Simpson describes his stay in the mental hospital in *North of Jamaica*, chapter 25.

It seems this does apply to me. I say "seems" because I don't remember doing this, but a man whose word I could trust once wrote me a letter in which he said that I thought "that technology had destroyed time so that all lives ever lived were being lived simultaneously, which was why you should ask Walter Adams for his watch, throw it out the window and remark that we didn't need such instruments any more."

This must have happened shortly before I had a "nervous breakdown"—the result of my experience during the war. There may have been other causes, but I think this was the main. I have no recollections of the months preceding the breakdown, and if people say I threw watches out of windows, OK. (HH 134)

It seems that, for a brief moment, Simpson too was one of the "angelheaded hipsters burning for the ancient heavenly connection." Like Ginsberg, for that matter, he was an outsider at Columbia, a native of Jamaica who was half-Jewish. But to become a *poet*, in postwar New York, meant to give up the "starry dynamo" in the "tubercular sky" in favor of the formal (and indeed political) correctness that would characterize the Hall-Simpson-Pack anthology. By the time Simpson published his first book, *Good News of Death and Other Poems* (Scribner, 1955), he had mastered the genteel mode almost perfectly.

If we want to understand just how extraordinary a poem "Howl" was at the time of its performance and publication, we might profitably read it against a poem like Simpson's "To the Western World." Sound is the first differentium: Simpson's poem is divided into three five-line stanzas rhyming *ababa*. The regularity of its iambic pentameter from

   /   /   /   /   /
A siren sang, and Europe turned away

to the final

    /   /   / /   /
And grave by grave we civilize the ground

distinguishes this midcentury poetry sharply from its more daring Modernist antecedents, whether the syncopated rhythms of Eliot, where "the ghost of a meter . . . lurks behind the arras," the open tercets of Stevens's "The Auroras of Autumn," the syllabics of Marianne Moore, or, of course, the free verse of Pound and Williams, the latter serving as a model for Simpson in his later poetry.

Within this tight form and its perfectly chiming and conventional rhymes ("same"/"came"/"name"; "found"/"sound"/ "ground"), the poet presents us with a carefully depersonalized capsule history of American imperialism. Irony and indirection are all: like Odysseus, "Europe," it seems, was seduced by a siren, and this Europe, the synecdoches of line 2 tell us, was turning away from the "high castle" of its medieval aristocracy as well as the "shepherd's crook" of its then dominant peasant population. The "three caravels went sailing" on a "strange ocean"—strange because it was the wrong one and also, no doubt, because the journey that led them not to the longed-for Cathay but to Mexique Bay took place on the stormy Atlantic.

In the second stanza, "they" merge with "we," as the poet compares the Conquistadors to "our" Pilgrim ancestors, who in their "early days . . . did the same," crossing the sea to "a shore in silence waiting for a name." To complicate things, Simpson introduces, in line 7, a buried allusion to Ferdinand in Shakespeare's *Tempest*, "weeping again the king my father's wreck," a line appropriated by Eliot in "The Waste Land," where it provides contrast to the tawdry present in the collage of "The Fire Sermon."

But despite the double allusion, "To the Western World" is perfectly straightforward thematically. "The treasures of Cathay were never found," we are told somewhat redundantly in stanza 3. But—and here is the moral—"we" are still at it: our "generations labour to possess" "this America, this wilderness." The poem's final line provides the punch line: "And grave by grave we civilize the ground." The only way we seem to be able to build a "civilization" is by killing, whether killing off the Indians who owned this wilderness or, by implication, killing our enemies in the recent wars. No wonder "the axe echoes with a lonely sound."

"To the Western World" is a well-made poem on a theme that no doubt resonated in the wake of the atomic bomb and the Korean War: the imperialist path that prompted the original discovery of America as well as its later settlement is still with us; ours is a civilization built on death. Truth, it seems, is accessible to the poet, the point being to express that truth with measured irony: "And grave by grave we civilize the ground."

Irony, indirection, third- rather than first-person reference, allusion, moral discrimination, tight metrical form: these constituted the Hall-Pack-Simpson signature, in contradistinction to the poems collected in Donald Allen's oppositional *The New American Poetry*, published just three years later and featuring the Beats, Black Mountain, New York poets, and the San Francisco Renaissance. But *The New American Poetry* unwittingly gave rise to another myth—the myth, put forward by Allen himself in his preface—that the central conflict of the day was between "closed" and "open" verse, between the formal and the improvisatory-spontaneous, the "cooked" and the "raw." I say myth because the irony is that Ginsberg (like many of the "New American" poets) was probably a much truer Modernist than were mandarin poets like Louis Simpson or Donald Hall. Indeed, Ginsberg had so thoroughly internalized the aesthetic of the Modernists he revered—Eliot, Pound, Williams, Hart Crane—that "Howl" unwittingly makes the case for *showing* rather than *telling*, for the inseparability of *form* and *content*, and even for Cleanth Brooks's theorem that "the language of poetry is the language of paradox."★ Even Ginsberg's fabled rejection of metrics for what was ostensibly the mere piling up of "loose" free-verse or even prose units can be seen, from the vantage point of the early twenty-first century, as formal continuity rather than rupture: the use of biblical strophes, tied together by lavish anaphora and other patterns of repetition.†

But in 1956, critics and fellow poets were sidetracked by the nasty subject matter of "Howl," its angry diatribes and metaphoric excesses, and its use of four-letter words and slangy diction. Not surprisingly, formalist poets such as John Hollander, another of Ginsberg's Columbia classmates and a poet included in *The New Poets of England and America*, took an instant dislike to "Howl." In his now infamous review for *Partisan Review* (1957), reprinted in Appendix 1 of the Harper facsimile edition, Hollander declares:

> It is only fair to Allen Ginsberg . . . to remark on the utter lack of decorum of any kind in his dreadful little volume. I believe that the title of his long poem, "Howl," is meant to be a noun, but I can't help taking it as an imperative. The poem itself is a confession of the

★Cleanth Brooks, *The Well Wrought Urn* (New York: Harcourt, Brace, 1947), p. 3.
†In its first draft, the poem that was to become "Howl" was called "Strophes." In 1956 Ginsberg told Gary Snyder, "These long lines or Strophes as I call them came spontaneously as a result of the kind of feelings I was trying to put down, and came as a complete surprise to a metrical problem that preoccupied me for a decade"(HH 154).

poet's faith, done into some 112 paragraphlike lines, in the ravings of a lunatic friend (to whom it is dedicated), and in the irregularities in the lives of those of his friends who populate his rather disturbed pantheon.

And, having quoted the poem's first two lines, Hollander shrugs, "This continues, sponging on one's toleration, for pages and pages" (HH 161).

Among the major critics of the period, Hollander's view was to prevail. In 1961, Harold Bloom pronounced both "Howl" and "Kaddish" "certainly failures," lacking all "imaginative control over the content of [the poet's] own experience." Similarly, Denis Donoghue declared that, in "A Supermarket in California," "Ginsberg has done everything that is required of a poet except the one essential thing—to write his poem." And in *Alone with America* (1980), Richard Howard observed that "Ginsberg is not concerned with the poem as art. He is after the poem *discovered* in the mind and in the process of writing it out on the page as notes, transcriptions."*

None of the above seems to have changed his mind in the intervening years. Meanwhile, other prominent critics—Frank Kermode, Hugh Kenner, Geoffrey Hartman, not to mention theorists like Adorno or Derrida or Julia Kristeva—have simply ignored Ginsberg's poetry. We have, then, the anomaly of a poem that has become iconic around the world[†] even as the book continues to be dismissed, or at least ignored, in discussions of postmodern poetics.

---

*See Harold Bloom, "On Ginsberg's *Kaddish*," in *The Ringers in the Tower: Studies in Romantic Tradition* (Chicago and London: University of Chicago Press, 1971), pp. 213–14; Denis Donoghue, *Connoisseurs of Chaos* (New York: Macmillan, 1965), p. 49; Richard Howard, *Alone with America* (New York: Alfred A. Knopf, 1980), p. 149.

[†]See Jonah Raskin, *American Scream: Allen Ginsberg's Howl and the Making of the Beat Generation* (Berkeley: University of California Press, 2004), pp. xxi–xxii.

To rectify this curious situation, we might shift the discourse from the biographical–cultural preoccupation, which continues to dominate most studies of Ginsberg's work, to a close look at the actual texture of "Howl," especially vis-à-vis its earlier drafts, as presented in Barry Miles's elaborate Harper & Row edition of 1986, lavishly annotated by Ginsberg himself and including a wealth of relevant documents.

Part I of the City Lights edition opens with the lines

I saw the best minds of my generation destroyed by
    madness, starving hysterical naked,
dragging themselves through the negro streets at dawn
    looking for an angry fix,
angelheaded hipsters burning for the ancient heavenly
    connection to the starry dynamo in the machin-
    ery of night,
who poverty and tatters and hollow-eyed and high sat
    up smoking in the supernatural darkness of
    cold-water flats floating across the tops of cities
    contemplating jazz, . . . (H 9)

Frank O'Hara, hearing Ginsberg declaim these lines in the Manhattan of 1956, evidently turned to his neighbor and whispered, "I wonder who Allen has in mind?"★ But extravagant as the poet's claim may be, we now know, thanks to Ginsberg's own annotations and those of his biographers, just whom he did have in mind, beginning with William Burroughs, Jack Kerouac, and Herbert Huncke. Again, the poet's careful choice of place names—Fugazzi's bar on Sixth Avenue in the Village or

---

★See Marjorie Perloff, "A Lion in Our Living Room," in *Poetic License: Essays in Modernist and Postmodernist Lyric* (Evanston: Northwestern University Press, 1990), p. 199, and chapter 10 passim.

the neighboring San Remo's or the "Paradise Alley" cold-water-flat courtyard at 501 East 11th Street, cited in line 10—give "Howl" its air of documentary literalism (see HH 125).

But O'Hara was onto something important: persons and places in "Howl" are so much larger than life that they come to occupy a mythic, rather than everyday, domain. The effect is achieved, I would argue, by a consistent use of tropes of excess—catachresis, oxymoron, transferred epithet—as well as rhetorical figures of incongruity such as zeugma and the catalog of seriatim items containing one discordant member, all these laced with self-mockery and deflation, as in "who plunged themselves under meat trucks looking for an egg" or "who scribbled all night rocking and rolling over lofty incantations which in the yellow morning were stanzas of gibberish." This peculiar paradox—the "lofty incantations" that are also "stanzas of gibberish"—is established at the very opening of the poem.

Consider, for starters, the adjective string "starving hysterical naked" in line 1. The first version read "starving mystical naked." Ginsberg notes:

> Crucial revision: "Mystical" is replaced by "hysterical," a key to the tone of the poem. Tho [sic] the initial idealistic impulse of the line went one way, afterthought noticed bathos, and common sense dictated "hysteria." One can entertain both notions without "any irritable reaching after fact and reason," as Keats proposed with his definition of "Negative Capability." The word "hysterical" is judicious, but the verse is overtly sympathetic . . . The poem's tone is in this mixture of empathy and shrewdness, the comic realism of Chaplin's *City Lights*, a humorous hyperbole derived in part from Blake's style in *The French Revolution*. (HH 124)

When I first read this commentary, I found it somewhat irritating: isn't it pretentious of the poet to inform us that the replacement of a single word is "crucial" and "judicious," creating the "mixture of empathy and shrewdness" found in Chaplin or Blake? But rereading "Howl" in 2005, I think Ginsberg's explanation is quite just. Paul Breslin, in an essay otherwise quite critical of "Howl," was perhaps the first to remark how odd the use of the phrase "starving hysterical naked" is in context, since all three adjectives designate bodies, not "minds."* "Hysterical" derives from the Greek *hystera* (womb), and Freud, who wrote so much about hysterics, considered it a somatic illness, usually of women. It thus is a more accurate term than "mystical," the three-adjective unit providing a graphic image of a mental hunger so intense as to seem literally physical. The consonance of "*star*ving" and hy*ster*ical," moreover, intensifies the coupling of these adjectives.

The second line underwent a similarly judicious revision. In the original version, it reads, "who dragged themselves thru the angry streets at dawn looking for a negro fix" (HH 13). Ginsberg's note tells us that he had in mind his pathetic friend Herbert Huncke, "cruising Harlem and Times Square areas at irregular hours, late forties, scoring junk" (HH 124). But the revision exchanges the adjectives so that it is the streets that are "negro" and the fix "angry." Why? Perhaps because "negro fix" resorts to the cliché that it is blacks who are drug users, and the streets are perhaps too predictably those of the "angry" poor. More accurately, the scene is the "negro streets" of Harlem, and now it is the "fix" that is "angry" in its defiance of the social order by which it is outlawed. And the third strophe sets up the paradox that permeates the poem. The "hipsters" are "angel-

---

*Paul Breslin, *The Psycho-Political Muse: American Poetry Since the Fifties* (Chicago: University of Chicago Press, 1987), p. 24.

headed," the starry sky a "dynamo in the machinery of night." On the one hand, the yearning for spirituality, for mystical knowledge; on the other, the clear-eyed recognition of the fallen technological world in which we live. And again, the sound structure is carefully wrought, "angel" chiming with "ancient," "hipsters" with "heavenly," "dynamo" leads to "night," the heavy trochaic rhythm revising itself in the anapests of

/   /   /   /   /   /   /

angelheaded hipsters burning for the ancient heavenly connection

And further, in the fourth line, Ginsberg introduces the syntactic peculiarity that becomes a kind of signature in "Howl." Instead of saying, "who poor and ragged and hollow-eyed and high," he ungrammatically juxtaposes nouns and adjectives: "who poverty and tatters and hollow-eyed and high." The shift underscores the artifice of the passage: this is hardly, as Ginsberg's critics have often complained, unformed speech. No one, whether rich or poor, sober or stoned, New Yorker or foreigner, talks this way; no one, to take another example, says, "who were expelled from the academies for crazy & publishing obscene odes on the windows of the skull" (line 7). Not "for crazy behavior" or "crazy pamphlets": "crazy" can apply to just about anything these "angelheaded hipsters" do. And, as in the case of "poverty and tatters," the syntactic distortion and ellipsis remind us that this is a poem, not real life, that this text is very much a made object.

Indeed, the unsettling clash of nouns and adjectives, with the heavy compounding of words like "angelheaded," "hollow-eyed," and "Blake-light tragedy," played out in the syncopated rhythms of the anaphoric "who" clauses, produces an air of gridlock. *Loading* and *oxymoronic jamming*: these give "Howl" its particular feel. Contrary to Hollander's stricture, the poem does not just ramble on and on, but, as perhaps that first audience at the Six Gallery in San Francisco understood better than Ginsberg's mentor, Lionel Trilling (who pronounced "Howl" just plain "dull," "all rhetoric without any music," HH 156), its larger structure depends on semantic-rhetorical suspension that produces continual *surprise* and hence demands rereading. Take strophe 7 again:

> *who were expelled from the academies for crazy &*
> *publishing obscene odes on the windows of the*
> *skull, . . .*

The allusion is evidently to Ginsberg's own sophomoric prank, his inscription on his dorm window of the phrase "Butler has no balls," with its reference to Nicholas Murray Butler, Columbia's revered octogenarian president.★ But in the poem, the "windows" oddly become those not of the Columbia dorm or storefront but of the *skull*, as if to say the graffiti permeate the very being of the poet. Such extravagant conceit characterizes "Howl" throughout. "Mohammedan angels stagger on tenement roofs illuminated," the "incomparable blind streets" are full "of shuddering cloud and lightning in the mind," and the "crack of doom" emanates from the "hydrogen jukebox."

The elaboration of such devices can be quite complex, as in strophe 57:

> *who jumped off the Brooklyn Bridge this actually hap-*
> *pened and walked away unknown and forgotten*
> *into the ghostly daze of Chinatown soup alley-*
> *ways & firetrucks, not even one free beer, . . .* (H 17)

★Raskin, *American Scream*, p. 60.

Again, Ginsberg is thinking of a real incident: in 1945, his friend Tuli Kupferberg made a drunken suicide attempt by jumping off the Brooklyn Bridge but was saved by the crew of a passing tugboat (see HH 128). But in "Howl," the victim who "walked away unknown" recalls not Tuli but the poet most significantly associated with the Brooklyn Bridge, Hart Crane, who was, of course, one of Ginsberg's heroes. The dreamlike "ghostly daze of Chinatown" gives way to the realism of "soup alleyways & firetrucks," and then to the absurd conclusion of "not even one free beer," as if such a state of affairs could actually prompt people to jump off bridges.

The literal ("this actually happened") bumping against the "ghostly": Ginsberg's "language of paradox" is found within lines as well as between them, as in strophes 59–60:

> who barreled down the highways of the past journeying
> to each other's hotrod-Golgotha jail-solitude
> watch or Birmingham jazz incarnation,
> who drove crosscountry seventytwo hours to find out
> if I had a vision or you had a vision or he had
> a vision to find out Eternity, . . . (H 17)

Here "barrel[ing] *down* the highways" is juxtaposed to the ascent *up* Golgotha, literally, the hill of the skull, where Christ's Crucifixion took place. "Hótród-Gólgótha jáil-sólitúde"—a nine-syllable unit that has seven primary stresses and intricate alliteration of *l*'s and assonance of *o*'s—describes the suffering of "hotrod" drivers, who have been placed in "jail-solitude watch." But the phrase also juxtaposes the hotrod speed and pleasure of the open road and the quietude of Christ on the Cross. And further: the "Birmingham jazz incarnation," far from being parallel to the "jail-solitude," is its antithesis: if you're lucky, the poem says, you may achieve the former rather than the latter. The word "incarnation" is carefully chosen: it is the afterlife of Golgotha, the redemption that follows the Passion.

But—another opposition—this densely packed, clotted, allusive passage now gives way to the simplicity and ease of strophe 60, the poet chuckling, so to speak, as he recalls the mad scramble of the Beats to *get* away, to transcend the daily round, to find "if I had a vision or you had a vision or he had a vision to find out Eternity." The desperation is almost comic, but, as the catalog continues, the poem darkens, turning to the world of the mental hospital:

and who were given instead the concrete void of insulin
    Metrazol electricity hydrotherapy psycho-
    therapy occupational therapy pingpong &
    amnesia, . . . (strophe 67)

In the notes, Ginsberg tells us that "Author received hydrotherapy, psychotherapy, occupational therapy (oil painting) and played Ping-Pong with Carl Solomon at N.Y. State Psychiatric Institute, July 1948–March 1949" (HH 131). The poem complicates this list by the absurd inclusion of Ping-Pong as well as by the addition of particular drugs ("insulin," "Metrazol"), the substitution of the neutral term "electricity" for "electro-shock-therapy," and the nonparallel item "amnesia," as if to suggest that the final result of the terrifying treatments cataloged will indeed be no more than this.

The mental hospital thread continues, culminating in the listing of "last" things ("the last fantastic book flung out of the tenement window" and the "last door closed at 4 A.M. and the last telephone slammed at the wall in reply"), only to explode suddenly with a parenthetical address to Carl:

ah, Carl, while you are not safe I am not safe, and
  now you're really in the total animal soup of
  time— (H 19)

Here, after all the hyperbole, all the anaphoric phrasing and hal-
lucinatory imagery, the poet interjects a low-key moment of or-
dinary intimacy between two friends, who know they're in this
"animal soup" together. It is the poem's epiphany, and so, in the
last few strophes, Ginsberg introduces his poetics directly:

and who therefore ran through the icy streets obsessed
  with a sudden flash of the alchemy of the use
  of the ellipse the catalog the meter & the vibrat-
  ing plane, . . .★

The "vibrating plane" and, two lines later, "the syntax and mea-
sure of poor human prose"—these give way, in Part II ("Mo-
loch"), to a simpler, incantatory invective against cultural and
political evil; but in Part III, the mode of the opening section
returns in the brilliant counterpoint of refrain and exemplum,
shifting from the comic burlesque of

I'm with you in Rockland
  where you've murdered your twelve secretaries . . .
I'm with you in Rockland
  where your condition has become serious and
  is reported on the radio

★In the Final Text, 1986, this line becomes "and who therefore ran through the icy
streets obsessed with a sudden flash of the alchemy of the use of the ellipsis catalog a
variable measure and the vibrating plane" (HH 6). "A variable measure" is Williams's
term, and "ellipsis" clarifies—perhaps overclarifies—the meaning of "ellipse."

to the pathos of

I'm with you in Rockland
   where fifty more shocks will never return your
   soul to its body again from its pilgrimage to a
   cross in the void (H 24–25)

and coming full circle, with the final Whitman reference, to the actual scene of writing in Berkeley:

I'm with you in Rockland
   in my dreams you walk dripping from a sea-
   journey on the highway across America in tears
   to the door of my cottage in the Western night★ . . . (H 26)

"Howl," I have been suggesting, is in many respects a poem that honors the principles of Modernism—*le mot juste*, the objective correlative, the use of complex semantic and rhetorical figures—even though the critics, put off by its "bad taste," didn't see how fully Ginsberg was working within the tradition. "It is a howl," wrote Richard Eberhart in *The New York Times Book Review*, "against everything in our mechanistic civilization which kills the spirit, assuming that the louder you shout the more likely you are to be heard" (HH 155). Here Eberhart reinforces Hollander's critique of the poem's "utter lack of decorum" (161).

From the distance of fifty years, the "bop kabbalah" "Howl" can be seen as a natural development out of Modernism. But there is another aspect of "Howl" that continues to be misunderstood. This so-called Cold War poem, with its "howl" against

★I am here discounting the "Footnote to Howl" (Holy! Holy! Holy!) as an unneeded add-on, an anticlimax to the great third part. The Footnote was not read at the Six Gallery in October 1955; it was written a few months later.

the Moloch of "skeleton treasuries! blind capitals! demonic in-
dustries! . . . monstrous bombs!" (H 22), must be understood, I
would argue, as very much a poem of World War II, the war
Ginsberg, born in 1926, narrowly missed. Unlike Simpson po-
ems such as "The Battle," which recounts how "At dawn the first
shell landed with a crack, / Then shells and bullets swept the icy
woods,"* "Howl" is not overtly about combat, but it is surely the
presence of that war, at its height when young Allen arrived at
Columbia in 1942 and studied in classrooms and dorms filled
with returning GIs, that accounts for the displaced violence at
the heart of "Howl."

Consider the strangeness of the poem's diction. Here human
beings don't walk: they "drag themselves," "stagger," "cower,"
"leap," "chain themselves to subways," "jump off the Brooklyn
Bridge," "pick themselves up out of basements," "plunge them-
selves under meat trucks," "barrel down highways,"and "crash
through their minds in jail." Again, these "angelheaded hipsters"
don't meditate or contemplate; they "burn for the ancient heav-
enly connection," "bare their brains to Heaven under the El,"
"hallucinate Arkansas," "listen to the crack of doom on the hy-
drogen jukebox," "howl on their knees in the subway," "sing out
of their windows in despair," and spend their days "yacke-
tayakking screaming vomiting whispering facts and memories
and anecdotes." And sex in "Howl" is always related to demonic
energy and violence: "who copulated ecstatic and insatiate with
a bottle of beer . . . and fell off the bed, and continued along the
floor and down the hall," "who went out whoring through Col-
orado in myriad stolen night-cars," "who balled in the morning
in the evenings in rose-gardens and the grass of public parks and
cemeteries scattering their semen freely to whomever come
who may."

*Louis Simpson, "The Battle," *Collected Poems*, p. 53.

It is usual to say that such violence—the violence of those "who burned cigarette holes in their arms" or "bit detectives in the neck"—was endemic to the protest against "the narcotic tobacco haze of Capitalism" (H 13). But in 2005, capitalism is more ubiquitous than ever, yet no one today writes this way; indeed, Ginsberg himself, in his later Zen period, wrote a much more muted poetry. Rather, from the distance of fifty years, we must understand "Howl" as at least in part a reaction to those, like Louis Simpson, who had *been there* and wrote odes to the "heroes" who "were packaged and sent home in parts."* If others could write of chained prisoners, Ginsberg would celebrate those "who chained themselves to subways for the endless ride from Battery to holy Bronx on benzedrine." If others, trained as war pilots, crashed their planes, the "heroes" of "Howl" "crashed through their minds in jail."

The violence of the war heroes was honored by the public; the violent acts of Ginsberg and his Beat friends, with their drugs and daredevil adventures, were often ridiculed. Indeed, the poet himself laughs at the exploits of those

who cut their wrists three times successively unsuccess-
    fully, gave up and were forced to open antique
    stores where they thought they were growing
    old and cried, . . . (H 16)

"Denver," we read a page later with reference to Neal Cassady, "is lonesome for her heroes." And not only Denver: "Howl" is itself "lonesome" for its heroes, those "heroes" willing to take on the "shocks of hospitals and jails and wars." Ginsberg's great hyperbolic-comic-fantastic-documentary poem thus memorializes that brief postwar moment when the lyric imagination, how-

*Simpson, "The Battle," *CP*, p. 54.

ever exuberant, wild, fanciful, or grotesque, was subject to the re-
ality check of actual events, the urge to assure the audience that
"this actually happened." The trope of choice continued to be that
of Ginsberg's New Critical contemporaries—paradox. But in
"Howl," paradox no longer goes hand in hand with the imper-
sonality and indirection of late Modernist poetics. Indeed, Gins-
berg's is a paradox curiously devoid of irony. The litany of Part
III—"I'm with you in Rockaway"—concludes, after all, with the
poet's extravagant dream that his friend Carl Solomon has crossed
the continent and arrived at the "door of my cottage in the West-
ern night." It is the mythic promise of that "arrival" that, fifty
years after its publication, continues to captivate its readers.

BOB ROSENTHAL

A WITNESS

———

Howl" is witness to a generation of strangers and lovers who live in these long strophes without fear. "Howl" is a loud communication but not disorganized and not without purport. The spine-tingling reality of hearing coyote howl in the cool night air is the clarity of the voice. Allen's howl wakes readers to use eyes and ears and tongues to strip the gauze away and perceive the world with clarity no longer hidden or denied.

The poem balances an orchestra of oral poetic and prophetic forms with the poet's voice at the apex of past and future. Poet and voice are suffused into a generational testimonial that skips one to the next, regularly opening up each generation anew. Not every reader stays in that moment of witnessing, but some of each group open. It's to become who you are; it's to allow you self-membership.

For so many, it was simply being able to say, "I'm Gay. I am Okay. I am Gay." I worked as Allen's secretary twenty years, 1977–1997, East Village, New York City. In the first ten years, I don't think a week went by without a fan letter from somebody who wrote, "Thank you for opening that door. Thank you for bringing me out of the closet." Now there are many organizations and groups to help sort out sexual identity. Versions of "Howl" arrived from the international ether of special fourth-class printed matter. A composer in Poland sent a giant musical score for "Howl" printed in a handmade book. Ragged samizdat Russian editions were smuggled out. Ten years past publication, the Albanian translation finally arrived at our door without much ado. Nothing could ever equal the excitement in July 1980 when, after signing for a piece of registered mail and trudging back from Stuyvesant Station Post Office, I held a nine-by-twelve-inch manila envelope addressed to Allen Ginsberg from John Clellon Holmes. I carefully sliced the envelope and pulled out a sheaf of papers. On the top of the first page, "Howl for Carl Solomon" was written in a faint pencil in Allen's hand. My first thought was that this couldn't really be "Howl," for the familiar long lines were arranged in William Carlos Williams's American triadic steps. But then I noticed Holmes's note in the upper right corner that Kerouac had sent him the manuscript. It dawned on me that I had just opened a normal manila envelope and now was holding an Ur-document in American literature in my hands! I sat slightly shaking and taking it in for many moments before running to find Allen. He had no idea that John ever had it. That thoughtful return by Holmes created the annotated *Howl* and became the cornerstone of the Allen Ginsberg collection now at Stanford University's Green Library.

"Howl" still helps young people realize their actual ambitions: not to become a poor poet living in a dump but maybe to become a physical therapist when you are expected to become a lawyer, or maybe to become a lawyer when everybody expects you to fail at everything. "Howl" transforms the losers into winners by offering a process of permission handed down from Blake and Whitman.

Although "Howl" won the right to be heard and was heard often on the radio for decades, the FCC later silently created a climate of fear in which radio stations would no longer take the chance of offending the invisible censors. Ironically, as "Howl" was eased out of the airwaves, it started to appear in high school texts. For the last several years of his life, Allen took informal polls of how many in the college-based audience had read "Howl" in high school. Most hands went up. Allen was often asked to read "Howl," but he mostly refused, not wanting to make the poem stale through overuse. But if he were reading in a state of the union in which he had not read before (i.e., Utah), he would include "Howl" to commemorate the occasion. He eventually read "Howl" in all fifty states and countless countries. An outdoor reading of "Howl" given on the steps of the U.S. Court of Appeals in October 1994 was one of the last readings of the poem. "Howl" has traveled steerage in many international travelers' back pockets. "Howl" has regularly been parodied to suit many moods and purposes. We collected file folders full of parodies. Allen's many hours of interviews with translators of "Howl" around the world taught the translators about American idiom and language. Recently "Howl" was read in a simultaneous global Internet communion. I am saving a copy for NASA when they call.

Letters of appreciation sent to the Allen Ginsberg Trust, the annual community festivals called Howl, the number of times the poem is lifted and placed on a Web site attest to the continuance of its long-term inspiration. "Howl" is a critique of repressive certitudes that renews hope through candor. The societal hierarchies we have known relentlessly resemble Moloch, embody Moloch, and out-Moloch Moloch. Invariably Moloch has been renewed, and so the poem "Howl" is made new.

ANDREI CODRESCU

"HOWL" IN TRANSYLVANIA

———

In 1963 a badly typed copy of an awkward translation into Romanian of "Howl" fell into our greedy little hands in Sibiu, Transylvania. "Our" was my friend Adrian's and my own, no others having been deemed safe enough to share this document brought by train from Cluj (a bigger city with more poets and a university) by Stoie, who was a student there. So hush-hush was this operation that Stoie, who at the time was translating Villon and Yesenin into mellifluous and drunken Romanian, forbade us to read the poem until he had gone back to school, and he would not divulge the translator's name under any circumstances, not even when Adrian took away the demijohn of wine. Most poets were studying how to be *maudits* in those days, taking their drinking very seriously, and Stoie was more than two-thirds there. He also had objective reasons to be afraid of what he had done by passing on to us what years later in Russia came to be known as samizdat. I am now wondering, from the safe distance of four decades, if we didn't exaggerate the dangers to enhance our youthful terribleness. (Our favorite adjective in 1963 was *"teribil!"* meaning both "incredible" and "scandalous," and certainly "terrible" in terms of bourgeois

taste.) It seems barely believable now that we could be terrified
of being found in possession of a poem. The danger was that a
snitch for the local Securitate organs might report to his supe-
rior that he'd espied a high school kid and his older (by six years)
friend reading an untranslated American poem, though it would
have taken a first-class literary superior to know just what to do
about it, and there was only one such man in the whole town,
and he was, I'm afraid, my best friend, Adrian, who—though I
didn't know it at the time—had some official reason to wear a
leather jacket and own a typewriter (verboten object in 1963, all
typefaces of all typewriters registered with the police, possible
disseminator of subversion, old commie awe of dank print shop
whence sprouts Revolution). Adrian was, like I said, six years
older and had never been a college student, which could mean
that he was in a Party Apparatchik Institute, although this is ret-
rospective. More to the point is that Adrian had taken me under
his wing and gave me what I wanted most: access to the poets of
the interwar era, the Romanian avant-garde, a mythic body of
work that was utterly unavailable (we called it "forbidden") and
that was neatly divided in two: the noisy, shameless, left-wing
deviant, border-busting internationalist (read: Jewish) notables
like Tristan Tzara, Benjamin Fondane, Eugen Ionesco, and Ilarie
Voronca, and the autochtonist, proto- (or full-blown) fascist,
myth-and-root nostalgists like Lucian Blaga, Emil Cioran, and
Aron Cotrus. In the mid-sixties the Party began stirring Roma-
nia right toward nationalism, and the prewar right-wing van-
guard was being slowly allowed to drip its bloodcurdling syntax
into the writing workshops. Our workshop in Sibiu was no ex-
ception; it was in fact the locus of the probatory rehabilitation
because Lucian Blaga and Emil Cioran, the most eminent of the
antebellum right, were both proud citizens of medieval Sibiu
(Hermannstadt in German, Nagyszeben in Hungarian). There
had been an influential Sibiu Circle, the outline of which was

still visible to us, and minor members of which ("memories") were still living in dignified poverty with the old books hidden but handy. Adrian had access to an old hunter who fed us wild duck and lent us Blaga's books, but then I stumbled accidentally on Tristan Tzara's poetry in French, and my attitude and my poetry took a decidedly antitraditionalist turn, due, no doubt, to my innate cosmopolitanism (read: Jewishness). At the time, the two major interbellic vanguards were indistinct; what they had in common was their unavailability, which shadowed by far their ideological differences. I understood Blaga's soulful longing for an Edenic past, his attraction to death, silence, mystery, and an otherworldly pantheon. His metapoetic spaces fit my adolescent gloom, the magic aura of Sibiu, and the general rainy gray of late Stalinism. But I'd also read Tzara, and I was no longer content to just die helplessly in the hope of joining some Germanic Elysium. I sensed the possibility of revolt, of action and gaiety, the potential of joy in the present, and the overwhelming, wondrous existence of reality itself. I became drunk with revolt and in love with a kind of journalism, the deliciousness of noting what was there, what surrounded me, what color Aurelia's eyes really were, what a ridiculous figure my school principal cut, the pathetic slogans peeling in my classroom, the oversize heads of the triple-chinned gargoyles of the Central Committee that menaced every pedestrian from damp old walls. I discovered comedy! Not just irony, or even satire, or the old standby of mildly subversive jokes, but wholesome, Rabelaisian, total, take-no-prisoners comedy. I was living in a ridiculous world! Everyone was absurd, including our long-suffering, scared parents and teachers! Everyone with their heads in the sand, their hands in their pockets, their greasy ties knotted like nooses around their tense necks. What I knew about Tzara, besides vertigo-causing spasms of liberty such as "des chants voraces ont embrouillé les plumes de leurs mourantes mésures / au pupitre du navire où le vent a ramassé le déluge de toutes les directions" ("the savage chants dimmed the feathers of their dying beats/on the lectern of the ship buffeted by the flood from all directions"), from *L'Homme Àpproximatif*, 1925–1930, and "il ouvre maintenant sa tente—un parapluie aù-déssus du poumon—et la chevelure de l'air qu'il aspire" ("he now opens his shelter—an umbrella under the lung—and the flowing mane of air that breathes him in"), from *L'Anti-Tête*, 1935, was that he had acted against war, boredom, and convention with dances, orgies, and new forms of music and art that horrified adults. I held the name of Cabaret Voltaire, birthplace of Dada, in a kind of sacred awe that made room only for Blaga's mystical Pan. I knew less about Dada and what had gone on at Cabaret Voltaire than I knew about Pan's nymph chases, but the facts were not relevant. The spirit of the new, the sense of generational revolt, was alive and causing vast upheavals in me. I was not alone, of course. All sensitive souls, including those of people working part-time and with decreasing enthusiasm in upholding the status quo, like, possibly, my friend Adrian, were sensing the coming of an *esprit*. Naturally, we read French and grew up in Sibiu knowing German, and we had a lot of school Russian (though we tried not to speak it for reasons of self-esteem, which didn't keep out Yesenin or Mayakovsky), and there was something wafting from all those languages that was at times overwhelmingly close to how the world really was. Close, of course, because we had no access to most real texts but only to what we believed them to be. How this worked is still a mystery to me: I read poetry in all those languages, written as clearly as these letters on my Mac G4 notebook screen, but not on any known surface. I read them in my mind and out loud often. There were times after the Wednesday night workshop when a small group of poets, maybe two others besides Adrian and myself, went to the Butoiul de Aur (the Golden Barrel) to drink wine and compose spontaneously in languages we sort of knew. At the conclusion of these gatherings, I would fly home full of wine and smoke, and recite out loud whole books by writers known or unknown whose work I had never read.

Extraordinary changes were taking place in the world. The Communist Parties of the USSR and the Republic of China had quarreled, and their division was made starkly apparent to us by the publication without comment one day of both points of view, side by side, in the Romanian Communist Party's official organ, *Scînteia* (The Spark). The lack of commentary by the Romanian CP spoke volumes: the days of unthinking allegiance to the policies of the USSR were over and, presumably, so was the unquestioning allegiance to the doctrine of socialist realism imposed on us by Moscow. Already, young poets were appearing who were feeding openly from the more surreal springs of folklore and using language in ambiguous ways. The de rigueur optimism of the Stalinist era was receding, and veritable strains of despair were being heard, albeit still muffled. The first poet-hero of our generation appeared in the person and work of Nichita Stanescu, an icon of the sixties complete with phlegmatic cigarette and bohemian mien. Following Nichita, the floodgates were partially open and there was a surge of metaphor-wielding poets, driving an imagery so obscure it could only mean open revolt. Which it wasn't, but it seemed that way in the rosy-fingered freshness of adolescence in what promised to be—and ended up being—the most adolescent decade of the second half of the twentieth century. To be sixteen "with your hand in Pamela's pants," as my later, late, lamented poet-friend Jeff Miller put it, was the best of all possible worlds when Pamela was a whole country, one's own furious heart, and the very *esprit du temps*, a Cupid blowing into our sleepy sails. I'm borrowing here from the exalted store of parlance available suddenly to us, but the picture, at least in Sibiu, wasn't quite as encouraging.

News traveled slow to the provinces, and, while we heard the Beatles on Radio Free Europe (shades drawn, played at whisper-volume), the first foreign movie to really speak to us, *The Loneliness of the Long Distance Runner*, directed by Tony Richardson, an Angry Young Man, didn't play at the Pacea Cinema in Sibiu until the autumn of 1964. We reinvented and danced the twist (no real models) and imagined a lot of things: rock 'n' roll, marijuana, jazz, disaffected youth, and poetry. The imagination that conjured poets out of the air and "read" their books, every line visible to me, caused me to write poetry so strange I kept my notebook on me at all times and, when I lost it, seriously considered suicide. I invented a poetics from whispers, fragments, hints, whatever seemed "modern," untainted by the stale clichés of stock proletcultist images. I don't think that the Romanian CP, after tentatively taking its nationalist stance, paid very close attention to poetry, though I might be wrong. It's clear now that, once the decision was taken, Adrian and the rarefied censor class turned instinctively to the prewar right because that's where the modern language of nationalism had been hatched. There were also Transylvanian issues, local ones, which had to do with the "purity" of the language and, by extension, that of the "race," notions which had circulated freely at these Carpathian altitudes, fed no doubt by medieval spirits still in Jew-hunting motion. "Anti-Semitism" was still a dirty word because the Communists forbade its expression, but it was all around me, and I had been privy to it since I'd become conscious of other people. It never occurred to me that the poetry I absorbed like a sponge might contain the germs of an ideology that intended my extermination.

After Stoie went back to Cluj, we locked ourselves in Adrian's room and read "Howl." When the dictatorship fell in 1989, it was said that half the country spied on the other half. What wasn't said was that the half that spied also had an obligation to interpret and discover exactly what was seditious about what was being read or said, and then had to reproduce the matter in simple and penalizable language. That was a much harder job. All I had to do was read and interpret. We didn't count on an experience that was beyond such concerns. "Howl" broke us both into pieces, and when we put ourselves back together, we were no longer the same. It was so, even though our understanding of what was being said was, in some instances, wrong. We were swept away by a force that burned through and beyond and above and below the words. Here was the new itself, moving in like a wave and sweeping away everything in its swell.

There was no way to translate into the Romanian language of 1963 the correct meaning of:

I saw the best minds of my generation destroyed by madness, starving
   hysterical naked,
dragging themselves through the negro streets at dawn looking for an
   angry fix,
angelheaded hipsters.

We knew about the destruction of "the best minds" of our country, though our generation was about to refuse (I hoped) the same fate; we knew about starving; I knew about hysteria (my mother's), about being out of your mind at dawn after a night of drinking; we even knew that we were "fashionable angels" (or "Îngeri à la mode," as the translator rendered this, which is ridiculous), but we certainly didn't know about needing "an angry injection" ("o injectie mînioasă," which brought to mind a stabbing), and "the negro streets" were an abstraction, unless we thought of them as those sinister streets pictured in our propaganda books, where black men and women in rags slouched in doorways with despair on their faces. We wouldn't have been wrong to think of them that way, but our Manichaeistic reason forbade us to think that anything the Communists told us in school might be remotely true. There were many things, in fact, in Ginsberg's poem that were not alien at all in those terms: "who burned cigarette holes in their arms protesting the narcotic tobacco haze of Capitalism . . . who demanded sanity trials accusing the radio of hypnotism." These things take place under Capitalism, we were told. What didn't take place under either Communism or Capitalism, however, was the prophetic voice of the poet shouting his contempt at the Moloch of all repressive ideologies: "Moloch the incomprehensible prison! Moloch the crossbone soulless jailhouse and Congress of sorrows!" Furthermore, this was the same voice as that of Dada to which "Howl" paid its respects: "who threw potato salad at CCNY lecturers on Dadaism." Clearly, we could no longer simply write obscure verses and hope that the masses would be illuminated by sudden understanding of our metaphors. We had to act as well as write.

I was convinced of this and heading for trouble. Our first reaction after reading "Howl," a poem I would reread throughout my life, returning to it at moments of doubt the way I return also to the early songs of Bob Dylan, such as "Masters of War," was one of self-defense. Adrian said he thought that Ginsberg lamented, and that "Howl" was in the epic tradition of Whitman's "Song of Myself," Nazim Hikmet's prison poems, Saint-John Perse's "Anabasis," and Mayakovsky's "Cloud in Trousers," but no greater than those and, unlike those, too uncompromising and bleak. Poetry in the epic and prophetic mode was admirable, but it wasn't native to our Romanian soil, a much denser, lyrical substance. I said I thought that Ginsberg celebrated even as he lamented. What I didn't say was that I had become instantly infected by an irresistible appetite for freedom, that I wanted to be epically, infamously bad, that I wanted to test the limits of my mind and the far reaches of liberty, that . . . I wanted to become American. I wanted to leave Sibiu that very minute to reach New York by morning. I was filled by disgust at the small and fearful world I inhabited, and I wanted to howl myself. Thus began what in two years was my leaving Romania and immigration to the U.S. There were other factors, of course, but "Howl" was there, primal, a sacred text. As it turned out, the poem made its way through the light-starved minds of my generation in all the countries of the so-called Eastern Bloc and was instrumental, along with Bob Dylan, rock 'n' roll, and abstract art, in toppling the rotten house of cards from within long before Reagan boasted of bankrupting the system with his arms race. After "Howl" did its work on the young, there was nothing to do but dismantle the armies. The fact that it took another quarter of a century is proof to the power of inertia and to the willingness, of course, of Soviet troops from the far reaches of the East to shed blood. "Howl" had not yet been translated into Kirghiz or Tajik.

On the surface, "Howl" became a matter of debate between myself and Adrian, connected with everything American, which was synonymous with everything modern and, for me, everything worth experiencing. We had a bet going on Coca-Cola, for instance: it was being served at a fancy hotel for foreigners in the capital. I thought it was alcoholic, Adrian didn't. We took the train there, spent all our money on Coke, and I got drunk, Adrian didn't. We debated whether American readers thought that Ginsberg celebrated or lamented. Did Ginsberg himself know? It was an idiotic question, and later I actually thought about asking Allen if he knew what he'd unleashed in "Howl," but by then, in 1967 in New York, the question seemed impertinent, irelevant. "Howl" had gone from being the subject of an argument between two young Romanian provincials five years before to being an attitude, a monument, a fact of life, beyond good and evil, beyond Ginsberg. It just *was*.

After leaving Romania in 1965 and spending some time in transit in Italy waiting for a visa, I made a beeline for Allen's apartment in New York in 1967. I presented myself as "the ambassador of poetry from the East," in French, a claim that made Allen smile. He was on his way to India for another of his vastly epic enterprises having to do with the spiritual well-being of the world, so we didn't talk long that time. I had his address from a hippie who'd given it to me on the Spanish Steps in Rome. I sat on the steps day after day writing, trying to conjure a voice that would be as powerful and undeniable as the one that had possessed all the poets I admired, including Ginsberg. I was aware that John Keats had lived in the house on my left and that I was called to an art that had high demands. At midcentury, in the twentieth century, something had given way, something vast was collapsing into the underworld, and a whole generation was doing its best to stay up until dawn hysterical and naked, and I was ready. In my first autobiography, written at the age of twenty-three and titled modestly *The Life and Times of an Involuntary Genius,*★ I tell the full story of meeting Allen Ginsberg, but this is the first time I've gone back to that first shock of reading "Howl" in Romanian, in a world that no longer exists, thanks in part to the effect that poem had on our minds. Right now, I'm interested in studying the Tristan Tzara moment, another crucial passage of the twentieth century, during the First World War, a moment like that in 1855 when Melville's "violet-hued force" escaped from its prison at the ragged core of the universe and opened a young man's heart to pour itself into the world. Allen called the crater a "diamond sutra."

★*The Life and Times of an Involuntary Genius* (New York: George Braziller, 1975). Reprinted with another memoir in *An Involuntary Genius in America's Shoes* (Santa Rosa, Calif.: Black Sparrow Press, 2001).

Your "Howl" for Carl Solomon is very powerful, but I don't want it arbitrarily negated by secondary recommendations made in time's reconsidering backstep—I want your Lingual Spontaneity or Nothing.
—Jack Kerouac, letter to Allen Ginsberg, August 19, 1955

"Howl" is a wild, volcanic, troubled, extravagant, turbulent, boisterous, unbridled outpouring, intermingling gems and flashes of picturesque insight with slag and debris of scoriac matter. It has violence; it has life; it has vitality. In my opinion, it is a one-side neurotic view of life; it has not enough glad, Whitmanian affirmations.
—Louis Ginsberg, letter to Allen Ginsberg, May 27, 1956

It is a howl of defeat. Not defeat at all for he has gone through defeat as if it were an ordinary experience, a trivial experience ... This poet sees through all the horrors he partakes of in the very intimate details of his poem. He avoids nothing but experiences it to the hilt. He contains it. Claims it as his own—and, we believe, laughs at it and has the time and affrontery to love a fellow of his choice and record that love in a well-made poem. Hold back the edges of your gowns, Ladies, we are going through hell.
—William Carlos Williams, Introduction to
Howl and Other Poems, October 1956

"Howl" is the most significant single long poem to be published in this country since World War II, perhaps since Eliot's *Four Quartets* ... "Howl" commits many poetic sins, but it was time.
—Lawrence Ferlinghetti, "Horn on Howl,"
Evergreen Review, Winter 1957

We have had smoking attacks on the civilization before, ironic or murderous or suicidal. We have not had this particular variety of anguished anathema-hurling in which the poet's revulsion is expressed with the single-minded frenzy of a raving madwoman . . . He has brought a terrible psychological reality to the surface with enough originality to blast American verse a hairsbreadth forward in the process.

—M. L. Rosenthal, "Review of Howl and Other Poems,"
The Nation, February 23, 1957

"Howl" proclaims, in a hopped up and improvised tone, that nothing seems to be worth saying save in a hopped up and improvised tone.

—John Hollander, *Partisan Review*, Spring 1957

I do not believe that "Howl" is without even the slightest redeeming social importance. The first part of "Howl" presents a picture of a nightmare world; the second part is an indictment of those elements in modern society destructive of the best qualities of human nature; such elements are predominantly identified as materialism, conformity, and mechanization leading toward war. The third part presents a picture of an individual who is a specific representation of what the author conceives as a general condition. "Footnote to Howl" seems to be a declamation that everything in the world is holy, including parts of the body by name. It ends in a plea for holy living. In considering material claimed to be obscene it is well to remember the motto: *Honi soit qui mal y pense* (Evil to him who thinks evil).   —Judge Clayton Horn, judgment, October 3, 1957

RICK MOODY

ON THE GRANITE STEPS OF
THE MADHOUSE WITH SHAVEN HEADS

———

Back in Providence, where I went to college, there were a lot of punk rock townies. The east side of Providence was their neighborhood of choice, and the epicenter of the collegiate east side was the wall in front of the Hospital Trust Bank. It was a low, comfortable wall, as walls go, perfect for long-term vagrancy. Seems like there's always a spot like this within the magnetic field of a college campus, a spot where the campus delights in displaying castoffs. There's Telegraph Ave., e.g., with its community of panhandlers. There are the dangerous sections of New Haven that lie just beyond the Yale campus. There is the old anarchist East Village, into which NYU inexorably stretches itself. Education can't be perfect, after all. Or maybe it's just that education, if it's doing its job, also includes its obverse.

One day on the Hospital Trust wall, I got into a vigorous back-and-forth with some evangelical guys. They had that wide-eyed look of evangelicals, that certainty. In fact, this was their one unmistakable feature. Otherwise they were dressed like anyone on the east side. In the company of these evangelicals, I was watching the better-equipped, more stable members of the student body amble past, the kids who had pennants mounted on their dorm room walls or shot glasses lining their windowsills. Eventually, one of the Jesus freaks turned to me. *Do you ever have one of those nights when you just feel as though you've given up all hope?*

Well, one of the reasons I hung around on the Hospital Trust wall was that I had lots of these nights. I was, if not *starving*, certainly *hysterical*, as on that evening not long before when the Quaaludes were getting in the way of my food service job. (I was briefly contracted to serve healthy items at one of the snack bars on campus.) The high point of that shift was tossing falafel balls into the boiling oil, where they were meant to be gently immersed, so that this oil then speckled the unprotected flesh of my forearm, instantly raising dangerous burns and blisters, to which I, in my heavily sedated condition, paid little mind. To the next patron in line, his or her mouth agape, I slurred the words *Anything else?*

The evangelical guy was trying to pick this scab. He knew there was a switch in me somewhere, a way to get me to come around, because I had *broke down crying in white gymnasiums naked and trembling before the machinery of other skeletons*. It did me no good that I didn't yet know the line from Ginsberg.

In my recollection, which isn't entirely reliable, one of the Hospital Trust regulars in attendance that day was a guy I'll call Mike Velocity, even though that wasn't his first name, nor was it his cool punk rock last name (he really had one). Mike Velocity carried around a briefcase, though he otherwise looked quite radical and punk rock with his spiky hair and his black jeans. In his briefcase, he said, were his poems. He was, it was said, one of the Briefcase Poets of Providence. There were a few others who apparently followed his example, and if you were on the wall at the Hospital Trust Bank, Mike Velocity would tell you about his poems and how it was a hard, coarse thing, this life. Mike had seen it all. Mike was a survivor—as were the other Briefcase Poets. And you, if you were a college student from up the block, were not.

This was the gray dawn of the Reagan inauguration. Maybe the hangover from election night was fresh. What we were doing that night was drinking and drinking and drinking some more, getting steadily more depressed about the moronic state of affairs. Like proper idealists (the moment, at least for me, had its share of idealism), we decided that there was no way we were going to let this thing stand, this election. It was arguably the end of the period in which you could say that there was a political vibe to the campus. We had the antinuke demonstrations, we had the antidraft-registration demonstrations, we had the pro-disinvestment demonstrations, we had the disruption of the Olin Lecture Series. People were pretty outraged about Reagan. So we piled into a little, beat-up four-door—there were maybe six or seven of us in this tiny little sedan—driven by an incredibly mercurial guy called Jody. Jody, who had been known to go into his bedroom and not come out for weeks (definitely one of those cowering *in unshaven rooms in underwear, burning their money in wastebaskets and listening to the Terror through the wall*). Jody, the guy who would emerge only to piss and get a bag of chips. Jody, who nonetheless had a smile that seemed to suggest an inexhaustible comprehension of the infinite. Jody was driving, and we were heading for Reagan headquarters, in the Biltmore Hotel of Providence, and we were going to crash the Reagan celebration, and we were going to tell the rich plutocrats in their motherfucking penguin suits what was what. Except that instead of crashing the party we crashed Jody's car. Sweet, mercurial Jody ran the red light on the hill by RISD, a very dangerous corner where many cars had no doubt been accordioned over the years. A car plowed into the center of ours, and I remember crying out, "We're going to . . . !" The perfect inaugural moment.

The car coming at us couldn't have been going more than twenty-five or thirty, and luckily no one was hurt; but we all got gingerly out of the car and skulked away, because we'd been drinking, and the cops were bound to turn up. I don't know who stayed with Jody. It was one of those things. We didn't wait around for the Man.

So: the Reagan years, with Mike Velocity holding forth on the wall of the Hospital Trust Bank, advancing his theories of the One True Poetry. What Mike Velocity was telling us, in the course of advancing his theories, was that Allen Ginsberg had tried to fuck him one time. He'd been at a reading of Ginsberg's and Allen had picked *him* out in the audience. Allen Ginsberg recognized, according to Mike Velocity, that Mike the Briefcase Poet was possessed of the one true poetic spark, the Gnostic comprehension of the true Buddha madness, and, Mike said, Allen had believed that the proper thing to do was to possess Mike Velocity carnally, to taste his delights.

Sounds a little like chicken-hawk-type activity, like it might have been *wild cooking pederasty and intoxication*, at least from this lofty vantage point of hindsight. I remember many years later having dinner with an august and *important* novelist, hero of mine, and this *important* novelist spent some of dinner railing against Ginsberg's poems about *alcohol and cock and endless balls*. I thought his point of view was curmudgeonly. I still would. So, actually, I didn't really think Mike Velocity's story was a chicken-hawk-type of thing, back on the Hospital Trust wall. Or maybe I just didn't give a shit. It was Mike's decision. He was a consenting adult, or very nearly so. Even though I was primarily a heterosexual example of the American college student, and even though Mike Velocity was primarily a heterosexual example of a badass punk rock townie (he kept hitting on a woman I liked), I had no trouble believing that Mike had been propositioned by Allen Ginsberg. In fact, it was possible that Mike actually *did* spend the night with Allen Ginsberg and just wasn't telling us because he wanted to preserve his badass punk rock reputation. He could also have made the whole thing up.

Poetry first, poetry above all, according to the Briefcase Poets. Questions about whether or not a seventeen- or eighteen-year-old street kid should be the lover of a fifty-four- or fifty-five-year-old poetry legend were secondary.

I didn't know much about Ginsberg. My own progress through the Beats started back a little bit. With the hippies. That was where I came into the story. The hippies were my older sister's friends. Maybe this is where the punk subculture of the seventies and eighties got its start, anyhow, in opposition to late sixties counterculture—the peace, love, and understanding that collapsed at Altamont or in 1974 or 1975, or whenever it collapsed. Punk was hippie ethics with torn fishnets and shorter hair and violent antipathies. Still, when I was a freshman in high school, I'd read *On the Road*, by Jack Kerouac, *new Buddha of American prose*, and like a couple of other books that I tackled back then, it taught me important things about American literature, like that you didn't need to have Big Mama Story dragging you along all the time. You could write with your feelings as your compass. Accuracy about your human emotions was material enough. Also, *On the Road* made jazz lovable to a white kid from the suburbs, and it started me thinking more about the virtues of spontaneity. These were not things that I had immediately learned from Kurt Vonnegut and Richard Brautigan and the pulpy science-fiction-type stuff that I consumed voraciously about the same time.

What Kerouac did, when you read him in the context of the seventies, was make clear that there were connections between the renegade cultural movements of the postwar decades. You had a sense that the jazz of the fifties, the bop that Kerouac loved, and the raps of Dean Moriarty led directly to the hippie ethos of the sixties. In fact, we knew this much, because we knew that Neal Cassady (another "Howl" dedicatee), a.k.a. Moriarty, had driven Further, the famous Day-Glo schoolbus of Ken Kesey and the Merry Pranksters, up and down the West Coast, to the early gigs of the Grateful Dead. We may have hated the Grateful Dead (this was among our most violent antipathies, although that didn't stop me from seeing them play a couple times), we may have thrown away, or at least hidden for many years, our Grateful Dead LPs, but we recognized that they represented one tangent of libertarian anti-authoritative counterculture, a counterculture that Kerouac, in his mad driving sprees with Cassady, partly sired.

Wasn't long after I got to college that I undertook my introduction to another of the great pillars of the Beat period, William Seward Burroughs, third dedicatee of "Howl," at the behest of my fiction-writing teacher, Angela Carter. She was responding, I figure, to my general bad attitude. According to her instructions, I went and fetched out *Naked Lunch* and *The Wild Boys* from the Rockefeller Library.*

The effect of Burroughs was different from that of Kerouac. Burroughs didn't depend on a Romantic-era methodology, at least not at first blush. With Kerouac, the prose wasn't perfect, but that was a matter of indifference. The belief system was perfect. The method actualized the belief system, which actualized the prose, and the name of this method was *instantaneity*, the recognition that what was conveyed instantly was, if not perfect, then at least *true*. First thought, best thought. What was instantaneous was somehow a riposte to the stylized, uptight fiction happening in more mainstream precincts, and there was something that I hated about that well-crafted mainstream naturalism, or at least distrusted, and Kerouac made the differences plain.

*We also read, in her class, "Why I Want to Fuck Ronald Reagan," by J. G. Ballard.

But with Burroughs it was all about the routine. With Burroughs, you could start the book anywhere. You didn't have to begin at the beginning (although the crime fiction parody that opens *Naked Lunch* is pretty great), and you didn't have to read through to the end. You could read the talking asshole routine, or the passage where the young man about to get hanged spontaneously develops an erection, etc., etc. Burroughs was like tarot cards or the *I Ching*. Wherever you landed said something about who you were and what you were after. Of course, Ginsberg is supposed to have arranged the pieces of *Naked Lunch*, or at least in one account. Maybe the structural smarts, such as they are, are all his. Anyway, Burroughs was hugely popular among the punk rock kids. He was a "lapsed idealist," as Mary McCarthy said, and this was probably what we liked about him. Burroughs's biomorphic horror seemed a perfect antidote to the feel-good sexuality of the hippies, even if this horror was at the same time consonant with any ongoing countercultural assault on bourgeois Americana.

But I had this resistance to poetry. Up till then, this resistance kept me from a trifecta in my esteem for the Beat Attitude. What I hated about poetry was Robert Frost. I hated having to memorize all that Frost in high school, and as far as I was concerned, Frost and his perfect rhythms and his nature scenes had nothing to say to me. Fuck Robert Frost. Fuck stopping in woods on a snowy evening. I hated Robert Frost. I hated bucolic imagery. I hated the reverence for nature, because what was nature anyhow but subdivisions in the suburbs and malls and nuclear power plants and petrochemical everything. On my own, I couldn't really afford to go anywhere untouched by man's pestilence. Fuck nature imagery. Fuck the sober and self-serious accounts of autumn leaves drifting lazily in a creek. I hated counting syllables in a line, because I knew from rock and roll that you could fit twice that many in if you needed to. Fuck meter. And there was no real reason to rhyme either. There'd been a resistance to rhyming in lots of the records I liked in those days. There wasn't much rhyming in *Remain in Light* by the Talking Heads, and there weren't too many rhymes on *Rocket to Russia*, or *Heroes* by David Bowie, which even employed the cut-up technique that Burroughs favored. Gang of Four rarely bothered with rhyming. Fuck rhyming, fuck meter, fuck nature imagery, fuck Robert Frost, fuck poetry. And fuck classical allusions, too. I didn't give a shit if I read another classical allusion in my life. It never impressed me when Ariadne or Poseidon or Cerberus appeared in a poem.

These aesthetic views were pretty consistent with those of my fellow would-be writers there on the Hospital Trust wall. I took a course in Dante in translation with one of my fellow loiterers, and we were in it mainly because we liked the imagination that dreamed up all those *punishments*—eyes stitched shut, suicides imprisoned in thorny trees. I took a class in *Paradise Lost*, too, and for one reason only: I liked Satan. Poetry, as conceived by the Briefcase Poets (and I say this despite the fact that Mike Velocity never actually showed me any of his poems—it's possible that his briefcase was entirely empty), should be written in the language of the *people*, and it should be comprehensible by the *people,* and this was, of course, a set of poetic principles that came, in part, from Walt Whitman. These principles were then amplified and expanded in William Carlos Williams, and they then rose to their zenith in the poem we have before us today, the epic in the language of the people, "Howl."

I was playing a lot of music at the time. I had a band called the Null Set, with my friend Jim Lewis, who later wrote *Sister, Why the Tree Loves the Ax*, and other stuff. After several months of rehearsal, I was ejected from our first gig for losing my voice, putting my fist through the tambourine, and bleeding all over everything. But this was not, in truth, a failure. I liked the idea that the band would break up after one gig. It was possible that I had said everything I needed to say in the rock band format. Anyway, at that same time I was learning how to improvise on the piano. I didn't really have any brilliant harmonic ideas yet. I stuck to the obvious majors and relative minors. But I could make my way around a rock-inflected improvisation. At a certain bar on campus, I played two or three times, noodling around while people drank or played Asteroids.

One night Jim came along to hear me playing. Something sent him hustling back to his room for his copy of "Howl." What he did, of course, was to read the poem aloud while I played. If you have never read "Howl" aloud, you have a treat in store, because the rhythms of the poem are so close to spoken rhythms that it really *needs* to be read aloud. I was lucky, because I was hearing "Howl" for the first time, and it wasn't until this moment of the completion of my Beat trifecta that I began to understand what the whole thing was about. I mean, I was trying to play at the same time, and I had my doubts that I was going to be able to play along with him as he read twenty pages of poetry. I wasn't sure we weren't going to drive a lot of people out of the campus bar. Still, it was a turning point, because this poetry didn't sound like the emotionally fraudulent, artificially constructed bullshit Robert Frost poetry, it had an epic cry, in its *vast sordid movies*, its *gyzym of consciousness*, its *romance of the streets*. Maybe I'd been wrong about poetry all along!

Jim had one of those little City Lights Pocket Poets copies, of which there are now apparently 915,000 in print. Take that, you *fairies of advertising* and you *sinister intelligent editors*! I'm pretty sure that our improvisational experiment dissolved in laughter and consternation and more beers, but the seed was sown. What I noticed about "Howl" pretty quick was the anaphora. It was a trick of Whitman, and it was a trick as old as poetry itself (Horace said that "things repeated are pleasing"), but to ears raised on the way

Johnny Ramone played barre chords—the same way every time in every song—or the way Steve Reich and Terry Riley repeated melodic phrases in the minimalist compositions of the period, the anaphora of "Howl" was unmistakably seductive and beautiful. The dependent clauses spliced together, beginning with "who" in the first section, there's something elegiac and impulsive about it all, as if the *angelheaded hipsters* cannot quite be pinned down, as if there's always more to say on the subject; the list can be expanded infinitely, and I liked this idea, like those Coltrane solos where he just couldn't figure out how to stop. I liked that the grammar of some of these Ginsberg phrases was almost impossible to parse, as in *who poverty and tatters and hollow-eyed and high sat up smoking in the supernatural darkness of cold-water flats floating across the tops of cities contemplating jazz.* This bit is meant to modify *angelheaded hipsters burning for the ancient heavenly connection to the dynamo in the machinery of night*, but it's difficult to figure out how to make it read smoothly, well, if smooth is what you're going for, if you're the traditional English department grammarian. "Hollow-eyed" and "high" are both adjectives, after all, but "poverty" and "tatters" are both nouns. Who cares! I didn't care! I liked it how it was! Because "tatters," "sat," and "flat" created an internal assonance, and because anyone who had sat up late high knew that it *did* feel as though you were floating above the city. If we were more obsessed with Patti Smith than with Sonny Rollins, if we were using Patti Smith metaphors, or Tom Verlaine metaphors, they weren't inappropriate in the context of the Beats, since Patti was pals with Burroughs, of course, and later recorded a free-wheeling reinterpretation of the "Footnote to Howl," which was just as beautiful as the poem itself, just as seductive. *The world is holy! The soul is holy! The skin is holy! The nose is holy! The tongue and cock and hand and asshole holy!*

And maybe it bears saying something about the Ginsbergian allusions to, you know, the alternate lifestyles in "Howl" (*who let themselves be fucked in the ass by saintly motorcyclists, and screamed with joy)*, from the point of view of those bygone days, which suddenly seem unaccountably distant in the Fundamentalist Now. The poem's allusions to mostly undepicted sexual practices are, natch, part of a larger iconography of gay male experience that undergirds the poem. But allow me the additional context of the punk rock years: This process of transubstantiation, through which what was perhaps considered *unspeakable* or *unclean* in straight America became the *most* beautiful, was like unto the desire, on the part of the badass punk rock townies, and on the part of the fellow travelers, to frequent dilapidated industrial spaces, to love the homely among our compatriots, to wear the plaids of the Salvation Army bins, to desire everything neglected or spurned or forgotten. One of my favorite activities used to be to drive over the industrial wharf of Providence, a really grim, smoky place full of tankers loading and off-loading and generators generating, semis pulling in with their unlabeled freight. No one bothered you over there, and the disconsolation of the reeds and grasses and ailanthus trees springing up everywhere was somehow powerful. If we were stuck with the cast-off, as indeed we were, we needed to find a way to love it and affirm it, to see that what we were stuck with was holy and worthy.

Ass-fucking in Ginsberg, in "Howl," was (and is) *holy* precisely because it has existed in Western culture as long as there has been Western culture. Its repression was an attempt to repress part of the story, and of this the author of "Howl" would have no part. In a similar way, in the Moloch section of "Howl," the alien qualities of advanced capitalism and enterprise are, despite their horrors, still to be seen as part and parcel of human imagination—*Moloch whose love is endless oil and stone! Moloch whose soul is electricity and banks! Moloch whose poverty is the specter of genius! Moloch whose fate is a cloud of sexless hydrogen! Moloch whose name is the Mind!*—so that humankind and nature are continuous and not so easily divided into the either-or dichotomies so favored by American literalists: all you guys over there are *not* real humans! We are! This contrary celebration of *all* the works of man in "Howl" was not unlike another popular writer of the period, popular among acquaintances of mine, namely the inexhaustible Marquis de Sade. The Grove hardcovers of *Philosophy in the Bedroom, Justine,* and *The 120 Days of Sodom* were being passed back and forth right then, and Sade makes an argument about sexuality not at all unlike that to be found in "Howl." Sex is love is a field is a dichotomy is innumerable ideas and positions available to anyone who might inhabit them, such that Mike Velocity might one day tryst with Ginsberg and the next day chase after the girl I had the crush on, and he might do these things among myriad possibilities, *for me to miss one would seem to be groundless.*

Beyond the admirable use of anaphora, "Howl," in both method and concerns, also managed to collapse some of the distinctions between prose and poetry. "Howl" thumbed its nose at any generic requirements or expectations, and in this way too I was totally into it. The one thing I was bad at, back then, was taking instruction. "Howl" didn't instruct, it sang, it celebrated, refusing to cooperate with ideas about what made prose prose and what made poetry poetry, and in it, therefore, a middle space could be exploited. If Ginsberg's lines had the swing, then they had *the thing*, and they did, and the semantic category into which we were meant to slot the poem was unimportant. (Or to put it another way: the right to pronounce categories was given back to the common reader, back to me and mine, as opposed to the academic poets and their critical apologists.) Other dichotomies—mad-sane, heavenly-earthly, male-female, Christian-Buddhist, heterosexual-homosexual, comic-tragic, high-low—got collapsed along the way too.

What's left? For good or ill, it's the human imagination and its faithfulness as a vessel for unpreconceived human experience: *with mother finally ******, and the last fantastic book flung out of the tenement window, and the last door closed at 4 A.M. and the last telephone slammed at the wall in reply and the last furnished room emptied down to the last piece of mental furniture, a yellow paper rose twisted on a wire hanger in the closet, and even that imaginary, nothing but a hopeful little bit of hallucination—*

I can't prove that I accepted these Beat lessons immediately. I can't deny that it was in the nature of youth to be skeptical of anything that had the veneer of respectability. And regardless of what Ginsberg did after "Howl"—helping to levitate the Pentagon, extolling the virtues of *wild cooking pederasty*, popularizing the harmonium—he had become a little bit respectable, in that "Howl" was already understood as a masterpiece (as was "Kaddish," another poem that became important to me). Sure, lots of academic types sneered about it, and still do, but by the time I got to "Howl," it was already twenty-five years old. Older than I was.

But maybe I can measure its effect, its eternal concordance with youth, in a tally, or a completely unscientific comparison of bad scrapes gotten into by this one "Howl" enthusiast. Mad? Starving? Hysterical? Naked? Poor? High? I stood outside the Store 24 waiting for my enamorata to get off her job selling pornography to the guys who came in every month and bought one of each. I lingered at the bottom of the downspout, trying to figure out how to climb the gutter to her room. I sat out on the edge of the railroad bridge, high on amphetamines, nattering on about philosophy and Brueghel and Bosch. I simulated fornication with my roommate in a production of Artaud. I sang ecstasies over Beckett and Derrida. I wrote reams of fiction that wasn't any good and wouldn't be for another ten years, if then. I scribbled song lyrics on napkins. I went to innumerable rock and roll shows. I slept with anyone who'd have me, just because. I drank and drank some more and searched out the mad ones, the ones *listening to the crack of doom on the hydrogen jukebox*. I laughed and wept and despaired and held off the evangelicals. I believed I'd never amount to anything. I was sure I was made for great things. I doubted I was made for anything good at all. Throughout it all, there was Mike Velocity on the wall in front of the Hospital Trust, mandarin, inscrutable, telling anyone who gave him enough time how the author of "Howl" had tried to pick him up, or that he'd spent the whole weekend drinking brandy and reading Ferlinghetti. Youth calls to youth! Did we identify with the Byronic excesses of the author of "Howl"? We hadn't done one thing, not one, he hadn't been compiling for us twenty-five years before!

The last way I can indicate how "Howl" was a great article of constitution of the punk rock years, part of a counterculture that stretched from the late fifties right up to when Kurt Cobain lay down on the floor with his shotgun—a counterculture manifestly in opposition to powers military and political, in opposition to tyranny and oligarchy—is to point out that the last good record of my college years, at least until the indie rock movement rehabilitated music seven or eight years later, was *Combat Rock*, by the Clash. One of the great songs on that album, "Ghetto Defendant," featured guest vocals by none other than—Allen Ginsberg! (*"Slamdance cosmopolis," "enlighten the populace," "hooked in metropolis"* . . . *"addicts & metropolis."*) He sounded great. Not dated in the least, laconic, funny, ominous. He snuck in passages about both Rimbaud and the Salvadoran death squads. And when asked about it later, Ginsberg said that the Clash had never paid him, but they did give him some really good hash.

Not long after I left Providence, Hospital Trust Bank tore down the wall.

SVEN BIRKERTS

NOT THEN, NOT NOW

———

I remember with that stunning focal resolution reserved for certain key events the exact moment—where we were sitting, what the light was like—when my high school girlfriend Lisa Petrides reached into her brown crocheted hippie bag and set out on the table between us a copy of Lawrence Ferlinghetti's *A Coney Island of the Mind*. It was the fall of 1968, and though City Lights Books had been around for a while, something about the occasion—probably it was my trust in Lisa's infallible discerning cool—blazed the idea of these books directly into my seventeen-year-old being. Picking up the slight, almost square little package, thumbing through it, I felt an immediate rush of covetousness. This same have-to-have feeling would a few years later deform into an almost indiscriminate acquisition mania, but back then it was still fresh and specific. I wanted that particular book—that shape, that cover, that sense it gave me that here was not a public property but an intimate artifact: a personal communiqué, an expression that had moved rapid-circuit out of the poet's brain and straight into my hand. A thing to have and keep, to hold as a shield.

Against what? Well, almost everything, though the situation

was not yet completely clear. Sitting across from each other that day in Alban's Delicatessen on Woodward Avenue, a few miles north of Detroit, Lisa and I were two disaffected teenagers tee-tering on a brink, very much aware of ourselves as living in a culture where the flame has been lit and the heat has begun to build but with the rush of full combustion still pending. Or so it seems to me now in the retrofit of years later. What could we have known then—Lisa, me, and our like-minded friends, the ones who were just then resisting their parents about getting haircuts, about turning down the music, about wearing some-thing other than the same ragged-looking jeans?

1968. Fall. The aftershock of vibrations from the Chicago con-vention were still traveling outward, merging with the bass-line buzz of the Doors, Jefferson Airplane, and for us in Detroit, the shrill feedback leads of MC5's Wayne Kramer. The typography of posters in record shop windows, but also on the announce-ment boards at school, was just starting to pick up that Avalon Ballroom acidhead look, bubbled letters melting together and peace-sign insignias filling all available white space with a kind of manic insistence that art history professors would later call "fear of the void." Of course, not a school assembly now went by without some self-anointed agitator standing up to question this or that hitherto sacred protocol. And after hours and at night in out-of-the-way gathering places, marijuana was quickly moving from rumor to verifiable possession, those first seed-heavy joints popping in their papers as we passed them back and forth down to the gluey roach.

But still we were waiting, unsure of what for, living in the "not quite yet," but never doubting that something very big was on the way. Critical mass. Who can say when it arrives or what combination of things finally allows one big panel of private or public stage scenery to be replaced by another? Was there a moment? If there was, I can't pinpoint it. But I do know that between the fall of 1968, when so much was still in active suspension, and the summer of 1969, which culminated, of course, in the Woodstock explosion, a huge, pervasive shift took place. I mean at the deep-down level—a change in the look and feel of things. It was as if Time, momentarily personified, had shaken its newly ringleted head and, taking a deep breath of deliberation, abruptly turned in a new direction. People talk about things being "in the air," and cliché be damned, that was how it felt. The light was brighter, more transparent, and the face and façade of things was somehow less locked in place. A projection? Of course it was, but what power such projections have when we don't know that that's what they are, and when all around us people are having the same experience, what the writer Blaise Cendrars once called "congenital hallucination."

Into this new felt and projected reality, this unforeseen world-in-the-making, arrived the City Lights booklet of Allen Ginsberg's "Howl," with its bold black lettering on simple white, and its dedication to "Jack Kerouac, new Buddha of American prose." The edition had been around for a time—I may have even seen or handled it, I don't remember. But this is the thing about connection and influence—it happens when it needs to, when the moment of Shakespearean ripeness has been reached. Oddly, I now have to confess that I don't recall the where and when of my first encounter, only the how and the what—the fact that a few lines of prosy poetry straightaway burned off much of the acreage of what had been there before, nullified it almost instantly. A whole worldview of easy alienation and disaffection, all those moody protagonists of the books I'd been reading, by Thomas Wolfe, William Goldman, C. D. B. Bryan, the Benjamin Braddock consciousness of Mike Nichols's *The Graduate*—all this practiced disaffection fell away before the blade of this new upped-ante assault. The opening lines did to the mind precisely what those first revolutionary guitar solos of Jimi Hendrix did to the pent-up and armored physical body of this teenage boy. They broke everything wide open.

I saw the best minds of my generation destroyed by madness, starving
    hysterical naked,
dragging themselves through the negro streets at dawn looking for an
    angry fix.

Can I possibly convey how those words moved in me, how that cadence undid in a minute's time whatever prior cadences had been voice-tracking my life? "Starving hysterical naked"—no commas, no pausing for qualification, no nod to the gram-marian (who by that feint quickly became a figure of the opposition), just that forward-march compression, that Boschian tangle of limbs, and the completely urban jolt. I'd known noth-ing like it in my leafy neighborhood, but the sensation now trumped everything, those "negro streets" pulling the white boy like rap pulls other white boys now, coding a whole panorama of the "real" before which nothing in my life could hold a plea. That was part of it right there, the deficit of the actual driving me, driving us all—we had built up such a backdraft of the un-expressed that it took only the lit match of "negro" or "tene-ment" touched to the right place.

I read just a little bit, a page or two, that first day, and then I had to close the book. The voltage was actually too great. This was something I would have to move up to slowly. But at first encounter it was enough to know that I owned it, that it fit in my pocket.

———

Allen Ginsberg. It's hard now to peel back the images, like decals pasted one over the other, to get back to the first shock of the man. Ginsberg before the diminishing impacts of the later books, before the lotus position and the bells and the chanting, when he was still a dangerous Beat guru, bearded and druggy, the plausible source of those lines that stripped the whitewash from my whitewashed world. The Ginsberg I postered on my dorm-room wall as soon as I got to Ann Arbor that next fall, wearing the mockery of his Uncle Sam hat on his Rasputin hair—as if no further word needed be said about where I stood.

And so it happened that "Howl," that mighty excrescence, came to me not as a poem—certainly not as a poem I read and knew start to finish—but rather as a series of bulletins. The lines arrived filtered through the image and subversive authority of their mysterious maker. I was avid for the Word, looking for the real and incendiary. I'd been searching for a sign in all the shadowy commotion of the new culture, with its heroic outcasts, its music, its ideology of wandering, its jagged us-them shadow play, its push for ecstatic connection, and it was suddenly there, distilled, in a booklet that was not much bigger than a passport.

The distillation was the thing, the supercharged chanting lines with their clustered telegraphing phrases that took no work of memorizing: "the starry dynamo in the machinery of night," "the supernatural darkness of cold-water flats," the hipsters "who got busted in their pubic beards," who "sank all night in submarine light of Bickford's . . . listening to the crack of doom on the hydrogen jukebox," who "vanished into nowhere Zen New Jersey," and who "lit cigarettes in boxcars boxcars boxcars racketing through snow toward lonesome farms in grandfather night" and "disappeared into the volcanoes of Mexico leaving behind nothing but the shadow of dungarees and the lava and ash of poetry scattered in fireplace Chicago."

It's hard to stop quoting, a fact that testifies like nothing else to what I'm talking about here, which is the phrase quotability that was the thing, over and above reading the work as a poem, an entity conceived and structured and developed according to any lyric plan. Indeed, for me Ginsberg's phrase brilliance at every point undermined my taking in the work with any larger poetic directionality. I jumped back and forth through the lines, flashing with every corroboration of my fantasies. Here was the jumbled headlong existence I'd first found in Kerouac, but raised to a pitch now, administered directly, its energy over and over shorting out the circuit pattern of lines in sequence. The characters were stripped of particularity and fired up into archetype, those angel-headed hipsters a kind of mantra of collective possibility, their dooms and ecstasies the amplification of everything I was feeling, never mind that I was a product of suburban privilege with no knowledge at all of cold-water flats or endless boxcars. Such is the combustion of image and emotional avarice, and such is the power of the projective imagination. I was planning my life around that little book, merging my unknown future into Ginsberg's phantasmagoria. And in a very real way, every experience I then launched myself toward, every edgy test I administered to myself—all the hitchhiking to unknown cities and courting of exhaustion, the eager attack on drugs and drink—so much could be traced to those few hundred lines. That was my template America, laid down and very soon echoing back through the surrealism of Bob Dylan, my other master, the two twining together so intimately at times that I was not surprised at all to see Ginsberg pop up in the background of D. A. Pennebaker's Dylan documentary, *Don't Look Back*.

I want to extend the kinship here, using it to try to clarify how it was that I knew the poem less as a poem and more as an extended dreamscape, for I connected to "Howl" very much in the way that just a few years later I would connect to Dylan's magnificent ballad "Sad-Eyed Lady of the Lowlands." "Howl" was an experiential panorama, the more evocative and compelling for not being in any sense linear. Poem and ballad were both hypnagogic in their reiteration, their stacking of vivid predicates around a simple, if enigmatic, subject. It was not an argument or development one followed so much as a procession of images—"with your mercury mouth in the missionary times," "with your sheet-metal memory of Cannery Row, / and your magazine-husband who one day just had to go," "and your cowboy mouth." And, as with Dylan, I needed only to know that it was a cloud of adoration and loss I moved inside, so with "Howl" it mattered to me only that here, at last, was the true wounded soul of America erupting, crying out—everything banished by the right-thinking functionary, by Dylan's Mr. Jones.

Among the many things that are now so hard to call back, the mood—the atmosphere—of those times is the hardest, for to get this one has to reexperience the feelings themselves. And to reach these, one has to get in past hindsight, past the subsequent narrative that is shaped at every turn by the knowledge of turns taken, corrections administered, outcomes achieved. The counterculture project, or whatever we choose to call it, went belly-up. Excess exacted cost, libertarian folk economies imploded, and political and corporate venality prevailed. Who knew? There is no innocent way to reconstruct the impact of "Howl," for the poem came to us in the before moment.

Ginsberg's scenarios of destitution, desperation, and insanity were unambiguous. These were, don't forget, "minds destroyed," tormented beings "who broke down crying in white gymnasiums naked." And trembling before the machinery of other skeletons, "who bit detectives in the neck and shrieked with delight in policecars for committing no crime but their own wild cooking pederasty and intoxication."

But my ear heard first the cadenced energy, the thrust, and

my untutored romantic imagination translated this obvious tor-
ment into excitement and possibility, as if these writhings were
just the birth pangs of visionary arrival, as if all these scenarios
were achieving apotheosis in our historical now, finding release
and redemption in the youth movement I saw exploding all
around me. Shameful as it is to admit, I glamorized the psychosis
Ginsberg was chanting in his lines. I believed in the simple—
preposterous—idea that desperation was the royal road to exalta-
tion. The excess, the pushing past, and then the attainment. Of
what? Well, of "Mohammedan angels staggering on tenement
roofs illuminated," of "incomparable blind streets of shuddering
cloud and lightning in the mind leaping toward poles of Canada
& Paterson, illuminating all the motionless world of Time be-
tween," of "whole intellects disgorged in total recall for seven
days and nights with brilliant eyes."

There was much evidence in "Howl" of transcendent con-
sciousness, what in later, gentler Zen days became satori. And
for an interval, a few years, it seemed the end of all journeying,
the one way out.

More than three decades have passed since that original injec-
tion was administered, three decades that have seen the fantasy of
that transformation come to nothing. I don't pretend to under-
stand how that impulse toward visionary completion, that Aquar-
ian thrust that was for a short time undeniably there, just fizzled.
That it did argues for its essential anomalousness, almost as if it
had been, if only in a metaphoric collective sense, one of those
evolutionary accidents, one that did not "select." But that sounds
fuzzy and grandiose, and doubtless there were innumerable con-
crete factors determining that one outcome prevailed over others.
There was a powerful shared mood; it discharged itself and disap-
peared. Full stop. And if I theorize even at such length, it's because

"Howl" expressed so much of it—to me, never mind that it was first published thirteen years before it reached me.

But when that inchoate dream, that dimly defined possibility collapsed, in the early 1970s, many things receded. The spirit of the harsh morning after was now, likewise, "in the air," and much of my music and many of my writers and poets were implicated. "Howl," like *On the Road*, like most of my rock and roll collection, lost luster. I couldn't reinsert myself into its desperate headlong music, its drama, anymore, and if I tried I felt mocked, exposed in all of my crude adolescent credulity. I had become deeply disenchanted, and it hardly helped matters that the poet himself, that fierce icon breaker, had grown into an avuncular pop icon, all finger cymbals and rolling waves of "Ommmm" that I could not take seriously. And as the years passed, his great outburst acquired its crown of thorny footnotes and worked its way into the canon, the Moloch imprecations sidling up to Walt Whitman's "barbaric yawp." The ultimate indignity: it had become possible to read "Howl" as a poem, in a classroom setting, with all of the discussion such reading entails.

But the fate of true expression isn't finally so simple, and going back to the poem has allowed me to recognize this. When I opened that little book again recently, I fully expected to find the familiar vision deflated to quaintness, a hippie-era curio, and the image of my outgrown younger self haunting the margins like some tiresome revenant. Oddly, hearteningly, it didn't happen that way. What I found instead, right away, even on first glancing exposure, was the same unruly power of line and image, the old unmuffled hammering. It rang again. Differently, and for different reasons, but it did ring again, even though now it sounded—necessarily—in the echo chamber of memory. Reading again, I couldn't help reconnecting with the life of the younger man who had taken that jagged dictation the first time. I was short-circuited back. But here was not the familiar memory trick, laying the then athwart the now. For it was at the same time new—as the words echoed, so they also blazed through afresh, direct. At the level of language, there was fission all over again. My exposure felt new, original, the words and rhythms doing what the best words and rhythms do, which is re-creating the event, the reality, overpowering the more reflexive operation of memory with the immediacy of occasion. Those lines, now as then, cantilevered out in open defiance of poetic closure.

And once again I was plunged into that implicit, almost forgotten subject—those "best minds"

who dreamt and made incarnate gaps in Time & Space through images juxtaposed, and trapped the archangel of the soul between 2 visual images and joined the elemental verbs and set the noun and dash of consciousness together jumping with sensation of Pater Omnipotens Aeterna Deus

to recreate the syntax and measure of poor human prose and stand before you speechless and intelligent and shaking with shame, rejected yet confessing out the soul to conform to the rhythm of thought in his naked and endless head,

the madman bum and angel beat in Time, unknown, yet putting down here what might be left to say in time come after death,

and rose reincarnate in the ghostly clothes of jazz in the goldhorn shadow of the band and blew the suffering of America's naked mind for love into an eli eli lamma lamma sabacthani saxophone cry that shivered the cities down to the last radio

with the absolute heart of the poem of life butchered out of their own bodies good to eat a thousand years.

There it was again, the power of the phrase, overturning the memory and the received idea of the phrase—back-to-square-one. Seizing its freedom as it did, as it does, from the very first line, "Howl" restored for me the sense of annunciatory risk. As before, I found I was reading in bursts, as if it were something glowing up spasmodically in a grate, lit bright and quickly burnt through. I couldn't take it as a poem. Not then, not now. For to read it as a poem, knowing what I know, how I invested myself once, would have been to finish it off, four-corner framing an agitation that would always run deeper than my idea of art.

EILEEN MYLES

REPEATING ALLEN

---

who lit cigarettes in boxcars, boxcars, boxcars racketing through snow
toward lonesome farms in grandfather night

Whenever I teach "Howl," I jump on this line. It's my favorite because the thingness of the word ("boxcars boxcars boxcars") is exactly what you see at a light while a train is passing—all throughout this poem Allen wrote cinematically but never more succinctly than he did in this line. Boxcars, boxcars, boxcars. It was what you saw, is all. "Howl" is remarkable because Allen did the complete thing—he wrote both a poem and a culture to put it in. Poetry went to the movies here and it never came out. I think the poetry world (something that probably shouldn't exist) is ever more cursed with public events that ask is poetry political, relevant, over, commercial, popular, etc. because in this poem it was all those things at once. Many of us write poems that are some of those things for *some* people, we write for "a" culture, not for "the" culture. Allen wrote "Howl," that's who he was, and "Howl" changed things. How? And I'm looking *in* the poem, not out and around it, because the poem is the theater of "Howl," the movie theater, I mean. It's replete with trailers: "who sang out of their windows in despair, fell out of the subway window, jumped in the filthy Passaic."

Somebody knows how many "who"s there are in "Howl" (and someone even knows who all those whos are). I considered calling Bob Rosenthal, Allen's longtime secretary, or Bill Morgan, the archivist-painter who sold Allen's papers to Stanford, to find out who was that guy "who jumped off the Brooklyn Bridge" and lived. I remember the story and people laughing that there actually *was* such a guy, like he was even pointed out one night in the bar: That's him. But my point actually just is that the poem functions so often literally like a trailer. The announcer voice of the poem keeps folding all those lives in as preview of the spectacle the poem will produce, meanwhile it's producing it *now*, and so much of the excitement of "Howl" is its capacity to produce those two effects at once. You're rubbing your hands as you read—ooh, this is going to be really good—but the experience is already happening.

And were all those whos poets, or poetlike people? It seems to me that Allen actually pluralized the identity of the poet by means of these wavelike lines, announcing the poet's arrival again and again. He (or she) wasn't exactly a poet, didn't need to be. The poet came in this cascade of people. Allen made the poet's identity something vague and postmodern. He was one of them, not which one. They were more like the barnacles on the poet's boat as he surged forward carrying them, or them carrying him, because they "who drove crosscountry seventytwo hours to find out if I had a vision or you had a vision or he had a vision to find out Eternity . . ."

Well, it's a little Pete Seeger, isn't it, the singer in the broad room inviting us to join in a cause whose vision is this after all? Or maybe Mitch Miller: "America, sing along!" Authorship (or poetness) seems really secondary in the poem-spectacle that everyone seems to be writing here (in "Howl"). It's Allen's identification bringing all those lives in close that works, and it also occurs to me (and Allen I think said this often) that it works a little bit like it did for Christopher Smart, Ginsberg's other great literary predecessor, besides Blake (and Williams), and I'm thinking of the Smart of "Rejoyce in the Lamb," which begins

For I will consider my Cat Jeoffry . . .

"Rejoyce in the Lamb" is a long (about eight hundred lines) and obsessive poem, which goes on in a stiff but attentive evocation of catness:

For he rolls upon prank to work it in.
For having done duty and received blessing he begins to
    consider himself.
For this he performs in ten degrees.
For first he looks upon his forepaws to see if they are
    clean.
For secondly he kicks up behind to clear away there.
For thirdly he works it upon stretch with the forepaws
    extended.
For fourthly he sharpens his paws by wood.
For fifthly he washes himself.

The poem ends like this:

For by stroking of him I have found out electricity.
For I perceived God's light about him both wax and fire.
For the Electrical fire is the spiritual substance, which God sends from
    heaven to sustain the bodies both of man and beast.
For God has blessed him in the variety of his movements.
For, tho he cannot fly, he is an excellent clamberer.

For his motions upon the face of the earth are more than any other
quadruped.
For he can tread to all the measures upon the music.
For he can swim for life.
For he can creep.

Christopher Smart was living in a madhouse in restraints when he wrote this poem, never published in his lifetime. I mention it because it's entirely structured of repetitions, a poem in chant form, much like "Howl," and the cumulative effect of the slightly recoiled paw of the final line is the cat practically moves. A poem that uses repetitions throughout, a standard of religious verse (which both Smart's and Ginsberg's poems are), ultimately has the effect of being a flipbook, a kind of low-tech predecessor of film (as Ginsberg knew it, and increasingly not as we know it now—since film's gone digital), and an equally good producer of altered states, and bliss. Like when you jumped up and down in childhood saying "taxicabs, taxicabs, taxicabs," the words started to sound strange, but you also got "high."

I turn to Kenneth Anger too in search of this mode, a euphoric one, considering *Scorpio Rising* (1964) to be another epoch-changing work of art. Anger's method was referred to in one description as "semiotic layering," which works just as well for "Howl." Kenneth Anger was relentlessly cultish, and though his accomplishment and influence weren't any smaller than Allen's, maybe the scope of who he was aiming the work for, audience-wise, was more precise. But his film employed the same biker boy references, and fanatical love for a number of American subcultures of the fifties was homoerotic, and in the context of the film, the effect of its culture was totalizing, in the extreme. The building repetition of belt buckles, motors, flashing signs, and flags finally produced a world that triumphed by its end—the case was made. Allen's ambitions were messier and planted more wildly. "Howl," like a Brian De Palma film, ends again and again. And even in the mostly nonspecific and linear-feeling Moloch section:

Moloch in whom I sit lonely! Moloch in whom I dream Angels! Crazy in Moloch! Cocksucker in Moloch!

And later

Moloch who entered my soul early! Moloch in whom I am a conscious-ness without a body! Moloch who frightened me out of my natural ecstasy! Moloch whom I abandon! Wake up in Moloch!

then finally

Light streaming out of the sky!

Where did that last one come from? Allen was such a diligent student of ecstasy and vision that he knew that as the swastikas and belt buckles flicker, something happens, the road opens, and a space opens up as well inside the poem, the cat creeps, or perhaps you just stayed up all night, praying to Moloch, and dawn *is* its mystical reply.

"Howl" is a poem full of miracles and events, not the least of which is its own machinery. Because you are in it, witness, and you watch the poem grow. The only promise in this poem is more, and it makes good, not in some other world but in this one that you read in.

Yet aren't these all photographs—or stills?

*with mother finally ****** . . .*

What do those asterisks mean? Fucked? Fried? What? Such a place
to begin a stanza, which then turns into a passage of endings:

> *and the last fantastic book flung out of the tenement window, and the
> last door closed at 4 A.M. and the last telephone slammed at the
> wall in reply and the last furnished room emptied down to the last
> piece of mental furniture, a yellow paper rose twisted on a wire
> hanger in the closet.*

All those "last"s feel like the sorts of things you'd see in, say, the
Holocaust Museum, or a museum of the American Indian, or
even in the anonymous family album that turns up in a thrift.
Tragic or no, after each of these "last"s I hear a click of the
shutter—it needs to preserve. Williams in his introduction to
the City Lights version of "Howl" makes passing reference to
the resemblance between this poem's hell and that of Jews in the
last war. I never thought about "Howl" as a Holocaust poem,
though I've been aware rereading it that it has Holocaust phras-
ing, the trauma of the Holocaust is all over it. So why not allow
the overt thought to surface, that maybe this poem forced Amer-
ica to experience, in an indirect fashion, something it otherwise
felt compelled to refuse? The sheer madness, the total horror of
the Holocaust. Pictures of emaciated corpses, the same pictures
again and again, is one version, but what is the invisible horror of
"Howl" that all the angelheaded hipsters are running from? Is it
the world we now know? Allen drops the loving leash of friend-
ship around his own neck when he repeatedly promises his insti-
tutional war buddy, Solomon, I'm with you "in Rockland/where
we hug and kiss the United States under our bedsheets the United
States that coughs all night and won't let us sleep."

Carl Solomon is a Jew, and he sounds more and more like
Allen's mother ("you imitate the shade of my mother"), whom

Allen may've needed to affirm his attachment to, and her own stay in a mental hospital. Through Solomon, he did.

I haven't touched the especially poignant and relentless flavor of Allen Ginsberg's misogyny. There are so many incidents of it here: "the one-eyed shrew of the heterosexual dollar, the one-eyed that winks out of the womb"—actually all three fates are pretty bad. And elsewhere in the poem, women provide opportunity for male bravado—"you've murdered your twelve secretaries"—or holy self-abasement—"you drink the tea of the breasts of the spinsters of Utica." Yuck, right? And he must've been singing the hipster virility of Neal Cassady when he referred to someone "who sweetened the snatches of a million girls trembling in the sunset." I guess male = sugar. No sweet pussy on its own? Not in this man's howl. In the Beat canon in general (see Kerouac), thanks to birth, we're blamed for life. It's a belief that might be as old as Buddhism, or Judaism. At best, we (females) are occasions of reflected light, practically the walls of the womb itself, the home and the office. You light up my life, we sing.

Yet in reality, I knew Allen for twenty-five years, and he was to my own female self a generous friend, though admittedly the fact that I looked like a boy when I was young helped. I passed. And still he tried to fix me up with his boyfriend, Peter Orlovsky. The bonds of sex and family were all mixed up, in a way that used to be considered good.

All of this somehow brings me to the boxcars line again. If women at best reflect male light, what is the entire concept of America doing in "Howl"? Isn't it some big moon, too? An imaginary space? In a poem or a country where female agency is repressed or erased, doesn't it return as structure itself? The poem is a woman we're gathering in? What is this dream?

who lit cigarettes in boxcars, boxcars, boxcars racketing through snow toward lonesome farms in grandfather night

I keep wondering about that grandfather night. The "lonesome farms," of course, are a case of attributing how you feel sitting in the car to the farms, and they're *out there*. But "grandfather night" seems very old. Older than America. I wondered if this poem's train isn't speeding through a night in which people are being yanked out of the beds, never to be seen again. Are on the train being carried to an unspecified destination. America? A country of incarcerated black men and smiling blond women. Is the pederast the new Jew? Ask Nancy Grace. For Ginsberg, pederasty was just another one of his happy crimes. Yet look at the Michael Jackson trial. Right now it's the only one, pinned mostly on homosexuals, for Christ's sake, though statistically most pederasts are heterosexual dads. The train is traveling through time, the effluvia of "Howl," taking pictures as it goes. It's a gift to look at this American poem at this moment in time, to wonder where it was really coming from, and where it went.

GORDON BALL

WOPBOPGOOGLEMOP: "HOWL"

AND ITS INFLUENCES

I grew up six thousand miles from San Francisco, nine thousand from New York, in Tokyo 1950–1962: only in bits and pieces did I come to learn of a strange new phenomenon taking place across the Pacific. When I was fifteen a classmate told me of a group of people on the coast of California who spent their days painting and reading and writing poetry; they were called "beatniks." I came home from school that afternoon and told my mother about them. "After all," I added, "what else is there to do?" "If you don't know," she answered, leaving the room in tears, "I won't tell you."

Later the same year, with my parents on furlough in the United States, we had a couple of days in San Francisco: the bank my father worked for put us up at the elegant St. Francis Hotel on Union Square, we saved money by eating at the nearby Foster's Cafeteria, and on my own I searched the granite blocks of Grant Avenue for beatniks.

Several years later, just graduated from a provincial men's college in the South, I bought the small black-and-white City Lights Pocket Poets Series Number Four, *Howl and Other Poems*, for seventy-five cents. I read some of the title poem and wasn't sure I understood it. But I kept it.

Two years later still, on hearing the poet declaim it, I began to sense the enormous power it would have, both in my life and in our culture.

A key to the Beats, and to the fact that they've given us a large, multidimensional, and ever-growing legacy, is their ability to absorb the form and vitality of many different literary and aesthetic traditions. It's as if they took to heart Henry James's dictum "be one of the people on whom nothing is lost"—and so we find ourselves today, still in the midst of opening, discovering, their gifts. Allen Ginsberg, in particular, drew richly (sometimes to the point of apparent contradiction) from an almost unlimited range of source and inspiration. And he left a legacy bountiful and diverse, in shape and subject.

What were the greatest influences on Ginsberg? At the heart of Ginsberg there's Kerouac: Ginsberg was inspired to write spontaneously (and frequently) by Kerouac's example, as well as by his manifesto, "Essentials of Spontaneous Prose," and his *Book of Dreams*. Equally important, he was inspired by the *sound* of Kerouac's prose and poetry, the "wopbopgooglemop," which Kerouac derived in part from *his* eclectic mix of interests: William Shakespeare and Thomas Wolfe, the American workaday vernacular he heard and used, the American musicalized vernacular of Lester Young and Charlie Parker, as well as his model for vocal phrasing—for full-mouthed enunciation of individual words—Frank Sinatra. When we read, in Ginsberg's "Notes Written on Finally Recording *Howl*," that the poem was "writ for my own soul's ear and a few other golden ears," we know the most golden of all were Kerouac's.

In mid-fifties San Francisco, Ginsberg and Kerouac and other young poets were reading R. H. Blyth's four-volume collection of haiku; for Ginsberg, in his own words, "the crucial discovery of haiku and ellipsis [omission of unnecessary connectives] in the haiku . . . serves as the [syntactic] base in *Howl*." Or, as he wrote in his journal from that period,

> Study of primary forms of ellipse, naked haiku, useful
> for advancement of practice of western metaphor
> —"hydrogen jukebox."

At the same time, his study of the ellipse—or ellipsis as he later called it—may also have evolved from his study of Paul Cézanne. As he once noted, "I am like Cézanne, sketching." "Howl," Ginsberg later claimed, was "an homage to Cézanne's method," and his study of Cézanne returned him to another influence, his 1948 William Blake epiphany, as he sought to convey in words and the spaces between them a sense of the transtemporal state of his Blakean "auditory illuminatons." Ginsberg has also spoken of the importance of his Buddhist studies and surrealism to his use of ellipsis.

So this signal stylistic feature of "Howl" may well have evolved from several quite different points of contact. *And* the fact that the spirit of something as radically condensed in form as the haiku appears on page after page of a *long* poem of *long*, Whitman-like lines is extraordinary.

Numerous other influences, sometimes almost violently joined, abound in this epoch-making poem. Dozens of important sources are identified in the annotated "Howl," from Christopher Smart, Vladimir Mayakovsky, and Kurt Schwitters through numerous Beat colleagues and their personal anecdotes and "eyeball kicks," Fritz Lang's *Metropolis*, peyote, and the Sir

Francis Drake Hotel. Ginsberg's inclusion of anecdotes is especially interesting, not only because it challenged 1950s critical bias against writing directly of personal experience, but also because he gave us, let's say, Herbert Huncke shoulder to shoulder with Herman Melville.

And the poem takes as its first locus for its "best minds" the "negro streets" of what was then an even more segregated America. In part through Kerouac's influence, there is in much of the rest of Part I a subtle presence of African America, which is later yoked with a different ethnic tradition in the phrases "bop kabbalah" and "eli eli lamma lamma sabacthani saxophone cry."

So Ginsberg has taken much, from many sources. What are we taking from "Howl"?

To begin with, American poetry. American poetry as composed, presented, and received is not as it was in the 1950s.

From the Beats' insistence on talking to each other in the 1940s and 1950s, intensely and without qualm, and their resulting coffeehouse and gallery declamations in the 1950s, came a revival of our recognition that poetry is *not* principally something that exists flatly, two-dimensionally on a printed page, but is something projected from within a human organism, within a human community. Allen's electrifying public readings of "Howl" are legion, as Kerouac's *Dharma Bums*'s depiction of his very first one reveals, with the poet "wailing his poem . . . drunk with arms outspread everybody . . . yelling 'Go! Go! Go!' (like a jam session)." Poetry, as Ginsberg maintained, can be "composed on the tongue."

I don't mean to say that today all poetry is so composed, simply that it's no longer de rigueur to follow academic forms of the past. Today, a poet is less likely to be asked the question

a colleague of Robert Creeley's took at a reading a genera-
tion ago: "Was that a *real* poem, or did you just make it up
yourself?"

So I guess what I'm saying is that the Cold War of Poetic
Forms is over, and we—Open Form—won. Rather than domi-
nation by the New Critical preference for the short lyric, what
we have today is a great multiplicity of form and subject matter.
A simple measure might be the changing status of Walt Whit-
man: in "Notes Written on Finally Recording *Howl*," Ginsberg
stated that Whitman's form had "rarely been further explored,"
that Whitman was a "mountain too vast to be seen," that with
few exceptions his line was taken as "a big freakish uncontrol-
lable necessary prosaic goof." Today, as we survey poets from
Galway Kinnell to June Jordan to Ed Sanders to James Tate to
Antler, we find it's no longer so.

And poetry today is presented differently. Each of the long
lines of Part I of "Howl" is ideally a single long breath: Gins-
berg's locating a poem in human tongue and breath, as well as
his linking it to music, has helped give us verse with a much
greater emphasis on oral delivery and performance, mixing artis-
tic media: Patti Smith, Laurie Anderson, Anne Waldman, and
Arrested Development come to mind. Poetry is no longer the
nearly exclusive province of the academy, no longer just for
sissies and stiffs.

Consequently, poetry is received differently. Over a genera-
tion ago, poems were often studied by sober explication, as if
they were something like crossword puzzles. They might've
been scanned, sometimes laboriously, but I wonder how often
they were read out loud for joy. The Eliotic legacy of imperson-
ality, as appropriated by the New Criticism, was worlds removed
from Diane Di Prima's reaction on first encountering "Howl"
late in 1956. As she tells us in *Memoirs of a Beatnik*, "We read
Howl together, I read it aloud to everyone."

Today, Allen's works and those of his colleagues appear in numerous anthologies and syllabi, and classes specifically on the Beat Generation are found at many colleges, while even some high school classes are studying the Beats. Years before his death in 1997, Ginsberg became a member of the American Academy of Arts and Letters, an honorary fellow of the Modern Language Association. "Howl" and "Kaddish" were the subjects of two special sessions at MLA conventions, 1986 and 1991.

How much of this poetic shift was purposely engineered by the Beats? According to Ginsberg, "There was some conscious intention to make a cultural breakthrough, to talk in public as we talked in private. How we behave in private is actually the ultimate politics. So the original literary inspiration was to behave in public as we do in private."

Kerouac wrote Ginsberg early in the fifties that the distinguishing feature of the Beats was their practice of honestly confessing to each other their deepest feelings. I am sure that their open speech—in an age of denial!—has *something* to do with the fact that today national debate includes, as legitimate topics for discussion, things such as homosexuality and heroin addiction. And Ginsberg's long "practice" at confession with Kerouac was undoubtedly a wellspring for the revelations of "Howl."

Unashamed personal revelation in literature, particularly in the 1950s, risked violating not only critical canons but legal statutes. As it's happened, the obscenity trials of "Howl" and *Naked Lunch*, along with many other skirmishes of the Beats, have contributed to greater freedom of life and letters in the United States.

How has such influence been felt abroad? Let's consider Eastern Europe. In the eyes of certain poets and scholars, the Whitmanic candor of Ginsberg's life and works contributed to the peaceful downfall of Communist regimes at the end of the last decade. Ginsberg's being chosen King of May at the May

Day celebration in Prague 1965 (where already "Howl" was being translated into Czech) may have been a prelude. A young Polish student of Ginsberg's has written of how Polish academics were not idle (or "academic") in their appreciation of the Beats, whose literature gave them added heart to challenge the literary and cultural conditions they faced. In the personal experience of this young Pole, Ginsberg's poetry was a ballast against the Polish police state after his return home in 1986 from a year in the United States. After barely escaping Polish jail for reported illegal and immoral behavior—homosexuality—while in the United States, he wrote that only reading poetry, most especially "Howl," relieved some of the crush of his alienating homeland: he loved Ginsberg's poetry because "it created a little world of freedom for me." Such a comment is a microcosm of what Ginsberg meant to readers through much of Iron-Curtained Europe for the span of a generation. As Nobel Prize–winning poet Czeslaw Milosz said in a 1991 tribute, Ginsberg is a "great poet of the murderous century."

While in the Soviet Union in the early 1970s, Beat scholar Ann Charters had the opportunity to visit the dacha of the late Boris Pasternak. There on a bookshelf she found, to her delight, a copy of *Howl and Other Poems*. Additionally, poet Yevgeny Yevtushenko has reported,

> After the grim McCarthy era and the witch hunts in Hollywood, the appearance of the beatniks was that sigh . . . that had been trapped in the chest of American society . . . It was not for nothing that we were attuned to the slightest reverberation of that sigh. The young poets of Moscow passed around issues of *Evergreen Review*. The generation of beatniks and our generation in Russia are inseparable . . .

Finally, there's one specific element in the collective psyche of the Beats that I'd like to explore. Kerouac late in the 1950s gave "Beat" the sense of "beatific." Ginsberg in 1968, when a second American revolution seemed at hand, said, "If the revolution isn't spiritual, it's not worth it." This spiritual base, which I see at the heart of the Beat Generation, may offer a redemption of the woeful American legacy projected by Walt Whitman 125 years ago, as he considered manifestations of "Moloch" in his day. Whitman wrote, in *Democratic Vistas*, 1871:

> . . . I say of all this tremendous and dominant play of solely materialistic bearings upon current life in the United States . . . that they must either be confronted and met by at least an equally subtle and tremendous force-infusion for purposes of spiritualization, for the pure conscience, for genuine aesthetics, and for absolute and primal manliness and womanliness—or else our modern civilization, with all its improvements, is in vain, and we are on the road to a destiny, a status, equivalent, in its real world, to that of the fabled damned.

In closing I'd submit that the Beats *are* that "subtle and tremendous force-infusion" Whitman called for. Allen Ginsberg for over four decades wrote, spoke, agitated, meditated, dreamed, and sang to bring about the spiritualization of America. Richard Hell once said of Allen, "He's a one-man generation." At the center of that singular generation, not on paper only but in body, breath, and air, is "Howl."

BILLY COLLINS

MY "HOWL"

———

The year "Howl" was published was the same year that I leaped headfirst into the great swimming hole of adolescence. In my high school, the poets being taught as acknowledged masters were dead white males with beards and three names: William Cullen Bryant, Henry Wadsworth Longfellow, John Greenleaf Whittier. The Metrical Lads, bless their hearts.

But "Howl" closed the door on all that. Alive with hormonal energy and invigorated with the outcries of "Rock Around the Clock" and *Rebel Without a Cause,* I was a perfect target for the poem's wild tone, its delinquent spontaneity, and its revolutionary poetics.

I bought the little City Lights paperback at the Paperback Gallery on Sheridan Square in the Village, which was about the hippest bookstore around. My dream was to be able to be smart enough to work there. They were very clear in their refusal to hire me, but there was no one to stop me from writing poems in imitation of Ginsberg's wild rave. If it's true that the road to originality lies in imitation, then it wasn't an utter waste of time for a Catholic high school boy from the suburbs to try to sound in his poems like a downtown homosexual Jewish beatnik intimate in the ways of pot and Benzedrine. "Howl," so perfectly titled, was coolness, madness, anger, and some of the secular beatitudes all wrapped into one poem. And Ginsberg's poem, his best as it turned out, was also the hand grenade that bounced into the house of formalism and lay there for a few minutes before exploding. When the air cleared, poetry had changed for good.

ALICIA OSTRIKER

THE POET AS JEW: "HOWL" REVISITED

I. GINSBERG THE YID

It was the best of times; it was the worst of times. It was 1966. We were in Vietnam, but we thought in our antiwar innocence that we might be out soon. Medgar Evers and Malcolm X were dead, but Robert Kennedy and Martin Luther King were still alive. The Chicago riots, the invasion of Cambodia, the killing of four students at Kent State hadn't happened yet. Allen Ginsberg was giving a reading at Princeton University with Gary Snyder. In Princeton I lived at that time disguised as a young faculty wife and mother of two. Simultaneously at Rutgers University I went to work disguised as a promising young scholar of late eighteenth- and early nineteenth-century poetry and prosody. Officially I was a Blakean. My own poetry remained in the closet during the years of my assistant professorship; had my colleagues known of my folly, I would probably not have gotten the job, since most of them considered creative writing the equivalent of basket weaving, an activity for the retarded. Also in the closet were my two daughters in diapers. One did not discuss family in my department, where my senior colleagues were witty and charming men who all looked and behaved as if they had never in their lives laid eyes on a diaper.

I had already heard Allen once, at Rutgers, where he took off the top of my head in the standing-room-only vault of Voorhees Chapel by introducing as his opening act, of all people, his father, Louis Ginsberg. Louis, with considerable self-importance, read some of his own poetry—rhymed, refined, culturally anonymous lyrics—as if to say, This is how it should be done, here's the real thing, now you can listen to my son. Louis's condescension was not a joke, it was real. Equally real was Allen's affectionate graciousness toward his dad. As the daughter of a mother who also wrote rhymed poetry, of the same vintage as Louis's, I was overwhelmed. I couldn't *dream* of doing a reading with my mom. Embarrassing! Impossible! Couldn't dream of achieving the spiritual state that would make such graciousness possible for me. But what if . . . ? And indeed, a mere twenty years later, I found myself able to do it, give readings with my mother. Not often, not easily, but with a certain amount of grace, which would have been impossible for me without that distant model.

In Princeton, Allen read "Please Master," and I was scandalized. But I had a question to ask him, and at the postreading party I fought my way through the crowd of adoring boy undergraduates to ask it. It concerned his voice: that sonorous, sweet, deep, vibrant, patient baritone seemed to emerge from some inexhaustible energy source, manifesting the double sense of *spiritus* as both breath and spirit. But I had listened to an early recording of "Howl" in which, far from having the long lines express the poet's "natural" breath units, as he so often claimed, the voice was high-pitched and short-breathed—entirely *un*equal to the long lines. What about it? Did he really develop the voice to go with the lines, and not the other way around? Yes, he cheerfully agreed, he had written the lines to go with his *potential* voice. And how, I asked—for this was what I wished to learn—did he train his voice to do what it did now? Could I do

that? Allen smiled and suggested filling the bathtub and lying in
the water facedown reciting poems. Then he took another look
at me and said: It's not so hard. Just do the breathing exercises
you learned in childbirth classes.

The breathing exercises I had learned in childbirth classes.
How did this gay guy, who knew nothing about women, know
at a glance that the shy chick in front of him had taken child-
birth classes? How did he know that pregnancy and childbirth
had been, for her, peak spiritual experiences? I wanted to kiss
his sandals. I watched him then with the flock of Princeton boys
and saw how he listened to each one with the same focused at-
tention, responding to each according to his need. He didn't just
want to sleep with them. He wanted to love them.

There is a word in Hebrew for a virtue at the core of Gins-
berg's character and his writing, a virtue that's been noticed by
infinite numbers of people—*chesed*. It means kindness, or loving-
kindness.★ *Chesed* is one of thirteen attributes of God according

★Ted Enslin is succinct and typical: "Many years ago I wrote a collection of short takes
on various poets, attempting to capture an outstanding characteristic of each one.
When it came to Allen it was simply 'KINDNESS,' and I let it stand as that single
word. One does not enhance such a quality by modifiers or explanation" (Bill Morgan
and Bob Rosenthal, eds, *Best Minds: A Tribute to Allen Ginsberg* [New York: Lospeccio
Press, 1986], p. 159). Tuli Kupferberg, ex-Fug, accompanies a ditty to "Al the Gins/A
Jewish Prins" with a cartoon of self and Ginsberg, the balloon of the first saying, "Hey
Allen what's the good word?" and the second answering "Kindness" (*Best Minds*, p. 159).
Jane Kramer's *Allen Ginsberg in America* (New York: Random House, 1969) represents
Ginsberg as unfailingly generous, compassionate, and saintly. On the other hand, Bruce
Cook in *The Beat Generation* (New York: Charles Scribner's Sons, 1981), argues that the
young Allen was "an aggressive, savage young man . . . a great hater," whose anguish
was healed only by the satori experienced after his exhausting and fruitless stay in India,
on the Kyoto–Tokyo Express (cf. Everson, *Best Minds*, pp. 105–107). And at least two
commentators on "Howl" seem, interestingly, offended by the poem's swerve from the
"anger" they feel ought to be its core. Michael Rumaker in *Black Mountain Review* (fall
1957) claims that "the impact of the anger" was corrupted "by sentimentality, bathos,
Buddha." Clayton Eshleman appears to agree, complaining that "Howl III" "is very
close to being cute" instead of pursuing "the direction toward an unqualified attack on

to Maimonides (who gets it from Exodus 34:6); it is, in addition, a quality of Torah (a Jew expresses gratitude each day to the God who has given us a Torah of life, and lovingkindness, and righteousness, and compassion, and peace); it is a quality highly regarded among traditional Jewish men, whom Talmud praises as "compassionate sons of compassionate fathers."

In no way could the young Allen Ginsberg have *known* any of this in the secular family in which he grew up, which was not simply secular but adamantly atheist. And yet these ideals would have saturated the air he breathed, for Jewish atheism in its Eastern European sources is fueled by the dream of social justice, which is also a dream of human kindness. Among the Yiddish writers whose shtetl ethos was the mulch from which Louis Ginsberg's socialism and Naomi Ginsberg's communism fed, Irving Howe describes what he calls the value of "sweetness," "the tone of love . . . with which such masters as Sholem Aleichem and [Isaac] Peretz faced the grimmest facts about Jewish life." Howe's further remarks on the fictions of Mendele and Sholem Aleichem, Peretz, Singer, and Jacob Glatstein might well describe "Howl": "The virtue of powerlessness, the power of helplessness, the company of the dispossessed, the sanctity of the insulted and injured—these, finally are the great themes of Yiddish literature,"* in which, as well, we find the humor (self-deprecating, buffoonish, absurd), the acerbity, the irremediable pain and melancholy a millimeter below the surface that we find also in Allen Ginsberg. Sholem Aleichem's village of Kasrilevke and Greenwich Village? Singer's saintly Gimpel the Fool and Ginsberg's angelheaded hipsters? Or, still more appallingly/ appealingly, a "chosen people"—chosen for persecution, for

the sensibility-destroying aspect of North America" (Lewis Hyde, ed., *On the Poetry of Allen Ginsberg* [Ann Arbor: University of Michigan Press, 1984], p. 109).

*Irving Howe and Eliezer Greenberg, eds., *A Treasury of Yiddish Stories* (New York: Viking, 1954), pp. 37–38.

pogroms, for the chimneys—reincarnated as "the best minds of my generation"? Like the Jews of Europe, Ginsberg's "best minds" suffer for a stubborn adherence to their faith. Yiddishkeit and Ginsberg? A mere generation of partial American assimilation divides them. Ginsberg in "Howl" will record, in veiled fashion, the humiliation and crippling of a population of immigrants to shores that promised hope and produced despair. He will gather the threads dropped by the revolutionary poetry of the thirties, left dangling in the winter of McCarthyism. He will *spritz* shamelessly alongside Henny Youngman and Lenny Bruce. Think of his extraordinary language. Ginsberg's beat lexicon, his determination to write a *low* dialect opposed to the literary diction promoted by his onetime mentor Lionel Trilling, may have been supported by William Carlos Williams. But it is also a tribute to his Yiddish-speaking ancestors and the obscure longevity of their gift for juicy emotional tragicomedy.

II. GINSBERG THE PROPHET

"People have been comparing me to Whitman, and although I love and adore and am a child of Whitman, both of us come from the Bible . . . We are talking about the endless quarrel between the establishment and the prophets, and I hope to be forever on the side of the prophets."★

That is not Allen Ginsberg, it is Muriel Rukeyser, a poet half a generation earlier, sprung from an assimilated Jewish family of quite another class from Ginsberg's; but one feels it *might* be Allen. Here, I want to argue, is the second area of the poet's Jewishness: if his personal style is an American incarnation of

★Jan Wojcik and Raymond-Jean Frontain, *Poetic Prophecy in Western Literature* (Cranbury, N.J.: Associated University Presses, 1984), p. 13.

the Yiddish personality, his moral power descends in a direct line from the power of Hebrew prophecy. Certainly "prophet" and "prophetic" are terms that are freely used about his work,★ and that he often uses himself. Describing his 1948 Blake-inspired visions, "he realized," Paul Portugés tells us, "that his visionary experiences were not unlike the calling forth of the Hebrew prophets by their Creator" and that his task as a poet would be to re-create "a prophetic illuminative seizure."† But the notion of the poet as prophet is a loose one. From the Greek *prophetes*, "interpreter" or "proclaimer," or "one who speaks for a deity," the term has been used in the English tradition since the late eighteenth century to denote a variety of sublimities opposed to neoclassic rationality. Jan Wojcik and Raymond-Jean Frontain define a "prophetic" stance in Western art as implying private vision, an insistence on the righteousness of the prophet and the corruption of his society, passionate and hyperbolic language, social radicalism, stylistic obscurity or incoherence, and "obsession, fine or frenzied," as "with every technique of language he can muster, the prophet delivers a message that never arrives."‡ Herbert N. Schneidau proposes a definition of the prophet as one who forces people to "look at their culture and see a myth . . . they can no longer believe in, for it is a living lie."§ In his 1966 *Paris Review* interview, Ginsberg describes the

★A notable example is Kenneth Rexroth's defense of "Howl" in his trial statement: "The simplest term for such writing is prophetic, it is easier to call it that than anything else because we have a large body of prophetic writing to refer to. There are the prophets in the Bible which it greatly resembles in purpose and in language and in subject matter . . . the theme is the denunciation of evil and a pointing of the way out, so to speak. That is prophetic literature" (Hyde, p. 50).
†Paul Portugés, "Allen Ginsberg's Visions and the Growth of His Poetics of Prophecy," in Wojcik and Frontain, p. 161.
‡Wojcik and Frontain, pp. 9–10.
§Schneidau, *Sacred Discontent: The Bible and Western Tradition* (Berkeley: University of California Press, 1977), p. 17.

genesis of "Howl" as follows: "I thought I wouldn't write a *poem* but just write what I wanted to without fear, let my imagination go, open secrecy, and scribble magic lines from my real mind—sum up my life—something I wouldn't be able to show anybody, write for my own soul's ear and a few other golden ears." Beginning Part I, he found himself composing "a tragic custard-pie comedy of wild phrasing, meaningless images for the beauty of abstract poetry of mind," and got excited and went on, "continuing to prophecy what I really know, despite the drear consciousness of the world."* In Ginsberg's 1971 craft interview with William Packard, he discusses the genesis of "Howl": "The poetic precedent for this situation is like Ezekiel and Jeremiah and the Hebrew prophets in the Bible who were warning Babylon against its downfall . . . They were talking about the fall of a city like Babylon, or the fall of a tribe, and cursing out the sins of a nation."† Now, what is wrong with this picture is that it suggests a view of the Hebrew prophets that charity might call at best sketchy. Jerusalem, not Babylon, for example, is the city warned and mourned in Hebrew prophecy. Nonetheless, Ginsberg's loose sense of prophecy may well correspond not only to most laymen's sense of the genre but to its historical flexibility and capacity for metamorphosis within Jewish tradition—particularly when we consider that the "prophetic" work "Howl" most resembles is the Lamentations of Jeremiah.

Extremity is the ground note of prophecy. Condemnation and warning dominate preexilic prophecy, eschatological promises dominate postexilic. But whereas Isaiah, Ezekiel, and the other

---

*Barry Miles, *Ginsberg: A Biography* (New York: Simon & Schuster, 1989), pp. 187–89.
†William Packard, ed., *The Craft of Poetry: Interviews from the New York Quarterly* (New York: Doubleday, 1974), p. 65.

canonical prophets are spoken to by God, and become mouth-pieces or trumpets of a force intimately engaged in the life of a covenanted people, the voice of Lamentations howls in a void: God is terrifyingly present as an agent of destruction, yet terrifyingly absent from discourse. Invoked and prayed to out of the depths, he does not reply. But it is precisely the failure of divine response that has produced, as Alan Mintz argues, a literature of catastrophe which itself is an agent of survival: "Jewish society . . . has had many massive individual catastrophes visited upon it and still survived; and in each case the reconstruction was undertaken in significant measure by the exertions of the Hebrew literary imagination . . . It is the story of the transcendence of the catastrophe rather than of the catastrophe itself which is compelling."*

The Book of Lamentations was composed by one or several authors in the aftermath of the fall of Jerusalem in 587 B.C.E. It emerges from a Deuteronomic paradigm according to which "destruction is the sign neither of God's abandonment of Israel and the cancellation of His covenanted obligations to the people, nor of God's eclipse by competing powers in the cosmos" but "as a deserved and necessary punishment for sin," which "allows a penitent remnant to survive in a rehabilitated, restored relationship to God." Lamentations deviates from the paradigm in that confession of sin in this poem is vastly secondary to "the experience of abandonment and the horror of destruction." The task of the poet is "to find adequate language for the horror," and to this end a female figure is used to represent collective victimization, a male figure to represent the inconclusive struggle for theological reconciliation. Crucial to Lamentations—and to the genre that will succeed it—is that "God remains

*Alan Mintz, _Hurban: Responses to Catastrophe in Hebrew Literature_ (New York: Columbia University Press, 1984), p. x.

silent . . . but the sufferer's emergence from soliloquy to prayer enables him at least to recover God as an addressible other" and not merely a brutal enemy.★

Between Lamentations and "Howl" the parallels are numerous and uncanny, commencing with the one-word title promising a discourse in the semiotic register of meaningless sound. Outside, or prior to, the Law: the lament. Beyond or before the symbolic register, a howl. A language of vowels. A memory between or among the lines of the universal inconsolable infant for whom the umbilicus to the Absolute is broken. The infant without boundaries, the I who is Other, or infinite, or zero, witness and victim, betrayed by the word, unable to speak a word. The shriek of the powerless, feminized male.

In both poems the voice is exclamatory, impassioned, hyperbolic, intensely figurative, and virtually impossible to pin down, to locate, to identify. In both, the speaking or shrieking or wailing "I" oscillates between individual and collective identity. In the first chapter of Lamentations, the baffled third-person lament—"How doth the city sit solitary, that was full of people! how is she become as a widow!" (KJV, 1:1)—slides without warning, in midverse, into first-person: "All her people sigh, they seek bread, they have given their pleasant things for meat to relieve the soul: see, O Lord, and consider; for I am become vile" (1:11). Note that "pleasant things" in this passage is a euphemism for sexual organs; the image is of a starving woman prostituting herself. And again, "Is it nothing to you, all ye that pass by? Behold, and see if there be any sorrow like unto my sorrow which is done unto me, wherewith the Lord hath afflicted me in the day of his fierce anger" (1:12). Is this "I" the defiled and deserted Jerusalem speaking? Or a narrator identify-

★Mintz, Ḥurban, pp. 3–4.

ing with her? Impossible to say, and the whole opening chapter refuses to differentiate.

Chapter 2 is inhabited by a voice recounting, with horror, the hostilities of the Lord against his own—"The Lord was as an enemy, he hath swallowed up Israel, he hath swallowed up all her palaces, he hath destroyed his strongholds . . . And he hath violently taken away his tabernacle . . . he hath destroyed his places of the assembly" (2:5–6)—a voice that shifts into first-person to exclaim, "Mine eyes do fail with tears, my bowels are troubled, my liver is poured out upon the earth, for the destruction of the daughter of my people" (2:11), and then to bewail the impossibility of metaphor or comfort: "What thing shall I liken to thee, O daughter of Jerusalem? What shall I equal to thee, that I may comfort thee . . . For thy breach is great like the sea; who can heal thee?" (2:13). In 3:1 an "I" witnesses distinctly: "I am the man that hath seen affliction"—it is this line that produces Whitman's "I am the man, I suffered, I was there"—and almost immediately *is* afflicted: "My flesh and my skin hath he made old, he hath broken my bones" (3:4). Toward the close of Lamentations 4 and throughout chapter 5 the pronouns shift again, to a consistent first-person plural, a "we."

In the first moment of "Howl," we read "I saw . . . ," and the voice dissolves into what is seen. The "I" releases itself or is released into its surge of empathic madness. In Blakean terms, Ginsberg becomes what he beholds, an anaphoric catalog of self-destructive crazies whose search for the "ancient heavenly connection" that is simultaneously absolutely sacred and absolutely profane—revelation and dealer—fails to find the "fix" that signifies practical mending and drugged ecstasy. No further "I" enters the poem until the middle of Part II, where Ginsberg briefly interrupts his invocation/exorcism of the sacrificial deity of industrial capitalist rationality—"Moloch whose name is the

Mind"—with a spurt of self—"Moloch in whom I sit lonely! Moloch in whom I dream Angels! Crazy in Moloch! Cocksucker in Moloch! Lacklove and manless in Moloch!"—and almost immediately disappears from his own text again. Only in Part III, with the intimate and affectionate address to a friend that parallels the "we" of Lamentations, chapter 4, and the refrain "I'm with you in Rockland," does the poem at last imagine a possibility of coherent individual human identity, an "I" in relatively stable relation to a "you." In the "Footnote," personal identity is again transcended; no "I" interrupts the absurd utterance of ecstasy.

Geography in both Lamentations and "Howl" is likewise central and likewise paradoxical and contradictory. In both poems, identity not only is collective but requires rootedness in place. The city, Zion, the daughter of Zion, Jerusalem, the cities of Judah. Hallucinating Arkansas, poles of Canada and Paterson, Battery to holy Bronx. In both, the connection of place and people has been ruptured—by starvation literal and figurative, by conquest and exile: place does not *sustain* what should be its people.

The rhetoric of both poems relies on sexual figures and on body images—especially images of sexual humiliation and public disgrace. The pain of Jerusalem is also shame: "The adversaries saw her" (1:7). "They have seen her nakedness" (1:8). "Her filthiness is in her skirts" (1:9). "The adversary hath spread out his hand upon all her pleasant things . . . the heathen entered the sanctuary" (1:10). "Jerusalem is as a menstruous woman" (1:17). The male speaker experiences God as fire in his bones, a net for his feet, a yoke on his neck (1:13–14). In 2:11, "mine eyes do fail with tears, my bowels are troubled, my liver is poured out upon the earth for the destruction of the daughter of my people." In 2:16, Zion's enemies "hiss and gnash the teeth." In 3:4, "my flesh and skin he hath made old, he hath broken my bones." In 3:16, "he hath broken my teeth with gravel stones."

Likewise in Ginsberg, the body is constantly at issue, and the issue is commonly exposure, humiliation, deprivation: "starving hysterical naked" comrades "bared their brains to Heaven under the El," "got busted in their pubic beards," "purgatoried their torsos," "broke down crying in white gymnasiums naked," "were dragged off the roof waving genitals and manuscripts," "let themselves be fucked in the ass by saintly motorcyclists, and screamed with joy," "walked all night with their shoes full of blood on the snowbank docks," "cut their wrists three times successively unsuccessfully," and so on. Extremity of spirit is enacted through bodily extremity. In a moment of climactic horror after describing famine in the city, and accusing God of causing it, Lamentations asks, "Shall the women eat their fruit, children of a span long?" (2:20). At the close of "Howl," Part I, Ginsberg evokes "the absolute heart of the poem of life butchered out of their own bodies good to eat a thousand years."

What Lamentations and "Howl" share most crucially is the anguished and intolerable sense of a divine power that thwarts, punishes, and destroys, that seems absolutely cruel rather than merely indifferent to human suffering, that cannot be appealed to and that remains silent, and yet that must be appealed to because it *is* God. It is ultimately God who is cannibalistically gorging on the bodies of babies in Lamentations, as the poem makes clear in its images of mouth and hand: "The Lord hath swallowed up all the habitations of Jacob, and hath not pitied . . . he hath bent his bow like an enemy . . . he hath not withdrawn his hand from destroying" (2:2, 4, 8). The horrifying sublime prepares for, explains, and contains the horrifying pathetic: "The hands of the pitiful women have sodden their own children; they were their meat in the destruction of the daughter of my people. The Lord hath accomplished his fury" (4:10–11).

Ginsberg's generation has likewise been swallowed up by a more than human force, as the figurative conclusion of "Howl," Part I—the butchered heart of the poem of life "good to eat a thousand years"—is literalized in the opening line of Part II: it is likewise a God who "bashed open their skulls and ate up their brains and imagination." A pause here for Ginsberg's "Moloch," that sublimely elaborate invention of Part II:

> *Moloch! Solitude! Filth! Ugliness! Ashcans and unobtainable dollars! Children screaming under the stairways! Boys sobbing in armies! old men weeping in the parks!*
>
> *Moloch! Moloch! Nightmare of Moloch! Moloch the loveless! Mental Moloch! Moloch the heavy judger of men!*
>
> *Moloch the incomprehensible prison! Moloch the crossbone soulless jailhouse and Congress of sorrows! Moloch whose buildings are judgment! Moloch the vast stone of war! Moloch the stunned governments! . . .*
>
> *Moloch whose love is endless oil and stone! Moloch whose soul is electricity and banks! Moloch whose poverty is the specter of genius! Moloch whose fate is a cloud of sexless hydrogen! Moloch whose name is the Mind!*

The name is derived from the Canaanite god of fire Moloch, to whom children were offered in sacrifice and whose worship by the Israelites is condemned in Leviticus, 1 and 2 Kings, Jeremiah, Amos, and Ezekiel: "Moreover thou hast taken thy sons and daughters whom thou hast borne unto me, and these thou hast sacrificed unto them to be devoured. Is this of thy whoredoms a small matter, that thou hast slain my children and delivered them to cause them to pass through the fire for them?" (Ezekiel 16:20–21). As Israelite society for several centuries practiced human sacrifice, which in theory it rejected, our society does the same. William Blake's Moloch represents the obsessive human sacrifice of war, especially as connected with perversely suppressed sexuality. Ginsberg's mind-forged Moloch likewise has this aspect, and is a broadly Urizenic figure for the oppressiveness of a modern industrial and military state, exuded from Reason. Ginsberg's Moloch is also the modern version of Mammon, the capitalism of "unobtainable dollars . . . running money . . . electricity and banks!" But although you cannot worship both God and Mammon, Moloch is not an alternative to God, Moloch *is* God: "heavy judger of men . . . endless Jehovahs . . . They broke their backs lifting Moloch to Heaven!" Inorganic, abstract, Moloch is simultaneously whale's belly and incubus. Within us and without us: "Moloch who entered my soul early! Moloch in whom I am a consciousness without a body!" Inescapable Moloch parallels the God of Lamentations.

The contradiction of a God who is also an enemy leads to a deeper contradiction central to the genre of lamentation and, it has been argued, to Jewishness itself. Chapter 3 of Lamentations, its longest chapter, centers on a fusion of despair and hope. "He hath turned aside my ways, and pulled me in pieces" fuses with "The Lord is my portion, saith my soul; therefore have I hope" (3:11, 24). "Out of the mouth of the most high proceedeth not evil and good?" (3:38). When Ginsberg's manic "Footnote to Howl" announces the holiness of everything, it produces an absurd, irrational, extravagant inversion of Part I. Like the hope of the author of Lamentations, Ginsberg's celebration is not logical but willed:

Holy! Holy! Holy! Holy! Holy! Holy! Holy! Holy! Holy! Holy! Holy!
    Holy! Holy! Holy! Holy!
The world is holy! The soul is holy! The skin is holy! The nose is holy!
    The tongue and cock and hand and asshole holy!
Everything is holy! everybody's holy! everywhere is holy! everyday is in
    eternity! Everyman's an angel!

As in Blake's "Marriage of Heaven and Hell," which is clearly one of Ginsberg's most important models here, "everything that lives is holy." Further, as "Holy" inverts "howly," what has previously been interpreted as monstrous by the poet himself may now be reinterpreted:

"Holy the solitudes of skyscrapers and pavements! Holy the cafeterias filled with the millions! Holy the mysterious rivers of tears under the streets!" In a spurt of hilarity, even Moloch can and must be included: "Holy time in eternity holy eternity in time holy the clocks in space holy the fourth dimension holy the fifth International holy the Angel in Moloch!" And finally "Holy the supernatural extra brilliant intelligent kindness of the soul!"

Kindness again. That almost imperceptible Yiddish kindness. It is perhaps of interest that Ginsberg apparently thought the poem finished after Part III and mailed copies to numerous friends and critics, including Richard Eberhart, to whom he wrote an extended formal discussion of the poem without the footnote on May 18, 1956, and including his father. From Louis, Allen received the following comment: "I am gratified about your new ms. It's a wild, rhapsodic, explosive outpouring with good figures of speech flashing by in its volcanic rushing . . . It's a hot geyser of emotion suddenly released in wild abandon from subterranean depths of your being." Louis insisted, however, "There is no need for dirty, ugly words, as they will entangle you unnecessarily in trouble," and added his anxiety that the poem "is a one-sided neurotic view of life, it has not enough glad, Whitmanic affirmations."* Sweet, embarrassing Louis. And did Allen perhaps compose the "Footnote" under the invisible pressure of his father's admonition? Its exact date is unrecorded.

*Miles, *Ginsberg*, p. 204.

THE POET AS JEW: "HOWL" REVISITED

III. IT OCCURS TO HIM THAT HE IS AMERICA

To be a Jew in the twentieth century
Is to be offered a gift. If you refuse,
Wishing to be invisible, you choose
Death of the spirit, the stone insanity.
Accepting, take full life. Full agonies:
Your evening deep in labyrinthine blood
Of those who resist, fail and resist; and God
Reduced to a hostage among hostages.

The gift is torment. Not alone the still
Torture, isolation; or torture of the flesh.
That may come also. But the accepting wish,
The whole and fertile spirit as guarantee
For every human freedom, suffering to be free,
Daring to live for the impossible.★

That is, of course, Rukeyser again, the Rukeyser of "Letter to the Front," published in 1944, stylistically a generation away from "Howl," chronologically a decade away, morally shoulder to queer Jewish shoulder. How Jewish then is the Ginsberg of "Howl"? His ethnicity was never exactly invisible to others. "Naive, he was incredibly naive," recalled Lucien Carr of his fellow student at Columbia. "He was just an eager young Jewish kid from Paterson who wanted to know everything about books and writers and art and painting, who knew nothing about the serious things in life such as wenching and drinking."† Kerouac fictionalizes the young Allen in *The Town and the City* (1946): "Levinsky was an eager, sharply intelligent boy of Russian-Jewish parentage

★Janet E. Kaufman and Anne F. Herzog, eds., with Jan Heller Levi, *The Collected Poems of Muriel Rukeyser* (Pittsburgh: University of Pittsburgh Press, 2005), p. 243.
†Miles, *Ginsberg*, p. 42.

117

who rushed around New York in a perpetual sweat of emotional activity."[*] And in *Vanity of Duluoz*: "I was sitting in Edie's apartment one day when the door opened and in walks this spindly Jewish kid with horn-rim glasses and tremendous ears sticking out, 17 years old, burning black eyes, a strangely deep voice."[†] Introducing *Empty Mirror*, William Carlos Williams calls Ginsberg "this young Jewish boy," before going on to compare him with Dante and Chaucer, but then comes around to remarking, "When the poet in his writing would scream at the crowd, like Jeremiah, that their life is beset, what can he do, in the end, but speak to them in their own language, that of the daily press?"[‡] Richard Eberhart, describing Ginsberg's performance of "Howl" at the Six reading for the September 2, 1956, *New York Times Book Review*, writes, "My first reaction was that it is based on destructive violence. It is profoundly Jewish in temper. It is Biblical in its repetitive grammatical buildup. It is a howl against anything in our mechanistic civilization which kills the spirit . . . It lays bare the nerves of suffering and spiritual struggle. Its positive force and energy come from a redemptive quality of love."[§] M. L. Rosenthal, reviewing "Howl" in *The Nation* in 1957, wrote that the poem had "the single-minded frenzy of a raving madwoman" (rather nice guesswork, one might say; Naomi *is* that madwoman, but "Kaddish" hasn't been published yet) but that some of Ginsberg's early poems at the back of the book "have a heavy Yiddish melancholy."[**] Edward Albee remembers Allen in the late fifties as "young, a young old testament prophet."[††] For Hayden Car-

---

[*]Ibid., p. 74.
[†]Ibid., p. 44.
[‡]Hyde, ed., *On the Poetry*, pp. 17–18.
[§]Richard Eberhart in ibid., p. 25.
[**]M. L. Rosenthal in ibid., pp. 29, 31.
[††]Edward Albee, "Dear Allen," in Bill Morgan and Bob Rosenthal, *Best Minds: A Tribute to Allen Ginsberg* (New York: Lospecchio Press, 1986), p. 5.

ruth he is "mindpetal, spectre, strangest jew, cityboy."[*] Yevgeny Yevtushenko, who with a charm equal to Allen's own calls him the "Omm-issar of American Poetry," remembers the Beats as "the uprising of the garbage dumps of the suburbs, as if tin cans, broken bicycles, and rusted cars erupted with a roar like Vesuvius' lava at the smug Pompeii of soullessness. And riding bareback on a garbage can, careering wildly past the Plaza and the Hilton, like a Jewish Mowgli of the concrete jungles, came Allen Ginsberg, prophet of the outpouring."[†]

As to Allen's own testimony, "At 14 I was an introvert, an atheist, a Communist and a Jew, and I still wanted to be president of the United States."[‡] His family listened to Eddie Cantor on the radio, and "it was a . . . high point of the week, I guess because he was Jewish and a national comedian and everybody in the family identified with him."[§] In his last year of high school, Allen vowed to devote his life to helping the working classes if he got into Columbia University. The simplicity of these identifications and that identity failed to outlast his crossing the river to Columbia and his immediate attraction to the bohemian likes of Lucien Carr, Jack Kerouac, William Burroughs, Neal Cassady, all non-Jews, apolitical, amoral. What was a nice Jewish boy doing with these types? poor Louis kept asking. What did he have in mind by writing "Fuck the Jews" accompanied by a skull and crossbones on his dusty dorm window? Ginsberg's biographer Barry Miles takes Allen's word at face value that his little naughtiness was to catch the attention of an Irish cleaning

[*]Ibid., p. 53.
[†]Ibid., p. 298.
[‡]Allen Ginsberg, *Journals: Early Fifties Early Sixties*, edited by Gordon Ball (New York: Grove Press, 1977), p. 17.
[§]Barry Miles, *Ginsberg: A Biography* (New York: Viking, 1989), p. 19.

woman he suspected of being anti-Semitic.★ Trilling and his wife were utterly unable to accept that Allen was simply goading the anti-Semitic Irish cleaner, and years later Diana Trilling was still using the incident as an example of Ginsberg's "Jewish self-hatred."

A few chapters later, Miles observes that Allen "was unable to relate to his Jewish heritage."† How very Jewish. Carl Solomon, the dedicatee of "Howl," who introduced Allen to his hero Artaud, publishes his "Report from the Asylum: Afterthoughts of a Shock Patient" under the name Carl Goy. Allen's brother, Eugene, changes his surname to Brooks when he becomes a lawyer. It would be years before Allen started identifying himself humorously as a Jewish Buddhist.

Two interesting essays by fellow poets touch on this matter through meditating on the ancient heavenly connection of Allen-Naomi. To Clayton Eshleman, Ginsberg's "visionary panic over the destructiveness of North American society, the way it titillates the self and then cold-cocks it," derives from how "on a very personal level, North America had done the same thing to his mother . . . it is the agony of the son who escorted his mother when he was twelve to the asylum . . . that flows through the magnificent first movement of 'Howl' . . . Ginsberg would save Mankind since he was unable to save Naomi."‡ Supporting this intuition, we might notice that the nominal "secret hero" of Part I may be Neal Cassady, "N.C. . . . cocksman and Adonis of Denver"; but toward the close of Part I

★Ibid., pp. 59–61.
†Ibid., p. 210.
‡Hyde, *On the Poetry*, pp. 109, 112.

comes a set of lines whose reference is Carl Solomon, and in their midst like a bubble the mother finally asterisked and the "yellow paper rose twisted on a wire hanger" in the nameless Naomi's madhouse closet. Allen Grossman, in a partially skewed essay on Ginsberg, "The Jew as American Poet," argues that "the Jew, like the Irishman, presents himself as the type of the sufferer in history"★ but that for Ginsberg the Beat subculture "takes the place of the real ethnic and political subcultures which in the past succored and gave identity to the outcast by forming a community of outcasts."†

"In 'Kaddish,'" Grossman continues, "the archetypal female is a mutilated and paranoid old woman ('scars of operations, pancreas, belly wounds, abortions, appendix, stitching of incisions pulling down in the fat like hideous thick zippers') haunted by the image of Hitler and dying, obscene and abandoned, in the sanatorium. This is Ginsberg's version of the Jewish mother and, simultaneously, of the shechina, the wandering soul of Israel herself."‡ What is expressed in "Kaddish" is repressed but surely present in "Howl." If Naomi is the invisible mother-matter of Ginsberg's first great poem, there is an uncanny connection between this mother who almost devoured her son and the mothers who cannibalize their children in the streets of Jerusalem. Grossman goes on, however, to claim that Ginsberg "erects on [Naomi's] grave an image which is no longer ethnic and which therefore is no longer obsessed by the mystery of the Jewish people in history,"§ implying, I think, that Ginsberg is somehow or other not a *real* Jew because of this: "Throughout Ginsberg's writing there is an ambivalence toward Jewishness

★Ibid., p. 102.
†Ibid., p. 103.
‡Ibid., p. 105.
§Ibid.

which should be recognized as it seems to be an emphatic part of his public statement."★

But ambivalence toward Jewishness may be a basic ingredient of Jewishness since the fall of Jerusalem in 587 B.C.E. Alan Mintz, tracing "responses to catastrophe in Hebrew literature" from Lamentations to the post-Holocaust era, finds the theme of *shame* at Israel's humiliation before the nations suffusing rabbinic writing in the Middle Ages; it is partially replaced by the exaltation of martyrdom as a response to European massacres of Jews; suffering becomes "an opportunity awarded by God to the most worthy for the display of righteousness."† In the early modern period, from the 1880s to the early 1900s, writers like Shalom Abramowitsch, Saul Tchernichovsky, and Chaim Nachman Bialik respond to the devastating pogroms that swept Russia and Eastern Europe with a literature of profound and bitter ambivalence toward the masses of Jewish people.

To be a Jew in diaspora is to be ambivalent. It is common also to take on the colors of the host culture. To be more German than the Germans, like Heine; more French than the French, like Dreyfus, Sartre, and Simone Weil; more English than the English, like Disraeli; more Russian than the Russians, like Isaac Babel, who rode with the Cossacks. To *believe* in the host culture's own ideals about itself—and to write as a passionate social critic when the host nation fails (of course) to embody those ideals: this is all normal for the Jewish writer.

Allen as Jew: from his father's socialism, i.e., his tenderhearted materialism, Allen keeps and intensifies the tenderness, and rejects the materialism. From his mother's communism—her paranoid idealism—Allen tries to exorcise the paranoia (everything's holy, Moloch is holy, breathe deep and say Om) while

★Ibid., p. 109.
†Mintz, *Hurban*, p. 6.

holding fast to the idealism, free love and all, physical and emotional nudism and all. From Louis's poetry he keeps a devotion to form. From Naomi's madness he keeps the outrageousness and outgrows the self-destructiveness.

From America, Allen takes Whitman. The manly love of comrades, the open road, the democratic vistas stretching to eternity, and also the eyes of America taking a fall, which he plants, later, in his mother's head. America will always be, for him, infinite hope and infinite disappointment. That's very Jewish.

And from Judaism he takes the universal compassion and rejects the tribalism. Instead of professing victimization as Jew, his writing projects victimization onto the world and in the same moment proposes, through the force of rhetoric, to save it. The power of prophetic rhetoric in the genre of Lamentations is that it must wring cosmic affirmation out of despair. God is your enemy, and you must trust him. Moloch, whose eyes are a thousand blind windows, eats his children, but you must declare him holy. A decade after completing "Howl," Ginsberg at the climax of "Wichita Vortex Sutra" calls "all the powers of the Imagination" to his side and declares "the end of the War." Ridiculous, absurd, foolish, impossible. Daring to live for the impossible.

KURT BROWN

A THIRTEEN-YEAR-OLD CADET

———

We met covertly on the backseat of a bus. I was ready. I had heard of him and his obscene book, a long poem called "Howl," which I held in my hands with the greatest anticipation. Among the other boys my age, his name had been bandied about, and perhaps something of the media exposure that accompanied the rise of the Beats in the mid-fifties had filtered through the fog of my adolescent self-regard, the ordinary narcissism that marks anyone's teenage years. I was poised on that threshold between an earlier interest in normal boyish pursuits—hunting, fishing, fighting, sports—and a new obsession with sex, which was quickly eclipsing all previous activities and interests. "Howl" had been banned, had in fact been the subject of a trial for obscenity. I had gotten my hands on a cheap novel here and there, prurient tales of motels with hidden cameras or sensory-deprived small-town teachers gone wild. And, of course, *Playboy* and a few other glossy magazines had already begun to exhibit the slick, airbrushed bodies of women, odalisques stapled erotically in triptych. Of all the salacious literature I had been able to obtain before this, however, none had been banned. "Howl," I concluded, must be the best of the best, the paragon of perversity for which I longed, and which would undoubtedly enlighten me once and for all.

It is important—important for me and for the context of this writing—to remember where I was and who I was at the time in order to appreciate the full extent of my transgression in obtaining and reading a copy of "Howl." Not only was it the fifties, that stifling decade that we have nonetheless come to celebrate as one of the happiest moments in twentieth-century America, but I was a thirteen-year-old cadet in a military school in South Carolina, a Connecticut Yankee in a courtly, cantankerous, and decidedly alien land. How all of this came about is another story, but one further detail adds to the unlikeliness of the scene: it was Sunday, and I was sitting on the bus that drove us to church each week in a nearby town. Often, and this meant half the time, none of us—including the older cadet who drove the bus—wished to attend the service. Instead, we parked on an inconspicuous side street and merely slept or read or walked around the gritty neighborhoods for an hour or so before driving back to the school, punctual but unsaved. It was on one of these counterfeit forays to church, on a beautiful Sunday morning in April while the town hardly breathed in its collective piety and honeysuckle sparkled in the links of a rusty chain fence, that I first laid eyes on "Howl" and read Ginsberg's stirring but decidedly unpoetic opening lines:

I saw the best minds of my generation destroyed by madness, starving hysterical naked,
dragging themselves through the negro streets at dawn looking for an angry fix.

One of the older cadets, someone we might have described at the time as a "hood" for his bullying, antisocial behavior, had brought the book along and made a great show of drawing it out of his pocket and reading it. It was obvious he felt superior, smug in the knowledge that he alone possessed the wherewithal to obtain secretly and appreciate the forbidden, while the rest of us looked on in a torment of anticipation and erotic jealousy. Within minutes, though, his entire demeanor changed. He frowned. He sighed audibly, and with unconcealed dismay. Suddenly he threw the book down beside him on the seat. "What *is* this shit?" he proclaimed, glaring at the little volume as though it had bitten him, as though it had offended him in some direct but unaccountable way. "It don't mean nuthin.'" "Let me see!" someone else shouted. And quickly the book was passed from hand to hand until the last cadet pursed his lips, shut the black-and-white cover with its single declamatory verb, like a head-line, and laid it down indifferently before leaving the bus. This was my chance. While the others sauntered up the street and around the corner in search of whatever titillation the drowsy Sunday morning might offer, I curled up in the backseat of the bus with Ginsberg's anthem to libido and suppressed rage, and began to read.

At first I shared the disappointment of my companions, a feeling of betrayal, that something fabulous, something prom-ised and secretly delicious, had been withheld. The words and phrases danced before my eyes, sounded in my mind like so much intellectual gibberish, the kind of thing I had been forced to read in school, words joined together for no other purpose than to confound young people like me. Here and there, though, the forbidden flickered momentarily, like some shadowy ser-pent's tongue, then disappeared. I read of the poet's friend, "cocksman and Adonis of Denver," who "sweetened the snatches of a million girls trembling in the sunset," of being "fucked in the ass," of how his other friends had been "busted in their pubic beards," and so on. But these moments were few and far between, couched in unfamiliar, rhetorical terms. Mostly the poem documented frenetic comings and goings in cars, life in cold-water flats, and the screeching of industrial steam whistles. Where were the moans and groans of conventional pornography, the breasts and engorged members, the taut nipples and full lips of a thousand cheap novels and magazines that pandered to male fantasy? Where was the smooth, unblemished skin and rounded buttocks of dime-store fiction with which I was already familiar? Yet something in the writing compelled my interest, kept me groping from phrase to phrase in the hope of some payoff I could hardly imagine, but for which I still ardently longed.

The sermon that morning was all Ginsberg. While the surface of my thirteen-year-old mind languished in disappointment, something deeper in me responded unwittingly, soaked up the power of that provocative language. Though I never memorized a bit of it—not then or since—certain phrases stuck in my mind immediately, lodged there to resound for years, eventually informing my own sense of how words might be brought together to signify experience and make poetry. Phrases like "a wig of blood" and "listening to the crack of doom on the hydrogen jukebox" rang seductively in my ears, along with the surging, powerful rhythms driven by the effective use of biblical anaphora. Ginsberg's lines swept across the page unhindered, built upon themselves in crescendos of feeling and thought, seemed to gather into the poem more and more of the world's ten thousand unaccountable things. I was balanced on an edge: half ready to put the book down in disgust, like the others, half unexplainably drawn back, again and again, to the next unreeling sentence, and the next. I don't remember moving, though I wouldn't describe myself as enthralled. The sun pressed through the glass of the bus window and illuminated the pages. A wiry black script ranted and hissed and cajoled. I read the whole thing. I read from the "heavenly connection to the starry dynamo in the machinery of night" to "Ashcans and unobtainable dollars!" I read until my brain felt "bashed open . . . good to eat for a thousand years!"

Then Ginsberg took a long bardic breath, and began again. Now it was stories of throwing potato salad at CCNY lectures, lobotomies, Metrazol and insulin. I was vaguely aware of how funny this was but probably didn't laugh or even smile, as poetry in my experience had always been treated as something serious and venerable, something no self-respecting citizen would find funny. I recall feeling a bit annoyed at Carl Solomon: who was he, and why should I care? Weren't these men better off in the madhouse for writing such things and behaving in such zany and unconventional ways? Then, after another brief pause heavy with the sound of vatic breathing, Ginsberg was off again, chanting his holy chant, through a forest of exclamation points resonant with the effort of his strident howling. "Holy! Holy! Holy!" etc. "Holy cock and balls!" "Holy asshole! "Holy Allen! Holy Huncke! Holy Jack!" In short, all of his friends and everything about them was holy, and everything else in the world was holy too. Even me. Even that battered, suffocating school bus. Even the semidilapidated, offbeat, rural town full at that moment with humble worshipers petitioning their god to forgive them for their gray, quotidian sins.

It occurs to me as I write this that I might be entirely mistaken. A small but insistent reservation nudges me, slides and flickers in the back of my brain, suggesting that the first edition of "Howl" ended right there—with that last brainless sentence devouring the reader—before Moloch even entered the picture. Before parts II and III were ever written and appended in later editions. I don't know. I may be conflating, as memory often does, a number of different readings into one. It doesn't matter. I have refused to go downstairs and take my copy of "Howl" off the shelf to check because I wanted to see how much I actually *do* remember, how much of the poem has pervaded my consciousness, how much of it has contributed to my inner life and thought, continuing to influence me for almost fifty years. There have been breaks, quarrels, disenchantments, to be sure, some of them lasting decades. For a while, I thought Ginsberg had become the harlequin fool he claimed he was in that first printing of his seminal poem. Surely he wrote too much and too fast, often printing mere journal entries as if they were fully realized, completed poems. Surely he has written some of the most superficial doggerel penned by a major American poet in the twentieth century. But I don't think I ever got over the spell of that first acquaintance with "Howl." And when I came to read his other great poems—"Kaddish," "The Fall of America," "Wales Visitation," and "Plutonian Ode"—and some of his brilliant, shorter work—"A Supermarket in California," "Sunflower Sutra," "America"—I was brought back into the fold, and knew again I was in the hands of one of America's masters of modern free verse and ecstatic expression.

Soon the others came straggling back, some with bottles of birch beer or Dr Pepper, some with various candy bars, packs of gum and cigarettes. Their gray woolen coats were thrown open in the heat, the full dress uniforms we wore on Sundays with gleaming brass buttons and polished belts. They swore and spit and clambered aboard the bus for the short ride home. Around us, people were just beginning to spill out of the churches, full-skirted and necktied, bonneted and impeccably groomed. Whole families piled into Ford Fairlanes or Chevy convertibles and started back for home as well, to stifle in the spring heat and the postwar decorum of an oppressive decade. As for me: the mark had been made. I didn't know it then, but not only Ginsberg, Kerouac as well, Ferlinghetti, Corso, Cassady, and a host of other unholy loonies loomed in my future. Some liminal transformation in my sensibility had taken place, my ideas about life and language ever so slightly deflected from their conventional course. For the time being, though, I almost certainly forgot "Howl" and the odd, hopped-up excitement of its unusual strophes. I went back to listening to the pabulum of popular rock, went back to textbooks and *Bandstand* and bland Hollywood movies. I breathed easily as the red clay fields of the Carolinas swept by, headed for whatever illuminations and hotrod Golgothas lay hidden, not far beyond the horizon, in my future.

PHILLIP LOPATE

"HOWL" AND ME

———

I must have been fourteen and still in junior high school when I first encountered Allen Ginsberg's "Howl." How it crossed my path I'm not sure; probably my older brother Leonard, who was seventeen and mad about Federico García Lorca and William Blake, tossed it my way, as he did all of his poetic discoveries. We went around for weeks intoning favorite passages—the first two lines, of course, "I saw the best minds of my generation . . ." down to "looking for an angry fix," and "fucked in the ass by saintly motorcyclists" and "boxcars boxcars boxcars," which for some reason always cracked us up. We loved the poem for its phonic fireworks and flaming images, but we also mocked its solemn, oracular quality, opportunistically applying an adolescent penchant for parody to any target within easy reach.

I have to say that "Howl" struck me from the first as a little ludicrous and overblown. In retrospect, I think I may have been threatened by its intense emotions, and deaf to its more ironic registers. Then, too, much as we embraced Kerouac and Ginsberg as a retort to the "tranquillized fifties," we were not immune to the ubiquitous parodies of them in the popular culture. Who could not giggle at Bob Hope's beatnik routine, wearing a beret and a fake goatee, banging bongos, snapping his fingers, and crying "Yeah, man!" Still, we were much more pro-Beat than anti-; and "Howl," by virtue of giving America the finger, fit neatly into our bag of anarchic provocations, along with *Mad* magazine, the raunchier lyrics of rhythm and blues, and, a bit later, Lenny Bruce.

I have a feeling some shards of Ginsberg's dangerous shrapnel lodged more deeply into my subconscious than I realized, because, soon after reading "Howl," I wrote a poem called "I Hate It All" and turned it in to my English teacher for creative writing extra credit. This lurid rant enlisted every cliché about "gnawing rats," "crying men," and "the dirt of the slums," disguising my personal resentment, no doubt, at my parents for making us live in a ghetto, before coming to the noble realization "But I am of it, of this thing I hate." It was, if you will, a precociously Baldwinesque moment of identification with all I was trying to flee. My English teacher, Miss Loftus, responded with sour surprise: "Phillip, I thought you were our most well-adjusted student!" and sent me down to the guidance counselor.

You must understand that, for all my extracurricular dabbling in anarchic culture, I was pretty much a goody-goody, and had gotten myself elected student president, no mean feat in a mostly black school, so that when I began poetically denouncing the squalor of my immediate environment, the adults around me grew understandably chagrined. Getting sent to the guidance counselor was not the pat-on-the-head, extra-credit response I had anticipated. I found myself in a jam, needing to explain my ode to hate as somehow not really reflective of my true feelings, and I began describing it as a creative put-on, spouting showy-off references to the Dadaists and Surrealists (never mentioning Allen Ginsberg, which would have been too close to home). My dodge, I could tell, did not convince the guidance counselor; but she had no choice, given my refusal to be candid about what was bothering me, except to send me back to class.

The odd thing, I see now, is that I kept doing this, modeling the role of the perfectly calm, responsible, civic-minded A student, while sending out flares that something was not right inside, I needed help. In high school, I again got myself elected to office, this time chief justice of the student court, meanwhile writing a very provoking piece about my feelings of alienation for a citywide essay contest. When my high school English teacher, Mrs. Gold, accused me of trying to *épater le bourgeois*, I mocked her behind her back as a provincial ninny.

All this self-divided behavior culminated in my getting accepted to an Ivy League school on a scholarship, and trying to kill myself by my sophomore year. We do not need to revisit that incident. The point I am making here is that I knew more than I sometimes cared to admit about the screaming confusion, rage, and lostness expressed by "Howl"; I had my own personal howl going on inside my head much of the time, and I was trying to keep a tight lid on it.

Having sorted out, or anyhow survived, this adolescent crisis of yearning and negation, I would spend the rest of my life striving for skepticism and stoicism. You might say I turned away from "Howl," with its suicidal grandiosity, gutter ecstasies, and apocalyptic nightmares, trading them in for the smaller promise of humor, equilibrium, and the everyday. Allen Ginsberg, a fellow Jewish writer who also went to Columbia before dropping out, was like an older brother (exactly seventeen years older) who had courageously blazed the trail ahead of me, smoothing the road not taken. I would stay in college, guard my scholarship, nose to the grindstone, graduate in four years and get married, showing everyone what a mature, responsible fellow I was.

The strongest pull that "Howl" exerted on me thus was cautionary. If it seemed an advertisement for madness, drug addiction, vagrancy, homosexuality, and rhetoric as the road to enlightenment, I knew with a shudder that those were not for me. I had come close—too close—to ending up like Carl Solomon in Rockland State Hospital: having landed in the psych ward after my suicide attempt, I'd suddenly needed to convince the staff that I was perfectly all right, I did not need any shock treatment, thank you very much. Needles had always terrified me, so becoming a junkie held no appeal. I was dead-set on clawing my way out of ghetto Brooklyn and into the middle class, too close to the poverty line to entertain romantic notions about bums and clochards. Limited as my sexual repertoire was, I did not want to get fucked in the ass by anyone, much less "saintly motorcyclists." And why "saintly"? I'd seen Brando in *The Wild One* and the motorcycle gangs in *Scorpio Rising*, and real live Hells Angels menacing the Lower East Side, and not a scintilla of sanctity did they radiate. If Allen Ginsberg wanted to have an orgasm with a guy, fine with me, but why insist that it was saintly, or that the sailors who blew him were "human seraphim"; that part struck me as sentimental. Besides, why was a good Jewish boy like Allen bothering with all Christian imagery about saintly? Perhaps the "saintly" bothered me more than the "motorcyclists."

"Howl" proffered one more temptation I resisted mightily, and that was contained in the words "my generation." This may not be the proper occasion to explore what lies behind my distrust of that (to my mind) smug, self-mythifying notion. Oh, what the hell. To quote Ben Hecht: "It is, as I have long suspected, very difficult for a writer to write about anybody but himself." Certainly true for me. I find the words "my generation" stick in my throat. They seem presumptuous; I don't feel it's my right to generalize for all those who happened to be born the same decade as myself. Or perhaps it isn't humility but vanity that won't allow me to speak of myself in any but idiosyncratic terms, resisting sociological categories that would place me in a collective epoch. Or am I merely envious that I never belonged to a glittering bohemian set, like the Parisians around Picasso in Roger Shattuck's *The Banquet Years*, or the Harvard crowd who went on to constitute the New York School of Poetry? In any case, here was Ginsberg, lovingly canonizing his particular set of friends ("Holy Peter holy Allen holy Solomon holy Lucien holy Kerouac holy Huncke holy Burroughs holy Cassady") as not only a generation but "the best minds of" his generation. And what entitled them to this accolade? That they ran naked through "the negro streets," smoked dope on rooftops, dropped out of the academy—in other words, that they made a mess of their lives. Am I being too literal here? Are we supposed to think that they started off as the best minds of their generation, and then the evil capitalist Moloch society ruined them, or that their own exquisite sensitivity led to their collapse, like Wordsworth's couplet about poets in their youth who begin in gladness and end in madness?

Throughout the poem, Ginsberg seems torn between portraying his buddies as the divinely chosen damned and extending a more democratic laurel of beatitude to all the downtrodden and losers, as when he says "holy Cassady holy the unknown buggered and suffering beggars holy the hideous human angels!" What about all those working stiffs who would not end up raving lunatics, who could not afford to drop out, were we automatically judged mediocre and condemned to a lower status than "the best minds," by dint of neglecting or refusing to fall apart? Of course "Howl" is a young man's poem, and I ought not to be subjecting it to this querulous, middle-aged class analysis when

what it has most to recommend it is its jazzy, generative enthusi-
asm, and its wholesome desire for redemptive embrace. The
poem ends with these lines:

Holy forgiveness! mercy! charity! faith! Holy! Ours! bodies! suffering!
    magnanimity!
Holy the supernatural extra brilliant intelligent kindness of the soul!

Okay, I can buy that. Not sure what it means, but I'm all for
kindness and forgiveness. Where I have trouble is when the poet
says: "the soul is innocent." He invokes the word "innocence"
several times in "Howl," like a son pleading before a stern father-
judge, demanding amnesty for all acts of self-destructiveness,
and shifting the blame disingenuously onto Society, Moloch.
Why not accept that we are not innocent?

Well, that is one reading of the poem, and probably the
conventional one. A contrary reading would be that Ginsberg
himself was something of a detached observer, more stable than
the others, portraying clearly though with sympathy the screwups
of those around him, even envying them their loss of control,
yet in his own way being cautionary, undeceived by their pitiable
attempts to rationalize all that insane behavior. For instance, is
there not some irony when he speaks of those "who threw
potato salad at CCNY lectures on Dadaism and subsequently
presented themselves on the granite steps of the madhouse with
shaven heads and harlequin speech of suicide, demanding in-
stantaneous lobotomy"? Or when he refers to "Dreams! adora-
tions! illuminations! religions! the whole boatload of sensitive
bullshit!" Yes, the whole boatload of sensitive bullshit, indeed.
That is what "Howl" throws at us and also what the poem at-
tempts to surmount—even managing, at times, to have it both
ways.

I will always be grateful to "Howl" for the way it prepared me for the beauties of Whitman, whose cornucopia of inventories and one-line portraits struck me as both gorgeous and inevitable. These two American masters also shared a love of cities and public spaces, the undersides of bridges, the streets, rooftops, alleys—the whole consoling urbanistic shebang, which means more to me as I grow older. These days when I read "Howl," I forgive the Blakean seraphic bluster and am much more attentive to the superb atmospherics of place, the mise-en-scène, so to speak.

The poem of Ginsberg's that really floored me, of course, was "Kaddish." I could be indifferent, finally, to Carl Solomon rotting in Rockland's mental wards, indifferent to Neal Cassady's priapic triumphs ("secret hero of these poems, cocksman and Adonis of Denver—"), but I could not be indifferent to Naomi, given my own embarrassed love for a difficult mother.

Hats off to Allen Ginsberg! I will end with a few anecdotes. During my years as a fellow traveler of the New York School of Poetry, I would run into him at parties and readings. We gave each other a wide berth; he seemed much more interested in cute young boys or being in Bob Dylan's entourage than in my own person, and I, for my part, did not go out of my way to cultivate him, the more so as I drifted further and further away from a bohemian mind-set. Instead I added him to that list of famous writers I knew casually but was unable to bring myself to attempt a closer connection, which I now only partly regret.

Once, after the Stonewall riots, I volunteered my services to a benefit poetry reading for gay rights, thinking it important at the time for straight writers such as myself to show solidarity publicly with the gay community. I read a long, comic, mother-

PHILLIP LOPATE

son poem that night called "The Blue Pants," and Ginsberg
closed the reading. Afterward, he came up and told me I should
have read a little faster. My first thought, which fortunately I did
not utter, was "What a putz!" I especially felt that way because
here I was "magnanimously" going out of my heterosexual way
to participate in a gay rights reading, and he was criticizing my
delivery. Years later, I wonder if he may have been paying me a
compliment: recognizing a fellow entertainer, and giving me a
bit of professional advice. I probably *should* have read my poem
a touch faster.

In the mid-1980s, I was on a committee to select the
Pulitzer Prize in poetry. Unlike other awards, the Pulitzer is de-
cided in two stages: first the writers' committee goes through all
the books in its designated area that were published the previous
year and sends up three recommendations; then a group of
newspaper and magazine editors makes a final selection. Since
the editors are usually not as versed in poetry as one might wish,
they often pick the most unchallenging, user-friendly collec-
tion. In any event, Allen Ginsberg's *Collected Poems: 1947–1980*
was published in 1984, and I pushed hard for it to be named one
of the three finalists. Ginsberg's achievement as a major Ameri-
can poet seemed to me self-evident, but I did not succeed in
convincing the other two committee members to include it.
Outraged, I took the unusual step of filing a minority recom-
mendation to the editors, who were thus obliged to consider
Ginsberg's *Collected*, along with the other three finalists. As it
turned out, the editors also rejected Ginsberg for the Pulitzer
Prize. I phoned Allen at his home to tell him he had at least been
one of the finalists. He was philosophical about it, saying, "They
don't want to give the big prizes to me. They still hold against
me all that stuff from the sixties."

I suppose you can be either King of the May or Poet Laure-
ate, but not both in the same lifetime. By now he was elderly

and infirm, and we chatted for fifteen minutes, mostly about his ailments but also about teaching creative writing. I remember none of what he said—nothing except for the tone, which was extremely amiable. He struck me as a mensch, a sweet, elderly, realistic Jew of a sort I was familiar with from my youth, and I chastised myself for having misjudged him before as a show-boating putz. (The truth is that he was probably, like most of us, a putz and a mensch.) I had probably misjudged "Howl" all along as well, and am misjudging it still. But I can't be too hard on myself for that. How can anyone whose formative years had intersected so primally with such a storm of a poem be expected to judge it with objectivity? "Howl" is lodged in my psyche, at the crossroads of my adolescent confusions.

TALKING HOWL 2

"Howl" is the skin of Rimbaud's *Une Saison en Enfer* thrown over the conventional maunderings of one American adolescent, who has discovered that machine civilization has no interest in his having read Blake.   —James Dickey, *Sewanee Review*, Summer 1957

"Howl" is the confession of faith of the generation that is going to be running the world in 1965 and 1975—if it's still there to be run.   —Kenneth Rexroth, "San Francisco Letter,"
Evergreen Review, Summer 1957

The issue here—as in every like case—is not the merit or lack of it of a book but of a Society which traditionally holds the human being to be by its very functional nature a creature of shameful, outrageous and obscene habits.
          —Kenneth Patchen, testimony, *The People vs. City Lights*, 1957

How neat it is for Dr. Williams, pediatrician, to introduce "Howl" to the world.   —Donald Justice, *Western Review*, Spring 1958

It is a howl against everything in our mechanistic civilization which kills the spirit, assuming that the louder you shout the more likely you are to be heard. It lays bare the nerves of suffering and spiritual struggle. Its positive force and energy come from a redemptive quality of love, although it destructively catalogues evils of our time from physical deprivation to madness.
          —Richard Eberhart, *The New York Times Book Review*, September 2, 1956

"Howl" is a great long, desperate wail, a struggle to make poetry out of all the objects, surroundings and people he had known. At times it reached an American surrealism, a bitter irony; it had a savage power . . . It reminded me of Artaud.

—Anaïs Nin, *The Diary of Anaïs Nin, 1955–1966*, 1966

Because of "Howl" poets writing in the sixties became ill at ease manufacturing their tried-and-true delicate nuances. Fashion decreed that they howl instead. Ginsberg's poem had the effect of a natural disaster . . . "Howl" knocked the hell out of earlier images of what best minds say and do. Not only was it descriptive of a vast social-spiritual death; but it provided a villainous cause; the god Moloch who in the poem is simply the System. Not since the thirties had the System had such an inclusive raking over—in fact, "Howl" single-handedly did much to restore the thirties vogue of super-colossal system-damnation we are still suffering from, and it did so without providing a Marxist antidote. It was what D. H. Lawrence would perhaps have called a death-energy poem.

—Reed Whittemore, "Review of Indian Journals,"
The New Republic, July 23, 1970

The sign of Moloch is everywhere and all the cities are one city, all the highways are one highway, all the stores one store, and to travel a thousand miles becomes meaningless, for wherever you turn, you come up against the same moving wall.

—Czeslaw Milosz, "Visions from San Francisco Bay," 1975

ALLEN GINSBERG

I'VE LIVED WITH AND ENJOYED "HOWL"

———

I've lived with and enjoyed "Howl" for three decades, it has become a social and poetical landmark, notorious at worst, illuminative at best, more recently translated for understanding hitherto forbidden to the public in Eastern Europe, the Soviet Union and China. It seems helpful in this fourth decade of the poem's use to clarify its literary background and historical implications as well as its author's intentions. Few poets have enjoyed the opportunity to expound their celebrated texts. Usually it is the lamplit study of an academic scholar, as with Mr. J. Livingston Lowe's hard interesting work on Coleridge's "Rime." Wordsworth essayed explanations of his editions. Whitman early and appreciatively critiqued his own Leaves with modest anonymity for a generally hostile or indifferent literary society. Later, for a more sympathetic public, he expounded its purport through several prefaces unique in comprehension of his own appointments and disappointments. Still I've ventured my intelligence, neither modest nor immodest, for the general public, poetry lovers, scholars, breakthrough artists and future generations of inspired youths.

The appeal in "Howl" is to the secret or hermetic tradition

of art "justifying" or "making up for" defeat in worldly life, to
the acknowledgement of an

Unworldly love
that has no hope
   of the world

   and that
cannot change the world
to its delight—

after desolation

as if the earth were our feet
were
an excrement of some sky

and we degraded prisoners
destined
to hunger and we eat filth★

    Thus William Carlos Williams appealed to the "imagina-
tion" of art to reveal our deepest natural ground: love, hopeless
yet permanently present in the heart, unalterable. ("Love is not
love/Which alters when it alteration finds.") The worldly love
hypostatized through thick and thin with Carl Solomon rose out
of primordial filial loyalty to my mother, then in distress. Where
mother love conflicts with social façade, the die is cast from an-
tiquity in favor of sympathy.

    Blocked by appearances, love comes through in the free
play of the imagination, a world of art, the field of space where

★William Carlos Williams, "Rain" in *Collected Poems: 1909–1939, Volume I,* 1938.

Appearance—natural recognition of social tragedy & world
failure—shows less sentience than original compassionate ex-
pansiveness of heart.

It is in the poem, as WCW says, that we reconstruct the
world lost. The end verses of Part I hypothesize various arts that
reconstruct our original *"petite sensation"* of *"Pater Omnipotens
Aeterne Deus."* The classic art tactics cataloged there suggest a
shrewd humor that protects our unobstructed sympathy from
chaos. The matter is in objective acknowledgement of emotion.

"Howl" was written in a furnished room at 1010 Montgomery,
a few houses up from where the street meets Broadway, in
North Beach, and continues down a few steep blocks into San
Francisco's financial district. I had weeks earlier quit work as a
minor market research executive, had moved in with new-met
friend Peter Orlovsky, but as he returned to Long Island to visit
his family over the summer, I was alone. I had the leisure of
unemployment compensation for six months ahead, had con-
cluded a longish period of psychotherapeutic consultation,★ en-
joyed occasional visits from Neal Cassady, decade old friend,

★Ginsberg began seeing the therapist, Dr. Philip Hicks, at the Langley-Porter Institute.
According to Allen, at one point in the treatment, the following dialogue occurred:
"What would you like to do?" the doctor asked. "What is your desire really?" I said,
"Doctor, I don't think you're going to find this very healthy and clear, but I really would
like to stop working forever—never work again, never do anything like the kind of
work I'm doing now—and do nothing but write poetry and have leisure to spend the
days outdoors and go to museums and see friends. And I'd like to keep living with some-
one—maybe even a man—and explore relationships that way. And cultivate my percep-
tions, the visionary thing in me. Just a literary and quite city-hermit existence." Then he
said, "Well, why don't you?" Ginsberg discusses this encounter as the Great Break-
through. The doctor's acceptance of Ginsberg's untraditional desires encouraged his
own self-acceptance and his misguided attempts to please his teachers and father, the
poet Louis Ginsberg—all of which in turn generated the time and space for "Howl" to
be written.

now brakeman on Southern Pacific Railroad, and maintained energetic correspondence with Jack Kerouac in Long Island and William Burroughs in Tangier.

I had recently dreamt of the late Joan Burroughs, a sympathetic encounter with her spirit. She inquired the living fate of our friends. I wrote the dream as a poem ("Dream Record: June 8, 1955") about which in a few days Kenneth Rexroth, an elder in his literary city, wrote me he thought was stilted & somewhat academic. A week later, I sat idly at my desk by the first floor window facing Montgomery Street's slope to gay Broadway— only a few blocks from City Lights literary paperback bookshop. I had a secondhand typewriter, some cheap scratch paper. I began typing, not with the idea of writing a formal poem, but stating my imaginative sympathies, whatever they were worth. As my loves were impractical and my thoughts relatively unworldly, I had nothing to gain, only the pleasure of enjoying on paper those sympathies most intimate to myself and most awkward to the great world of family, formal education, business, and current literature.

What I wrote that afternoon was not conceived as a poem to publish. It stands now as the first section of "Howl." Later parts were written in San Francisco, and in a garden cottage in Berkeley over the next few months, with the idea of completing a poem.

In publishing "Howl," I was curious to leave behind after my generation an emotional time bomb that would continue exploding in U.S. consciousness in case our military-industrial-nationalist complex solidified into a repressive police bureaucracy. As a sidelight, I thought to disseminate a poem so strong that a clean Saxon four-letter word might enter high school anthologies permanently and deflate tendencies toward authoritarian strong-arming (evident in later-'50's neoconservative attacks on Kerouac's heartfelt prose and Burroughs's poetic humor).

Please with this Howl, I remain your yet living servant, etc. The author.

JANE KRAMER

THE BEST MIND

I was a student when I first heard Allen read "Howl," and a young reporter when I first met him, but by then I thought of Allen as someone I already knew. I was wrong. Once Allen Ginsberg actually came into your life, he settled there—intimate, indispensable, and so familiar that you could not imagine your life before him. It didn't matter if you became his reader or his lover or his old, close friend; it didn't matter if you lived halfway around the world from Allen or kept a toothbrush in his Manhattan flat. Allen belonged to the person you were, or hoped you were, or liked to think you could be.

Forty years ago, when Allen's mother wrote the letter that he quotes in "Kaddish," she told him: "The key is in the window, the key is in the sunlight in the window—I have the key—get married Allen don't take drugs." And while Naomi Ginsberg was mad and dying when she wrote that letter, she really did have, I think, the key to Allen. He was a born paterfamilias—nurturer, provider, the proud father of his tribe—which may be why, even now, people persist in calling him "the father of the Beat Generation" when in fact it is *his* generation they mean. He embraced the world. He thought that with love, sex, a good mantra, and what he called "the right spiritual information," anybody's bad boy could be turned around and put on a path to enlightenment. When I met him, a few years into the Vietnam War, he was trying out his theory in letters to people like Robert McNamara, telling them to stay calm, telling them that this thing called "enemies" was just a bad dream, something in their heads. He reminded me then of some television dad, writing his weekly admonishments to a son who's acting up because the boy in the next tent at camp has hurt his feelings.

I met Allen through one of the bad boys—a kid named Tommy who had got lost along the path to enlightenment and was helpless and homeless in New York. Tommy had arrived in New York from Nashville three years earlier, carrying a flute and the mothy remains of his father's football-stadium fur coat, all set to apply some southern charm and salesmanship to what he thought of as his new Aquarian principles. I remember that he once showed up at an editing room at CBS, where I was putting together a documentary, with fifteen dollars' worth of tickets to a Let's Legalize Marijuana rally in his pocket and managed to unload them all onto a station janitor and four Republicans from the news staff. I remember this because a few months later he was arrested for selling two pounds of marijuana, tried, convicted on the testimony of an informer posing as a pothead, and then released, pending an appeal. He broke the terms of his first bail bond and wound up in a cell at the West Street prison until he was released again, in his parents' custody. After a few penitent months at home, he packed a bag and disappeared and eventually turned up, with the police on his trail, back in New York—which is when he appeared at my door, one snowy December night in 1966, wrapped in that old fur coat. He was shivering badly, his teeth were chattering, his eyes were glassy, and from what I could make out he was just starting to come down from a long and ravishing amphetamine high. He said that he had been walking for hours. The four girls who lived in the apartment near Columbia where he had been bunking all week had finally thrown him out, and Tommy had grabbed his coat and started walking downtown. Passing my building, he decided that he wanted soup. I asked him where he was going, because I suspected that he might not be going anywhere. Tommy said, "Where else? Allen's house."

For me, in 1966, Allen Ginsberg was the name attached to "Howl" and "Kaddish" and a couple of other poems I liked— "Sunflower Sutra" I loved—and to a legend that was more often than not referred to as Allen-Ginsberg-Jack-Kerouac-Gregory-Corso. Allen was the one with the beard, the one who showed up everywhere with a harmonium, intoning his poetry or wailing something in Sanskrit while he leapt around a stage in what looked to be an ecstatic trance.

A few days later, I called Allen, asking to write about him. I was very nervous. Tommy had warned him that I might be calling, and Allen, by chance, had come across an old *Voice* story of mine in an anthology a friend had sent him. Allen announced right away that he hadn't much liked the story, but then he sighed and said, "Well, people change." He also wanted to know if any of the editors I worked with were closet queens—"closet queen," coming from Allen, was the ultimate insult—who, because of sneaky qualities of the soul, might be tempted to tamper with his persona in my manuscript. Finally, he indulged in some delicate questioning, which he then confessed was prompted by the suspicion that I was a "lady narc." By any ordinary standards, the things he said were rude, ludicrous, or both, but Allen had managed to make them absolutely friendly. He sounded like a nice man who happened to have a few reasonable misgivings about starting a project with someone from a magazine like *The New Yorker*—which, he pointed out, had never allowed the words

"fuck," "vagina," or "blow job" in its pages. We made a date for
the next morning. After I hung up, I knew that I liked him al-
ready for treating me to such a candid, peculiar conversation.

I arrived at his old apartment, in the East Village, at about
eleven. It looked like a cross between an underground news-
paper office and a Beat hotel. Half a dozen houseguests were in
the process of waking up—wandering around naked, yawning,
blinking, drinking coffee. A visiting San Franciscan, who was
going to publish Allen's South American journals, was sitting on
a mattress in the front room of the railroad flat, reading one
copy, and an old girlfriend of Allen's from New Jersey, who had
volunteered to set up a cross-referenced card catalog for his
notes and papers, was busy dumping the contents of a metal fil-
ing cabinet onto the dining room floor. There was a lot of noise.
Someone in a bedroom was chanting. Allen's television, radio,
and portable stereo sets were on. And the girl from New Jersey
was listening to a tape of an interview with Allen by a Nebraska
housewife. (The housewife was saying, "That's 'Howl,' I pre-
sume, as in 'howling with laughter.'") Allen himself was perched
on top of an old wooden desk near the publisher's mattress,
chewing spearmint gumdrops and talking on the phone to Tim-
othy Leary about the marijuana test cases that were due to be
scheduled that winter in the federal courts.

The next few months saw the brief, bright heyday of Love
in the Haight-Ashbury and Flower Power on the campuses.
LSD held promises of becoming, as Allen put it, a "useful edu-
cational tool." The instinct for community was high for the first
time, really, since Brook Farm. Tenderness had been taken up by
students as the lost chord in the political melody. Satori was en-
joying a revival as a kind of all-purpose spiritual spa. ("It's like,
if you're a *real* Bodhisattva," Allen was once instructed by a
woman in his favorite California sexual commune, "then . . .

ideally you should want to fuck everybody in the universe.") It was a nice moment, but the young casualties of the movement, like Tommy, were beginning to appear.

Allen had an incredible concern for those casualties. There was a good deal of discussion then in Allen's circle about what the proper attitude toward them should be, and I remember that some of his more doctrinaire friends, like the poet Gary Snyder—who for a while was Allen's coadviser to the Haight-Ashbury—argued that casualties were inevitable in times of profound social revolution and that, given their inexorable bad karma, it was useless for the revolution to worry too much about them. Allen worried. There were always a few lost souls attached to his rotating brood, and he looked after them all—so well, in fact, and so cheerfully, that many of them left his household quite unnerved by the whole experience. Watching Allen with the freak-outs and flip-outs and dropouts of the late sixties, I began to realize the extent to which what had at first seemed like a full-fledged rescue operation was really just a natural reflex of his own very special strength and sanity. His household worked (and so much of what he was prescribing for the rest of the world seemed eminently workable) largely because Allen himself worked so well as a personality. His household, wherever he happened to put it, was a communal prototype, though very few of the hippies' communes ever measured up to it. Emmett Grogan's San Francisco Diggers, who were around then and for a while considered the last word in togetherness, turned out to be more like an army of buck privates under a temperamental general than a hippie love nest. Most of the sacred-orgy societies, like the California commune, were oppressed by their various "Buddhist" mandates to share everything and everybody. And seekers in the acid conclaves, like Tim Leary's, often ended up preaching relentlessly to one another over the fine points of dogma, such as who should do the dishes and how many centigrams, precisely, a true believer needed to consume. By contrast, the ease and open-endedness of life at Allen's was even more remarkable. Too many of his critics—and followers—tended to forget, as I did then, the fact that Allen had put years, and a great deal of anguish, into his own freedom, and that he was a disciplined artist and a thoroughly educated man. He had worked for his mysticism, and it was bound to be different in its tenacity and substance from the quick-vision ecstasy of a runaway fourteen-year-old. I remember a talk in California between Allen and some of his friends in the communal family. One of them announced that with the right amount of LSD a person could save a lot of time getting insights, and he added, "The old yoga may guarantee that with enough discipline you'll reach certain states of mind and certain experiences, but an acid yoga makes *sure* you have the experience, the actual zap of the experience." Allen listened for a while and then said: "Just taking acid's no yoga." Finally he added, "Yoga is getting through acid, knowing what to do with acid. Yoga is knowing how to be *neat* when you're high."

For me, getting to know Allen was such a large, happy experience that months went by before I could piece together some impressions and actually begin writing. (I'm not sure what, exactly, I had expected of Allen, but coming home from our first day together I was astounded by the fact that he had gone to the bank to deposit a check and then slipped into a local diner for some bacon and eggs.) By the time I finished, over a year and a half had passed since the Greater New York Be-In in Central Park with which the book I eventually wrote about him ends; Vietnam was more and more on everybody's mind; be-ins had given way to campus sieges as the preferred form of communal enterprise; and I myself was living in a small, imperial city in the middle of Morocco, where all the hippies were tourists and where the last student reckless enough to complain about anything was wasting away in jail. The isolation I felt then from war protesters, student activists, hippie lovers, and virtually every other sign of young, revolutionary life was as much spiritual as spatial.

It was impossible to imagine Allen Ginsberg in Morocco, and thinking about Allen there, I began to understand how very much he belonged in and to America. Allen was often called a mystic, but despite his exuberant plunges into Eastern disciplines and forms, Allen's was that odd, optimistic, American brand of mysticism, which he traced, quite rightly, back to Whitman, and which was rooted in humanism and in a romantic and visionary ideal of harmony among human beings. That buoyant humanism, that vision of a felicitous and sexy life-in-the-world, that exceptional tenderness, had nothing whatever to do with the holy men I was encountering in Morocco, where questions of compassion and community and fellow feeling were considered quite irrelevant to the pursuit of a lively ecstatic life. In America, it had been easy and of course exciting to believe that Allen's vision could take hold and flower anywhere. But I was in a place where a good part of the population spent its time having visions, and there was no appetite for all of Allen's loving universe. By the time I finished writing, I was beginning to see, sadly, how much a redeeming vision needs a "community of the enlightened," as the Buddhists say, that is ready to receive it.

Allen once told me that he was "not as nice, not as easy" as my book made him, and that I had forgotten the Allen Ginsberg who howled with love and rage and grief, and in a way I had. "Howl," for me, was something over and done with, gone. I think that—being so young then, especially to Allen's forty-year-old paterfamilias, and so enchanted by the promise of that benign American moment which he represented and, for all intents and purposes, invented—I never really accounted for the cost to Allen of all that buoyancy and all that tenderness and all that syncretizing passion. I was a student of literature; I knew Allen's discipline as a writer and even his discipline as a person, but not really his exhaustion. Allen's father, Louis, who was a Sunday poet, used to shake his head at Allen's wanderings and his errant enthusiasms and say that his son was "restless." He thought (and in this he was not so different from Allen's mother) that all Allen needed to do was locate himself—in his head, in the world—and then Allen would be "cured" of too much seeking. What he missed, of course, was the purpose of his son's bardic mission. What Allen wanted to cure was America. He wanted to assimilate the world in its stupendous variety—for himself, for his poems, for his country—and bring it home and make America safe for somebody like Allen Ginsberg. He wanted America to understand why the Allen Ginsberg decked out like Krishna for a couple of hours chanting and the Allen Ginsberg dressed up in cummerbund and tuxedo for an uptown opening and the Allen Ginsberg wrapped in beads but otherwise naked for a tantric night in Marin County were the same person, and not some fatally divided psyche destined for another round with the doctors at Rockland State. He wanted America to embrace its own variety, which was after all the source of the rhythms and idioms and digressions of the language he chose as an American poet.

I saw Allen very little over the next several years. He was touring a lot then—sometimes to read his poetry, sometimes (in a kind of Bob Dylan–Allen Ginsberg road show) to chant the Blake poems he had set to Eastern music—and I was mainly in Europe, reporting. He showed up, though, for the important moments. He had come to Providence once to talk up the graduate student I was going to marry to my mother. ("He's cute,

Mrs. Kramer," Allen kept saying. "Maybe I'll take him.") And when I had a daughter, he arrived one night for dinner to chant his blessing—to "lay a good mantra on the baby" is the way he put it—and to make sure I remembered the mudra he had taught me in San Francisco, the one for chasing demons away. But after that I saw him mainly when he came to Paris to give a reading or to see his French publishers, Christian and Dominique Bourgois, who had been my own publishers and were our mutual friends. They always had a party, and Allen loved parties. He loved putting on his suit and being soft-spoken and agreeable and attentive. He loved to *épater la bourgeoisie* by being just like them, and actually he felt quite tender toward what he called "groovy rich ladies." I was never surprised to pick up the *Herald* in Paris and read, say, about Allen Ginsberg and Francesco Clemente arriving together at some fancy party, or about Allen Ginsberg joining a PEN benefit committee with Gayfryd Steinberg, because Allen did not discriminate when it came to sharing spiritual information.

About ten years ago, my husband came home from the Graduate Center at the City University of New York, where he teaches, to say that he had just run into Allen in another incarnation: Allen was now a Distinguished Professor of Poetry, and he remarked to my husband in passing that the two of them appeared to be the only professors in the building wearing ties. A few weeks later, we joined Allen at a memorial service for a friend named Ahmed Jacoubi—a Moroccan painter whom Allen had known in Tangiers in the late fifties and early sixties and had introduced to us when we were going there, ten years later. In spirit, Ahmed was as close to Allen as anyone I had ever known, despite the fact that for most of his life he was illiterate. Francis Bacon had taught him to paint; Bill Burroughs and Paul Bowles taught him to make stories; but it was Allen who understood the poet in Ahmed and saw in him a kindred spirit. When Ahmed died, he was living in a loft in Ellen Stewart's Cafe La MaMa annex, and Ellen, who considered herself Ahmed's sister, had arranged the evening so that his friends from both countries—poets and dancers and playwrights and musicians—could invoke their own version of Ahmed's world. Allen read a poem and played his harmonium and chanted, and for a moment he was the Allen I used to know, and not the Allen I had been getting used to—the Allen who was often ill and putting his life in order; the Allen who could talk your ear off about what his biographers were doing, what his archivists were doing, and what the people collecting his letters were doing; the Allen who was interested in posterity and seemed, sometimes, to be collecting his life instead of living it. In a way, that night at La MaMa marked the beginning of the end of a better time. Everybody there felt it, though nobody—and certainly not Allen—talked about it. But the last time I saw him—it was six weeks before he died, and we were having dinner together at the artists Alain and Ariane Kirili's loft—Allen spent the evening asking questions. He wanted to know about everybody's life, everybody's work, everybody's children; he wanted to know who was happy and who was miserable or disappointed, and why, and what he could do about it. I said to my husband later that Allen seemed "different"—as if he were going on a trip and collecting *our* lives, the lives of the people who in one way or another had touched his own, to carry with him in his head. People close to Allen say that he didn't know he had cancer until a week before he died, but I think that night he was getting ready to say goodbye.

The news of his death came this way: "Allen died." It was a Saturday morning in April, and I can't believe that anyone who picked up the phone and heard those two words, as I did many times that morning, had any doubt who "Allen" was. Allen changed a world, and even if that world has turned out to be much smaller than most of us hoped it was, or could be, back in the days when a boy on the run presented me with Allen's phone number, the change was indelible. Allen was indelible. He was enormous.

DAVID GATES

WELCOMING "HOWL" INTO THE CANON

———

I drove to the store the other day and parked next to an SUV whose sound system was booming out a rap song so loudly that the bass shook my Saab. The refrain was "Fuck you/ Fuck you/Fuck you," and I thought, *Who needs this fucking shit?* It wasn't that I don't cuss myself, as you see. It wasn't that I have a problem with rap; for a while there, N.W.A's "Fuck Tha Police" was my favorite piece of music. It wasn't that I felt threatened; the only person in the car was a blond teenage girl fussing with her lipstick. It wasn't that I think freedom of expression carries with it the obligation not to be stupid; it carries with it no obligation at all, and anyway, who decides what's stupid? It was just that . . . I don't know *what* it was just that. Maybe it was that I just wasn't in the mood.

But it made me think we'd come a long way in the half century since Allen Ginsberg's "Howl" was cleared of obscenity charges—by a San Francisco judge who happened to be a Sunday school Bible teacher—and that it's not been entirely to the good. Don't get me wrong here. My unimportant personal annoyance over a moronic rap song passed soon enough, and I'm not nostalgic for the days when the government actively suppressed books and threw authors and publishers in jail. (It happened to Ginsberg's publisher, Lawrence Ferlinghetti; the ACLU had to bail him out.) But over the years, the many victories over censorship, of which the "Howl" trial was one of the noblest, have diminished art's ability to affront, however much it may still annoy. And in Ginsberg's case that's a problem. Banned literary mandarins such as Joyce and Nabokov may simply have wanted to go about their hermetic work unmolested, but Ginsberg was a public poet and a provocateur. "Howl," for all its affirmations, is a profoundly oppositional poem, and it counts on *being* opposed.

The 1950s—homophobic, anti-Semitic, conformist, dominated by Cold Warriors and McCarthyites, censorious to the point of paranoia—provided all the opposition a poet could ask. The Bush era may be an even lousier time to be alive, but so far any form of artistic expression short of child pornography can be as transgressive as you want to make it, as long as you don't get your heart set on having your CDs sold in Wal-Mart, your books taught in red-state high schools, or your grant proposal approved by the NEA. True, "Howl" can't be read on the radio, thanks to an FCC decree that goes back to the Reagan administration, and in 2000 it was apparently bounced from an advanced-placement English class in Jacksonville, Florida. (Probably it's been banned elsewhere, though this was the only specific incident I could turn up; surely many teachers wouldn't even try to assign it.) But nobody's seizing copies of the poem, as U.S. Customs did with the first edition (which was printed in England), and nobody's been booked and fingerprinted over it since Ferlinghetti. Even the famous trial wasn't much of a contest. The prosecution (which Ferlinghetti thought didn't show much appetite for the case) called only two "expert" witnesses: some academic clown who claimed "Howl" was just a ripoff of Dadaism, and an elocution teacher who said reading the poem was like "going through the gutter . . . I didn't linger too long on it, you can be sure." Um, thanks—you may step down. They proved no match for the likes of Mark Schorer and Walter Van Tilburg Clark.

In fact, "Howl" has now become an American classic, like "Evangeline" and "Snow-Bound," except that people still read it. There it sits in *The Norton Anthology of Contemporary Poetry*, complete with sobersided footnotes. (Including one that explains that line I've wondered about all these years: "with mother finally ******." The word turns out to be "fucked," of course; according to Ginsberg, he substituted the asterisks "to introduce appropriate level of uncertainty.") The poem, saintly motorcyclists and all, is on somebody's syllabus in almost every American college except Bob Jones University, and nobody says boo. Toward the end of his life, Ginsberg himself was happy about this, as all right-thinking people should be, but if he'd known in 1955 how respectable "Howl" would become, I wonder if he'd have been so jazzed. Would the poem have fallen flat with nothing to push against? Much of its power comes from its sense of a censorious readership, which does not agree that, for instance, the "tongue and cock and hand and asshole" are holy, that butt-fucking motorcyclists are saintly and sailors giving and receiving blow jobs are "human seraphim." "Howl" deliberately assaults and inverts its readers' assumptions about what's holy or hellish, sane or mad. (Only the mad can hear "the crack of doom on the hydrogen jukebox"; the sane, we assume, must hear only a Patti Page record.) And those assumptions—thanks in part to the popularity of works such as "Howl"—are no longer as rigid as they used to be. Our gain, but maybe the poem's loss.

The first line, now quoted as much as "April is the cruellest month," announces that madness has destroyed "the best minds of my generation." But alongside the lurid images of those who "cowered in unshaven rooms in underwear" or "walked all night with their shoes full of blood" or "presented themselves on the granite steps of the madhouse . . . demanding instantaneous lobotomy," "Howl" also presents madness as a visionary state, and a condition of moral, spiritual, sexual, even political, superiority. Among the poem's best minds are martyrs who "burned cigarette holes in their arms protesting the narcotic tobacco haze of Capitalism," mystics "burning for the ancient heavenly connection to the starry dynamo," cocksmen who "sweetened the snatches of a million girls," and zealots who "fell on their knees in hopeless cathedrals praying for each other's salvation." Not the kinds of folks Eisenhower Republicans would have wanted around, but traditionally admirable figures in canonical literature—including the Bible itself.

In fact, the poem turns out to be as much a prophetic *celebration* of the mind's destruction as it is a howl of protest. The villain of the piece, don't forget, is "Moloch," that all-devouring entity of Part II, "whose name is the Mind!" By this, Ginsberg means the lifeless, bodiless, sexless, logic-chopping machine whose works include "Robot apartments! invisible suburbs! skeleton treasuries! blind capitals! demonic industries! spectral nations! invincible mad houses! granite cocks! monstrous bombs!" He diagnoses these topical horrors of the 1950s (which have only gotten worse in the ensuing half century) not as the results of illogical thinking—in which case, it would have made better sense for those "best minds" to be out pounding the pavement for SANE and Adlai Stevenson instead of "dragging themselves through the negro streets at dawn looking for an angry fix"— but as the hellspawn of thought itself, divorced from compassion, imagination, and vision. Presumably—and here's the Buddhist paradox that *really* makes "Howl" a provocation—the Mind that brought us LeFrak City and the hydrogen bomb is the same Mind the reader brings to bear on the poem itself, assuming that Mind was formed, as Ginsberg's was, under the tutelage of the New Critics. It must also be the Mind Ginsberg himself used, as we now know, to revise the poem as methodically as a formalist poet might have done—but that *is* too much to get your mind around.

"Howl," in other words, is a far more complicated and ambiguous poem than the straightforward work of social protest that its defenders presented in court, and that the good Judge Clayton W. Horn agreed was "an indictment of those elements in modern society destructive of the best qualities of human nature; such elements are predominantly identified as materialism, conformity and mechanization leading toward war." This was, and deserved to be, a winning argument in defending the poem against the charge of obscenity, in the legal sense. In a literary sense, though, Ginsberg *meant* the poem to be obscene: not merely offensive in its forbidden words describing forbidden acts but offensive to intellect, to common sense, to all our consensual realities, to all the boundaries we believe necessary to civilized life. This is not, at bottom, a poem holding up liberal, or libertarian, pieties against conservative pieties, although that's how it had to be sold to the judge and the public, and it's what Ginsberg himself sometimes seemed to argue when he put on his crusader-for-free-speech hat. It's a *radically* offensive poem, or used to be—offensive even to received notions of what poetry is, and it needs offended readers whose fear and outrage bring it most fully to life.

And it's hard to find such readers anymore, at least among the sorts of people who are apt to be exposed to "Howl" in the first place. (There'd still be hell to pay if somebody tried to teach the poem at a "Bible college" or a fundamentalist madrassa, but that's not going to happen.) While the text hasn't been bowdlerized, its subversive force has been vitiated by the receptive climate in which it now luxuriates. Mere cusswords can't shock us, and if saintly motorcyclists are still too gamy for a few mossbacks in the English Department, there's always Gay Studies. Thanks to its association with the Beat movement, "Howl" has largely managed to avoid the Gay Lit ghetto—which would ensure that straights would never read it—but if the lights start to go out, that could serve as a Bushproof refuge for a while. Actually, I doubt "Howl" is in much danger—once a work of literature starts to get revered, it's hard to get people to unrevere it— which suggests that the poem itself is no longer *seen* as dangerous. I think that's a misreading, but over time it happens to the best of 'em; after all, nobody's on Dickens's case these days for what Macaulay called his "sullen socialism." It would be madness, and not in Ginsberg's visionary sense, to hope for a new era of censorship just so "Howl" could get its street cred back— and, as an ancillary benefit, so civilized folks like me wouldn't have to hear another "Fuck you" cranked up to ten. Yet something's been lost by our welcoming "Howl" into the canon: the possibility of another "Howl." I'd gladly live in a Ginsbergian utopia of peace, tolerance, pansexuality, communitarianism, omnidirectional love, and good drugs just for the asking. Who wouldn't, if they could ever get over minding other people's business? The hitch is, Allen Ginsberg wouldn't be writing in it.

JOHN CAGE

WRITING THROUGH HOWL

———

for A. G. on his Sixtieth Birthday

WRITING FOR THE FIRST TIME THROUGH HOWL

I

sAw
themseLves
Looking for
hipstErs

starry dyNamo

hiGh sat
theIr
heaveN

Saw
puBlishing
odEs on
Rooms

listeninG to the terror

beArds returning through
Laredo

beLt
for nEw york
iN
druGs
wIth
alcohol aNd
ballS

Blind
in thE mind
towa Rd
illuminatinG
dAwns
bLinking
Light

thE
wiNter
liGht

endless rIde

broNx
wheelS
    Brought
thEm
wRacked
liGht of zoo
sAnk
Light
continuousLy
musEum to
brooklyN
bridGe

platonIc
dowN
    State
and eye Ball
wholE
    Recall

niGhts
brilliAnt eyes
Leaving
traiL of
picturE
atlaNtic

    Go and
lIt

sNow
farmS
    Bop

    thE
vibRated
seekinG

visionAry
onLy
supernaturaL
    Ecstasy
iN
streetliGht

spanIard
aNd
taSk

    But
    thE
dungaRees and
chicaGo
coAst

incomprehensibLe
capitaLism
distributEd
iN
deliGht

polIcecars
No
pederaSty
By
thosE
the sailoRs
the eveninGs
    And the

publLic
freeLy
comE

wouNd
   Golden
ecstatIc
   aNd
    Sweetheart
tremBling

   thE
   Red
flashinG
   bArns

   Lake
coLorado
hEro
cocksmaN

   Gaunt
waItresses
   loNely petticoat
   eSpecially
   Blood
on thE snowbank docks
foR
floodliGht
   &
obLivion

   Lamb
stEw
romaNce

bridGe
to buIld
   oN
   Sixth
   By
orangE
   cRates
of theoloGy
   And
   Lofty
animaLs
   hEart
   &
   veGetable
threw theIr
eterNity
outSide of
   Blasts
   thE
   iRon
intelliGent
   hAppened

the ghostLy
fiLthy
criEd
daNced

   German
whIskey
   aNd
earS
   Blast
   thE
hotRod–

JOHN CAGE

liGht

And
untiL
souL
crashEd
miNds
Golden
realIty
saNg
Sweet
haBit or
thE

oR
accusinG
rAdio
Left
saLad

thE
graNite
wiG
foetId halls
aNd
Solitude-
Book
thE
dooR
hanGer
And
hopefuL
carL
you arE

Not safe
i am
throuGh
theIcy
suddeN
flaSh of
viBrating
planE

dReamt
imaGes
juxtAposed
souL
2 visuaL
imagEs
aNd
toGether
wIth
aeterNa
deuS

madmanBum
and angEl
Rose
Ghostly
jAzz
in the goLdhorn shadow

eLi
Eli-
sabacthaNi

II

Good
theIr skulls

aNd
  Solitude

  Boys
armiEs
  paRks
  judGer of men

   And
moLoch
buiLdings
arE
stoNe of
  Governments
       moloch
  Is
moNey
whoSe
canniBal
whosE
  aRe
lonG
endless jehovAhs

  moLoch whose
  moLoch
  whosE
  aNd

sexless hydroGen moloch
  Is
  loNely
cockSucker
without a Body

III

  mE
my natuRal
liGht
streAming out of
moLoch

moLoch
industriEs
graNite cocks
Gone down
rIver
aNd
floodhighS

Bronx
scrEam

you'Re
losinG the
the Abyss
in rockLand
souL

diE
iN
all toGether

I'm
rocklaNd
that coughS

out of the comaBy
airplanEs
Roof

JOHN CAGE

anGelic bombs

illuminAtes
itseLf

eternaL war is
victory forgEt your
uNderwear

hiGhway
cross amerIca

the westerN
Footnote   iS

holy

everyBody's holy
angEl
soul aRe holy

anGels
in the insAne
hoLy

the
hoLy
thE
saxophoNe
diGs

los
Is los
New
San

the eyeBall

thE
chaRity
intelliGent

WRITING FOR THE SECOND TIME THROUGH HOWL

I

mAdness
coLd-water
fLats

thE
braiNs
throuGh
wIth
aNd
academieS
Burning

monEy

maRijuana
niGht

After
endLess
cLoud
thE
motioNless
Green

joyrIde

suN

aShcan

Brain
drainEd of
bRilliance

niGht

submArine
fLoated
Lost

thE
wiNdowsills

ambiGuous
cIty
easterN
heartS

Boxcars
rackEting
towaRd
niGht

telepAthy

instinctiveLy
angeLs who
angEls who
iN

throuGh
amerIca
eterNity

So
the f.B.i.
sExy
daRk skin
passinG out
Arms
whiLe
of Los
thEm
dowN

roseGardens
cemeterIes
semeN
turkiSh
Bath
whEn
with a swoRd
nothinG but
Ass
Loom who

aLong
thE
aNd

down
Gyzym of
sunrIse
uNder
Stolen

Backyards

rickEty
Rows on mountaintops

upliftinGs
&
soLipsisms of
suicidaL dramas

thE
baNks of
diGested
rIvers
aNd
muSic

Borsht

drEaming
puRe
kinGdom who
meAt

Looking for
aLarm

fEll
oN
Gave up

antIque
aNd
madiSon

By
thE
dRunken
who sanG
in despAir

Leaped
nostaLgic

finishEd
iNto
hiGhways

haIl–
crosscouNtry
Seventytwo
came Back
waitEd
bRooded
waitinG for
heAds

bLues
aLcatraz
mExico
mouNt
or Grave

sanIty
&
lectureS on
loBotomy
givEn
concRete

WRITING THROUGH HOWL

and finGers   stReets
                                         foG
the wArds of   smokestAcks
     piLgrim state's   cities
rockLand's and
     thE   moLoch whose
                                              oiL
     iN the   stonE
cataloG the   aNd
     tIme   moloch who friGhtened
     &   whom I
     Space
     verBs   skeletoN
and sEt   capitalS
                                                   Backs lifting moloch

     pooR
and intelliGent   thE
     And   miRacles
the souL to   Gone
     Lamma   epiphAnies
                                              Loves
saxophonE cry   the rocks of time reaL

     dowN to the   th E
                                         dowN to the river
II   judGement
                              III   lauGh
               moloch
                                              thIs
     Is   rocklaNd
     teN   writerS
armieS   Bang
     tomB
     whosE   thE

173

JOHN CAGE

immoRtal   Footnote   Bum's as holy as
unGodly   thE
An   aRe
                                       anGeles

rockLand
souL   frAncisco
thE   hoLy
iN

                                       hoLy
huG and   tangiErs
kIss
uNited   IstaNbul holy
uS

WRITING FOR THE THIRD TIME THROUGH HOWL

I   stArving   dreAms with
           fLoating   Lightning
       contempLating jazz   worLd
                                  of timE

       who barEd
           uNder   wiNe
           liGht   borouGhs of
                                     traffIc
           theIr   aNd
           aNd   Shuddering
       got buSted   Bickford's

           puBic   thE
       who atE   cRack of
           fiRe   jumpinG
                                     escApes off
                                     bLeak furnished
           niGht   raiLroad

grandfathEr
plotiNus
throuGh
Idaho
wheN baltimore
impulSe
followed the Brilliant
thE
fiReplace
with biG
pAcifist
hoLes

aLamos
thE
islaNd
Grass

theIr
bloNde
loSt
loveBoys
thE
thRee

a packaGe
A
fLoor
eLuding
thE
sNatches
throuGh
myrIad
Night—
carS

the craB

thE
stReets
couGhed
flAme

tubercuLar
Lung
thE
uNder
thouGht
crIed
burNed
verSe &
taxicaBs
rEality

bRooklyn
neGroes
bArefoot
bLoody
goLgotha
who drovE
to fiNd
throuGh
theIr
aNd
heartS

who
Buddha
locomotivE
naRcissus
& a hunG

JOHN CAGE

                    potAto   Body
      subsequentLy
            insuLin   its pilgrimagE
           mEtrasol
      occupatioNal   cRoss in
              Greystone's   lonG
           wIth   islAnd
           beNch   Living
           realmS of love   in rockLand
                                                     arE
                But   thousaNd
               littlE
              you'Re   cottaGe
           jumpinG   nIght
               sensAtion   Footnote   the toNgue
       you speechLess   iS
                                                     Burroughs
                Lamma
               thE   thE
               owN   maRijuana
                                                 anGeles

II   breakthrouGhs
                                                 peoriA
           the rIver   hoLy

           dowN   hoLy

III   yearS animal   timE
                                                 iN

WRITING FOR THE FOURTH TIME THROUGH HOWL

nAked

the eL and

angeLs

who passEd

uNiversities

traGedy among the

theIr

draNk

paradiSe

Backyard

thE

Rooftops

kinG

chAined

themseLves

hoLy

thE

Noise of

throuGh

fIre

mooN

Screaming

Boxcars

studiEd

cRoss

thouGht

mAd

gLeamed

okLahoma

thE

wiNter

ciGarette

theIr

Narcotic

pamphletS

naked and tremBling

thE

shRieked with

committinG

And

howLed

genitaLs and

bE

iN

ciGarettes

wIth

cuNt

laSt

But

thE

giRls in empty lots &

hunGover

tokAy

stumbLed

apartment cLiff—

thE

hudsoN

Gas

edItors or were   rIver they saw
ruN
abSolute   III carl solomoN
  Birmingham   muSt feel
hE   tomB
jouRneyed   mad comradEs
tanGiers   ouR
pAcific   niGht
bLack   And
woodLawn   Let
thE   rock Land
daisychaiN   wE
Gaps   owN
wIth
coNform to   Footnote   Grandfathers
hiS   hIpsters
Band   &
                  drumS
thE
foR love into   lamB of
                 thE
II   filth   cRazy
              anGel in moloch
uGliness
And   holy the seA
chiLdren
                hoLy
oLd   hoLy
thE   thE
prisoN   visioNs
lauGhter

WRITING FOR THE FIFTH TIME THROUGH HOWL

I

drAgging
cooL
schoLars of
thE
&
throuGh

wIth
aNd
of

Shuddering
viBrations
thE
fRom

listeninG to

from pArk to
Leaving
Lava
poEtry
iN
Gas—
sordId movies
oN
Sudden
Bottom

thE
pushcaRts
niGht

II

tortillAs
pLunged
cLocks
thEir
Next
bridGe
thIs
aNd
Soup

to Boys
thE
juRy
demandinG
And
eLectricity
onLy
onE
iN
throuGh
tIme

dowN here
to Say

Brains
scrEaming

staiRways
sobbinG in
moloch

the heAvy

                moLoch   rockla Nd
                                                    ha S
                moLoch   Footnote   holy the Bop
                thE   apocalyps E
                crossboNe

                                                      st Reets

III   where we are Great

          typewrIter

WRITING FOR THE SIXTH TIME THROUGH HOWL

I   At   aLso
                bLake—   brokE
              hoteLs   dowN
                dEath
                iNcomparable   Great
                                                wartIme
            hydroGen   mooN
            empIre   headS
                aNd   Bad
        memorieS and   thE
                Boxcars   daRkness
                                            stanzas of Gibberish

                poE
                                                    An egg

                    st. john of the
                stReets   successiveLy
                                                growing oLd

            midniGht
                rAin   thEir
                                                    oN
                Lounged   forGotten
                                                & fIretrucks

WRITING THROUGH HOWL

Not
over the Street

truly Bald
thE
dReam
flunG
And
Last
Last

thE
iN
thouGht
mIght
aNd
clotheS of
II Blood
arE
bReast

is a smokinG
A
bLind

moLoch
whosE
staNd

III a straiGhtjacket
I'm
oN
iS
Footnote JazzBands
thE
Rebellion

WRITING FOR THE SEVENTH TIME THROUGH HOWL

I dAwn
Leaping
dusks of brookLyn

battEry
oN
ciGarettes
theIr
who loaNed
viSionary
aBout
volcanoEs
shoRts

weepinG
And
skeLetons
wiLd
thEir
kNees

II

III   Game   Footnote   aByss
         wIth
     catatoNic   thE
       Should   bRilliant
                                  . . .

WRITING FOR THE EIGHTH TIME THROUGH HOWL

I   An   toBacco
        poLes   hazE of
        untiL   squaRe
         thE   cookinG
         i N
      throuGh   intoxicAtion
         It

                          Let
         oN   saintLy
    Smalltown   sEraphim
                     atlaNtic

WRITING FOR THE NINTH TIME THROUGH HOWL

       Angry   battaLion
    soLidities   thE
                     aNd

ELIOT KATZ

RADICAL EYES: POLITICAL

POETICS AND "HOWL"

To say that someone is a political poet does not mean that politics is the only thing the person writes about. In addition to social ideas and observations, Allen Ginsberg's work contains powerfully expressed psychological, spiritual, autobiographical, familial, sexual, and literary themes, as well as poems of daily life and perceptions. Often what is most striking about Ginsberg's poems is their lively exploration of the ways in which these varied concerns interrelate. But I think it is fair to say that what has resonated most in the minds and imaginations of readers across the planet for half a century has been the keen sense that here is a poet devoting considerable literary skills and talents to help envision and create a more humane world.

In the fifty years since the publication of "Howl," it has deservedly become one of the most widely read and influential poems of the twentieth century. As one can tell from early reactions, especially the bursts of laughter and applause on early recordings, "Howl" astonished even those familiar with Ginsberg's work up until that time, stunning readers and listeners with its linguistic and oratorical energy, its striking imagery, its mixture of empirical perception and surreal imagination, its extension of previously undervalued literary precursors, its dynamic willingness to explode widely accepted cultural and political dogma, its assertions of honest selfhood and sexuality against a repressive culture, and its relentless search for a more fulfilling lifeworld.

"Howl" is structured like many meaningful projects in politics, psychology, or science. A problem is first examined, so that it can be identified. Then a solution is proposed, and, if the solution seems like a potentially effective one, the participants celebrate.

The poem begins with one of the most quoted opening lines in American poetry: "I saw the best minds of my generation destroyed by madness, starving hysterical naked."* After the initial "I saw," the "I" disappears for a while into the substance of the poem, and the poet, tossing aside traditional poetic cautions, dives relatively unshielded into the social turbulence of his day. In psychological terms, we might read this descent as an attempt to work through difficult or painful emotional issues instead of avoiding or denying them. On the political level, by plunging the self into social turmoil at the beginning of "Howl," Ginsberg is able to look behind America's curtains of conventional propriety to see how repressive aspects of culture are actually affecting people, particularly young people around the poet's age who are longing for more fulfilling lives and a more welcoming society. The exploration includes an energetic examination of both worldly details and metaphysical imagination—in so doing, Ginsberg finds a dynamic way to conjoin his William Carlos Williams–influenced empirical-objectivist interests[†] with his Blakean visionary inclinations.

---

*Allen Ginsberg, "Howl," in *Collected Poems: 1947–1980* (New York: Harper & Row, 1984), p. 126. All subsequent references to the text of "Howl" are from this edition.

[†]Although, when it came to Williams, Allen seemed to focus mostly on the doctor's empirical verses, I would note that Williams himself was also interested in mixing perception and imagination, as can easily be seen in his long experimental poems like "Spring and All."

Diving into the world, the poet of "Howl" sees "the best minds" of his generation grappling desperately to overcome deep feelings of depression, frustration, and alienation. The Holocaust survivor psychiatrist Viktor Frankl had labeled this sort of spiritual crisis "existential frustration" or "existential vacuum,"* which Frankl believed was widespread in the twentieth century as a result of conformism and totalitarianism. Writing in 1945, Frankl claimed a survey revealed that 60 percent of his American students suffered from existential vacuum, which may help explain why "Howl" hit a nerve among such a broad section of American youth.

The various ways in which the "best minds" of "Howl" react to their existential frustration range from energetic and sensible efforts to achieve self-integration to rash and self-destructive acts to stifle the pain. To find a nonconformist fulfillment, Allen's compatriots look to alternative spiritual and literary traditions ("who studied Plotinus Poe St. John of the Cross telepathy and bop kabbalah"), to jazz ("who lounged hungry and lonesome through Houston seeking jazz"), to drugs ("Peyote solidities of halls"), and to sexual experimentation ("who copulated ecstatic and insatiate"). Impatience with status quo and self leads some of Ginsberg's best minds to frenetic travel, which in the dialectical spirit of Part I is clearly preferable to staying put, but which does not quite succeed in resolving the protagonists' weighty needs ("who journeyed to Denver, who died in Denver, who came back to Denver & waited in vain"). The intense and unpredictable energy and rhythms of Ginsberg's long lines perfectly undergird the vigorous endeavors described.

The long lines of "Howl" are in the tradition of Blake and Whitman, but Ginsberg makes his own lines even longer than

---

*Viktor E. Frankl, *Man's Search for Meaning* (1945; rept., New York: Washington Square Press, 1984).

these predecessors'. As the lines continually refuse to stop at the right-hand margin of the page, they imply an even more strenuous effort than his literary ancestors' to free the poetic line, and by extension the culture at large, from restrictive boundaries. Ginsberg was not the first to use lines of this length, nor even the first to utilize them with an implied political intent. In the 1930s, some of the left poets (e.g., Kenneth Fearing, Mike Gold) being published in journals like *The New Masses* and in proletarian poetry anthologies had often used lines whose length extended Whitman's. But the long lines of "Howl" somehow seemed new and different. Infused with the rhythms of Kerouac's recent prose and bebop jazz—the latter carrying, among other things, an implicit rejection of 1950s racial segregation through its embrace of an African-American-invented musical form—as well as an expert use of traditional poetic elements like alliteration and assonance, the long lines of "Howl" sparkled with vitality, and held together as fully energized units densely packed with a mix of lively perceptions, dazzling imagination, humor, and resourceful wordplay capable of keeping readers and listeners thoroughly engaged. It is significant that most of the main poets whose work provided the foundation for "Howl"— Blake, Whitman, Williams, the French surrealists and Russian futurists—were not being read much in academies of the time and have become far more widely acknowledged in part because of the way a poem like "Howl" reshapes our ideas about literary history.

In her essay "On the Edge of Darkness: What Is Political Poetry?"★ Denise Levertov rightly insisted of political poetry— of all poetry—that questions like "whether it is poetic" and not simply "versified ideas," and whether it succeeds in "engag[ing]

★Denise Levertov, "On the Edge of Darkness: What Is Political Poetry?," in *Poetry and Politics,* edited by Richard Jones (New York: Quill, 1985), pp. 162–74.

our aesthetic response" were paramount. Ginsberg, too, was highly cognizant of the need to develop aesthetically effective strategies to turn his social ideas and observations into memorable poetry. In a postcard he generously sent my friend Danny Shot in May 1976, after we had each sent him our earliest work, Allen wrote: "Another thing you gotta remember is each line should have some haiku or double joke or image or mad sound or Poetry in it, not be just flat prose." In "Howl," Allen made sure his lines were filled with poetic tools like powerful imagery both real and surreal, mythification, comedy, and improvisational rhythms, so his political verse would not read anything like "flat prose." Emily Dickinson famously said that she knew a poem was a good one if it made her feel that the top of her head had been taken off. What Dickinson was, I think, getting at is the element that probably does more than any other to make a poem feel aesthetically vital—the element of surprise. Surprise in poetry can come in any number of ways: thought-provoking insights, surprise phrasing, startling imagery, an unexpected way of looking at an object or event, an odd line break, novel wit or humor, an innovative sense of rhythm or form, a provocative extension or subversion of previous literary traditions. As poets like Pope and Dryden well knew, even politically didactic poetry, so often disparaged by mainstream reviewers, can be effective when it is accompanied by surprise insight, phrasing, or imagery. It is partly the inventive and endlessly surprising linguistic mix of "Howl" that enables the poem to continue sounding relevant and timely to so many successive generations.*

*The surprise quality in Ginsberg's poems is what Helen Vendler seems to observe when she writes: "His mind roams widely, in unpredictable ways . . . One can't widen consciousness in poetry by having it follow a programmed path." In Helen Vendler, "American X-Rays: Forty Years of Allen Ginsberg's Poetry," *New Yorker*, November 4, 1996, pp. 100–101.

Amid the torrent of the long lines, it only makes sense that perceptions would often seem blurred. Although the poem begins with a declaration of witness ("I saw"), even a cursory glance at the imagery of Part I ("who disappeared into the volcanoes of Mexico leaving behind nothing but the shadow of dungarees and the lava and ash of poetry scattered in fireplace Chicago") reveals that the witnessing of "Howl" is rather an expressionistic one. This is not mere literal testimony but a fusing of the real and the surreal. The "I saw" of "Howl" looks at the actual world, but it also looks beyond ("their heads shall be crowned with laurel in oblivion"). It witnesses the outward acts of real people ("who jumped off the Brooklyn Bridge this actually happened"), but it also impressionistically attempts to transmit a compendium of inner psychic adventures ("who ate the lamb stew of the imagination or digested the crab at the muddy bottom of the rivers of Bowery").

In the decades before "Howl," left theorists had engaged in spirited debates about the social implications of surrealism and other forms of international modernism. While some theorists argued in favor of one side or another (e.g., Georg Lukacs for realism, Theodor Adorno for high modernism), the philosopher Ernst Bloch asserted the importance of modernist literature in a nondogmatic way that (unlike, say, some of the language-poetry theorists of the 1980s) did not devalue the also important contributions of more representational modes. According to Bloch, since the project of the left was to create a better world out of the present one, reality for the left ought to be viewed as "reality plus the future within it."★ Because the desired human world had not yet arrived, it could not be reduced to empirical per-

★Ernst Bloch, "Marxism and Poetry," in *The Utopian Function of Art and Literature: Selected Essays*, translated by Jack Zipes and Frank Mecklenburg (Cambridge, Mass.: MIT Press, 1989), p. 162.

ception or narrative realism. Experimental montage or surreal imagery, by creating meanings that did not yet exist in the actual world, could, in Bloch's compelling phrase, offer "anticipatory illuminations"*—hints or sketches of future potential—in a way that realist work could not. The powerful mix of realistic description and surreal imagination in "Howl" lends itself to a kind of witnessing intended not solely for the goal of investigating the present but also for the aim of anticipating a more humane future.

In the mixture of realism and surrealism in Part I, a few of Ginsberg's "best minds" try left-wing protest in order to overcome their growing sense of social alienation: "who distributed Supercommunist pamphlets in Union Square weeping." An endnote in the *Annotated "Howl"* published in 1986 indicates that this line refers to a 1955 peace rally with participants like Dorothy Day, Bayard Rustin, Judith Malina, and A. J. Muste.[†] Additionally, some best minds "burned cigarette holes in their arms protesting the narcotic tobacco haze of Capitalism." Yet, overall in Part I, political protest seems only a small part of his protagonists' struggles to obtain self-fulfillment, and there is little explicit emphasis in this part on political repression as a root cause of his friends' despair, loneliness, impatience, and rage.

Indeed, "Howl," Part I, is not heavily political in a traditional pre-1950s leftist sense. The group that Ginsberg unites under the banner of "best minds" is not a class-based collective. Rather, he has poetically developed—by symbolically connecting people through the anaphoric repetition of "who"—an alternative basis for unity, an aggregate of young people desperate for more meaningful lives. Significantly, this new assemblage—

*Ibid., p. 160.
[†]Allen Ginsberg, *Howl: Original Draft Facsimile* . . . , edited by Barry Miles (New York: Harper & Row, 1986), p. 128.

ELIOT KATZ

based on generational concerns about spirituality, psychology, and culture, as well as politics and the economy—prefigures what would a decade later become a widespread American youth counterculture and a youth-led New Left. A number of the founders and leaders of 1960s movements have cited the influence of Allen and the Beat Generation in their politically formative years. On a politics panel at Naropa Institute in 1982, Abbie Hoffman said that he'd memorized "Howl" for two years,[*] and in his autobiography Hoffman wrote: "Jews don't have saints, they just have Ginsbergs every once in a while."[†] In a February 2005 phone conversation, one of the founders of Students for a Democratic Society (SDS), Bob Ross, who was known at the time as a fan of Beat literature, told me that he had read Ginsberg in high school and that Allen's poems provided a "certain dissonant, dissident mind-set" that carried forward and helped him prepare for being an activist. The Port Huron Statement, SDS's 1962 manifesto written mostly by Tom Hayden (who was deeply influenced by reading *On the Road*[‡]), even began with a line whose rhythm and generational focus, although written as expository prose, seem in some ways to recall the first line of "Howl": "We are people of this generation, bred in at least modest comfort, housed now in universities, looking uncomfortably to the world we inhabit."[§] Allen's work also influenced musicians like Bob Dylan and the Beatles, without whom

[*]Quoted in Paul Krassner, "Allen Ginsberg's Greatest Poem," in *Best Minds: A Tribute to Allen Ginsberg,* edited by Bill Morgan and Bob Rosenthal (New York: Lospecchio Press, 1986), p. 155.
[†]Abbie Hoffman, *Soon to Be a Major Motion Picture* (New York: Perigee, 1980), p. 123.
[‡]Tom Hayden, *Rebel: A Personal History of the 1960s* (Los Angeles: Red Hen Press, 2003), p. 17.
[§]Port Huron Statement of the Students for a Democratic Society, 1962. Posted online courtesy of the office of Tom Hayden at http://coursesa.matrix.msu.edu/~hst306/documents/huron.html.

the 1960s would have looked far different. With good reason, in their book on the 1960s, *America Divided*, the historians Maurice Isserman and Michael Kazin begin their chapter "The Making of a Youth Culture" by describing the October 1955 evening when Allen Ginsberg first read "Howl" in San Francisco's Six Gallery.*

Whether political, spiritual, or cultural, the energetic attempts to find fulfillment in the first section of "Howl"—although viewed largely by the poet with considerable empathy or admiration and as far preferable to passive acceptance of a toxic status quo—ultimately prove unsuccessful. People get "busted in their pubic beards" and end up experiencing "waking nightmares" in their search for redemptive dreams. Attempts at escapism prove fruitless, as those who bid to remove themselves from society's material restraints end up with alarm clocks falling "on their heads every day for the next decade." As for the peace activists in Part I: "the sirens of Los Alamos wailed them down."

Near the end of Part I, the last shred of hope for improved conditions seems to disappear: with the "last fantastic book flung out of the tenement window," "the last door closed," and "mother finally ******." It is at this moment, when the poem's narrative exudes a dire pessimism, that the poet shifts focus, turning attention directly to the problem at hand, in this case toward the explicit issue of poetic technique. At the end of Part I, Ginsberg begins to recognize the possibility of hope in poetry's wide-ranging stylistic toolbox, which includes the imagination's ability to create "incarnate gaps in Time & Space through images juxtaposed." In other words, surreal imagery ("the ghostly clothes of jazz") and modernist montage ("hydrogen jukebox") can create "gaps" within dominant culture by making images that do not yet exist in the actual world (but only in the "arch-

---

*Maurice Isserman and Michael Kazin, *America Divided: The Civil War of the 1960s* (New York: Oxford University Press, 2000).

angel of the soul"). This is Ernst Bloch's "anticipatory illumination," portending the possibility of a future world transformed out of the present.

For the author of "Howl," in appropriating William Blake's notion of a poet's prophetic role, the literary imagination is thus understood to be a potential means to envision healthier social and psychological possibilities. In addition to providing anticipatory illuminations, the act of modernist montage invites audience participation in the creation of meaning. Because montage does not contain a clear narrative logic, it requires, as Ginsberg states in the liner notes to *Holy Soul Jelly Roll!* a "mind interpreting sense to it."[*] Or, in the words of the theorist Stephen Bronner, modernist forms of art can "foster individual responsibility insofar as the audience is made to take part in the active construction of something new."[†] The poem's modernist elements thus work to urge readers to see themselves as part of a kind of dialogue that helps shape the ultimate meaning of the poem. Ginsberg's "best minds," after all, refer only in part to his personal friends and acquaintances—and to his own autobiography, as Marjorie Perloff observes.[‡] Because the catalogs of Part I do not name names, readers are free to find places in which to insert their own identities and desires in the text. We might even say that because it encourages reader participation, the poem implicitly entreats its audience to choose whether to sympathize with the countercultural community Ginsberg is creating or with the dominant institutions from which that community rebels.

---

[*]Allen Ginsberg, liner notes to *Holy Soul Jelly Roll! Poems and Songs, 1949–1993* (Los Angeles: Rhino Records, 1994), p. 8.

[†]Stephen Eric Bronner, *Of Critical Theory and Its Theorists* (Cambridge, Mass.: Basil Blackwell, 1994), p. 175.

[‡]Marjorie Perloff, "A Lion in Our Living Room: Reading Allen Ginsberg in the Eighties," in *Poetic License: Essays on Modernist and Postmodernist Lyric* (Evanston, Ill.: Northwestern University Press, 1990), p. 228.

Some readers may even see how the poem's vast progressive energies can carry beyond its own author's comprehension in some areas, which may partly help explain, for one example, why this poem has been cited by many contemporary feminist poets as inspirational even though it clearly did not explore dominant gender dynamics with the same energy that it explored so many other important issues of the day. By nurturing readers' subjectivity and sense of choice, the poem's modernist elements offer additional challenge to the sorts of institutional pressures toward conformity that have been driving the poem's protagonists mad.

Just what is it that has been driving them mad? From where have these institutional pressures originated? Now that Ginsberg has undertaken a full-immersion tour of his contemporary society, exploring symptoms of alienation and desperation among his generation, he is able to define the social source of those symptoms. Part II displays a radical shift in the poet's approach. Rather than continue to narrate or describe, here he analyzes and declares. Part II is also more explicitly political than the first section. In the process of narrating the experiences of his protagonists in Part I, Ginsberg created a countercultural community. Now that the poet is uncovering the cause of a community's maladies, the focus moves to an even more collective and public level.

In this section, various sources of repression are aggregated and named Moloch—after the Canaanite fire god who was worshiped by sacrifice of children. As many have pointed out, there are clear similarities between Allen Ginsberg's Moloch and William Blake's Urizen ("Times on times he divided, & measur'd / Space by space in his ninefold darkness"*): Each is a figure that em-

---

*William Blake, "The Book of Urizen," in *The Complete Poems*, edited by Alicia Ostriker (New York: Penguin, 1977), p. 242.

braces an instrumental reason divorced from human emotion and imagination. Some insightful critics like James Breslin and Tony Trigilio have claimed that this section shows Ginsberg in opposition to "authority"* or to "system-building."† But I think it would be a mistake to try to fit his meaning into a kind of postmodern theoretical framework. Rather, it seems to me that it is the particularly repressive characteristics of actually existing authority and systems that are criticized. Along these lines, the radical social psychologist Erich Fromm in *Escape from Freedom* had distinguished between "rational authority" (as in a healthy teacher-student relationship) and "inhibiting authority," in which "superiority serves as a basis for exploitation."‡ Ginsberg, I would argue, does not rule out the utopian possibility of developing far more humane and democratic systems in the future. Indeed, in many ways it is the vision of just such a long-term possibility that seems to drive so much of "Howl," as well as Allen's later work. In a 1965 interview with Tom Clark, Ginsberg makes this point about system-building explicit: "Another century has gone, technology has changed everything completely, so it's time for a new utopian system."§ It is the instrumental and exploitative character of present institutional structures that leads to both social injustice and self-fragmentation.

Many writers have described the repressive Cold War political and cultural climate in our country during the era in which the poem was written: a militaristic foreign policy that included engagement in the Korean War and covert foreign interventions

*James E. B. Breslin, *From Modern to Contemporary: American Poetry, 1945–1965* (Chicago: University of Chicago Press, 1984), p. 101.
†Tony Trigilio, *"Strange Prophecies Anew": Rereading Apocalypse in Blake, H.D., and Ginsberg* (Madison, N.J.: Fairleigh Dickinson University Press, 2000), p. 174.
‡Erich Fromm, *Escape from Freedom* (New York: Henry Holt, 1941), p. 163.
§Allen Ginsberg, *Spontaneous Mind: Selected Interviews, 1958–1996,* edited by David Carter (New York: HarperCollins, 2001), p. 33.

as in Iran (1953) and Guatemala (1954), a growing stockpile of nuclear weapons routinely described as part of war's standard arsenal, the chilling of democratic dissent with House Un-American Activities Committee hearings and hundreds of domestic groups appearing on federal watch lists, the 1953 execution of the Rosenbergs, homophobic Senate investigations into the employment of gays and lesbians in the federal government, the persistence of racist Jim Crow laws until 1954, and the acquittal of Emmett Till's murderers in 1955. One hundred years after "Song of Myself," Whitman's vision for an enlightened American democracy was a far cry from the view one saw on the nation's streets.

Fewer writers on "Howl" have noted the way in which progressive ideas were evolving in 1950s America in response to domestic and world events. The modern civil rights movement was growing in numbers and influence, and 1955 would see the start of the historic Montgomery bus boycott inspired by Rosa Parks. In his illuminating look at the 1950s left, *If I Had a Hammer,*★ the historian Maurice Isserman examines the fifties as the decade that saw the essential end of the Old Left in America and the creation of the New. With revelations mounting about the repression and murders that had taken place under Stalin, many groups on the U.S. left—including democratic socialist organizations led by folks like Max Shachtman and Michael Harrington, new journals like *Dissent*, the nascent antinuclear movement, and even the Communist Party—were debating new philosophies and strategies that might extend the original left ideals of bringing more political democracy, economic fairness, and peaceful cooperation to society. Many key figures on the left, from the psychologist Erich Fromm to the political writer

---

★Maurice Isserman, *If I Had a Hammer: The Death of the Old Left and the Birth of the New Left* (New York: Basic Books, 1987).

Dwight MacDonald, were also focusing more attention on the social role of culture and psychology than had the more orthodox left of previous eras. French existentialists like Sartre and Camus were being read. These new philosophical and activist energies were in the air—and in books and left journals—in the years immediately preceding Ginsberg's writing of "Howl." Allen's poem beautifully captured the oppositional energies of the time and, through his highly personal literary skills and imagination, helped amplify those energies for generations to come. The poem also, of course, created new progressive energies in the poetry world by challenging the New Critics' more impersonal and politically conservative aesthetics.

One of the most influential social analysts of the mid-1950s was the radical sociologist C. Wright Mills, author of popular "Howl"-era volumes such as *White Collar* and *The Power Elite*. Although Allen mentions reading Mills in a letter to his father in 1961,★ I am not sure whether he had read Mills by the time of "Howl." But Mills's political ideas were circulating in progressive publications, and it was Mills who is largely credited with popularizing the term "New Left" in the United States. It is interesting that Mills was the subject of graduate theses written by two of the founders of SDS, Tom Hayden and Bob Ross.

Many of the ideas of C. Wright Mills parallel those found in "Howl," especially Part II. Mills rejected, as inadequate for the 1950s era, much of orthodox Marxism's economics-privileging language and analysis, including the Old Left idea that the working class would necessarily be the main agent of social change. Yet Mills simultaneously insisted on the need for more radical ideas than those offered by the tradition of American liberalism. In his opinion, a broad "power elite" was now "in com-

★Allen Ginsberg and Louis Ginsberg, *Family Business: Selected Letters Between a Father and Son*, edited by Michael Schumacher (New York: Bloomsbury, 2001), p. 145.

mand of the major hierarchies and organizations of modern so-
ciety. They rule the big corporations. They run the machinery
of the state . . . They direct the military establishment."[*] Ob-
serving post–World War II pressures toward conformity, Mills
described a new white-collar class, in which "the malaise is
deep-rooted" and in which capitalist bureaucracies had usurped
human freedom in the name of instrumental reason: "rationality
seems to have taken on a new form, to have its seat not in indi-
vidual men, but in social institutions which by their bureaucratic
planning and mathematical foresight usurp both freedom and
rationality from the little individual men caught in them." As a
result, average people become "alienated from work and, on the
personality market, from self" and "politically apathetic."[†]

Mills, who believed that young people would play a crucial
role in new movements for social change, contended that "to be
politically conscious . . . is to see a political meaning in one's
own insecurities and desires."[‡] In this sense, it is the exploration
of the psychological effects of contemporary society on his gen-
eration in "Howl," Part I, that enables Ginsberg's more politi-
cally conscious verse of Part II. Cornel West writes that Mills
believed "the ruling elite—political, economic, and military big
shots—live and revel in a cultural form of life that cements them
into a group characterized by coordinated actions, unified inter-
ests, and a highly limited range of opinions and outlooks."[§]
Ginsberg, like Mills, believed the power elite were cemented
by common interests into a group, and he named this group
Moloch.

[*]C. Wright Mills, *The Power Elite* (New York: Oxford University Press, 1957), p. 4.
[†]C. Wright Mills, *White Collar* (New York: Oxford University Press, 1951), pp.
xvi–xviii.
[‡]Ibid., p. 327.
[§]Cornel West, *The American Evasion of Philosophy: A Genealogy of Pragmatism* (Madison:
University of Wisconsin Press, 1989), p. 129.

Of the Moloch section of "Howl," Alicia Ostriker writes:
"In Blakean terms, Ginsberg is 'giving a body to Error.'"* In
this poet-prophet tradition, one cannot cast out error until one
has defined it and given it material shape. In "The Four Zoas,"
Blake's poet-prophet figure Los "began the binding of Urizen
day & night in fear / Circling round the dark Demon with
howlings dismay & sharp blightings / The Prophet of Eternity
beat on his iron links & links of brass."† (It is interesting that
Blake's Los is able to bind and transform Urizen through "howl-
ings.") Ginsberg acknowledges that he learned from Blake the
poetic technique of mythification, of taking "political details"
and "magnif[ying] roles into cosmo-demonic figures."‡ For
Ginsberg, Moloch becomes a literary figuration capable of car-
rying a determinate social critique through its assembling of
existing social forces, and capable also of mythologizing that
critique to suggest a more universal and timeless relevance.

If "Howl" were a piece of political or philosophical prose,
the use of such mythic metaphor might suggest a root element of
ahistoricism at the core of the poem's social criticisms. The
philosopher Jürgen Habermas has written: "Demythologization
that does not break the mythic spell but merely seeks to evade it
only brings forth new witch doctors."§ But Habermas was speak-
ing here about political essays, and he sensibly, at least in my
view, embraces a concept of sphere-differentiation,** in which the

*Alicia Ostriker, "Blake, Ginsberg, Madness and the Prophet as Shaman," in *William Blake and the Moderns*, edited by Robert J. Bertholf and Annette S. Levitt (Albany, N.Y.: State University of New York, 1982), p. 121.
†William Blake, "The Four Zoas," in *Complete Poems*, p. 340.
‡Allen Ginsberg, liner notes to *Holy Soul Jelly Roll!*, p. 15.
§Jürgen Habermas, *On Society and Politics: A Reader*, edited by Steven Seidman (Boston: Beacon, 1989), p. 45.
**See Jürgen Habermas, "Excursus on Leveling the Genre Distinction Between Philosophy and Literature," in *The Philosophical Discourse of Modernity: Twelve Lectures*, translated by Frederick G. Lawrence (Cambridge, Mass.: MIT Press, 1992), pp. 185–210.

boundaries between spheres (e.g., politics and culture) are seen as drawn in dotted lines, or something like semipermeable membranes. The left literary critic Terry Eagleton describes this view as maintaining a "necessary differentiation of the cognitive, moral and cultural spheres," which are seen as "interrelated but not conflated."* In other words, this is a dynamic view that sees politics and culture interacting in different ways in different historical contexts—in various times and places, art and politics can overlap to differing degrees, bounce off each other, embrace, or stand apart. Under this philosophy, the criteria for judging art and the criteria for judging politics can be distinct,† and with different criteria used, one can appreciate each field without reducing the intrinsic possibilities or demands of either field to the other. In this way, we can even learn to appreciate the work of quality poets who advocate a politics with which we disagree. If the spheres of politics and poetry are seen as "interrelated but not conflated," then the energetic complexity of those interactions becomes fascinating to study when a skilled poet crosses heuristic boundaries by writing political poetry.

In the case of "Howl," the mythic element helps give the poem a long-term resonance to such an effective degree that the "Moloch" section continues to echo with readers fifty years after it was written. (It is interesting that other poems by Ginsberg, such as "America" or "Wichita Vortex Sutra," employ the technique of demythologization, providing progressive news and analysis in interesting ways to debunk dominant government or media myths about politics or history.)

In addition to long-term resonance, the mythification of Part II carries identifiable social criticisms. By "giving a body" to

---

*Terry Eagleton, *The Ideology of the Aesthetic* (Oxford: Basil Blackwell, 1990), p. 406.
†Habermas: "The false assimilation of one enterprise to the other robs both of their substance," in "Excursus on Leveling the Genre Distinction," p. 210.

Moloch, Ginsberg is able to reveal the cause of his compatriots' existential frustration to be a set of intertwined, oppressive aspects of religious, sexual, familial, political, artistic, historical, and economic institutions. As Moloch ate children, unaccountable modern institutions devour healthy human subjectivities and bodies. Pointing out the chasms that remain between American reality and American ideals one hundred years after "Song of Myself," the poet of "Howl" declares that the country which presumes to nurture individuality and informed political citizenship actually obliterates these: "bashed open their skulls and ate up their brains and imagination." America has not groomed liberal subjects but has allowed industrialism to fashion nonhuman, conformist mentalities ("Moloch whose mind is pure machinery!"). Professing to promote the rule of law and universal moral values, America actually imprisons people for irrational reasons ("Moloch the incomprehensible prison!") and reveals its immorality through its lust for militarism ("Moloch whose fingers are ten armies!"). The United States creates deleterious governing structures ("Moloch the stunned governments!") and builds factories that pollute its natural beauty ("whose smokestacks and antennae crown the cities!"). And furthermore, the supposedly freedom-loving America actively suppresses healthy sexuality ("whose fate is a cloud of sexless hydrogen!") It is interesting to note that "Howl" adopts some of the imagery of T. S. Eliot ("Here is no water but only rock"*), associating the signs of a sterile society in "Howl," Part II, with images of dryness and rocks ("granite cocks!" "down on the rocks of Time!"), but by the poem's end Ginsberg will subvert T. S. Eliot's project by using this imagery to convey a more progressive political vision.

And, while the Moloch section of "Howl" highlights the

---

*T. S. Eliot, "The Waste Land," in *The Waste Land and Other Poems* (New York: Harcourt, Brace & World, 1934), p. 42.

gap between America's ideals and its reality, it also implies that our founding ideals are in need of a more radical update: "Howl," Part II, derides nationalism ("spectral nations!"), challenges a core value of liberal individualism by equating Moloch with "Solitude," and takes consistent and energetic aim at profit-oriented, capitalist economics and the financial hardships that result—"Moloch whose blood is running money!" "Moloch whose soul is electricity and banks!" "Moloch whose poverty is the specter of genius!"

The social ills and hyperrationality evident in the 1950s technological age have become objectified in the new atomic weapons of mass destruction, the "monstrous bombs!" No longer is the fear of a life-annihilating apocalypse purely specu-lative or allegorical. As the SDS students at Port Huron would write just seven years later: "Our work is guided by the sense that we may be the last generation in the experiment with the living."[*] Thus, while the use of a metaphor, Moloch, to iden-tify the source of multiple social oppressions can be said to elide historical specificity, we can see that the mythification simulta-neously enables Ginsberg to present a long-reverberating social critique that illuminates a new multidimensional field of politi-cal, psychological, cultural, and militaristic repression.

Once the source of repression is identified, the possibility of transformation can be envisioned. And, in the tradition of Blake, Ginsberg writes with the assumption that what a vision-ary poet imagines can potentially be made real. As he says in "Death to Van Gogh's Ear!" about good governments: "they have to begin existing they exist in my poems."[†] Or, as William

---

[*]Port Huron Statement, p. 2.
[†]Allen Ginsberg, "Death to Van Gogh's Ear!," in *Collected Poems*, p. 168.

Blake had said in "The Mental Traveller," "For the Eye altering alters all."⋆ Although Carl Solomon at the end of Part III physically remains in Rockland, Ginsberg's optimistic gesture in this section is to envision alternatives to the existing world that one day might be actualized, a keen assertion that—although changing society is not easy—the world is mutable and dependent on human actions. Or, as the recent global justice movement puts it: "Another world is possible."

"I'm with you in Rockland" is Part III's anaphoric assertion of solidarity, the tonic to Moloch's "solitude" that will help free the confined Carl Solomon, and by extension oppose the existential and material suffering of America's repressed subjects. In Part I, a countercultural collective had been implicitly envisioned through formal means—the syntactic parallelisms and the anaphoric repetition of "who." In Part III, the desire for solidarity is made explicit and becomes a model for the sort of collective social effort, or movement building, that could potentially improve human conditions by challenging Moloch's multilayered rule.

Carl Solomon is detained in an "armed madhouse," an instrumentally rational institution where "the faculties of the skull no longer admit the worms of the senses." In America's psychiatric hospitals, as in society as a whole, authoritarian solutions are no solutions:

I'm with you in Rockland
where fifty more shocks will never return your soul to its body again from
its pilgrimage to a cross in the void.

Social institutions have wrenched body from mind, and the medical establishment's prescriptions are mean-spirited and ineffectual. The expression of interpersonal solidarity asserts a

---

⋆William Blake, "The Mental Traveller," in *Complete Poems*, p. 501.

view of the self in relational terms, a view of healthy subjectivity as healthy intersubjectivity, of healthy independence as interdependence.

The poet's empathy in Part III of "Howl" is largely articulated in a personal way, but it does include broader political references as well. Carl Solomon plots "the Hebrew socialist revolution," and "twentyfive thousand mad comrades all together singing the final stanzas of the Internationale" are envisioned before Solomon's ultimate redemption can occur. This is not to claim that Ginsberg implies a specific political program or ideology. There is no sorting out varied left traditions like anarchism, syndicalism, progressive populism, or democratic socialism. (By the mid-1950s, there was overwhelming information available about the crimes of Stalin, long emphasized by Allen's Debsian socialist father, so that Soviet-style communism was seen by Ginsberg not as falling within the honest arena of left traditions but as a betrayal of those traditions. This is why his activists in Part I distribute "Supercommunist" rather than "Communist" pamphlets, why he later in "Howl" praises the "fifth" International, why in "America" he inventively proclaims "what a good thing the party was in 1835,"* and why his poems could be embraced by young dissident writers in Eastern Europe.) There is no choosing in "Howl" among particular anarchist, labor, or democratic socialist groups, parties, or platforms. And yet, while no fixed ideology or specific program is advanced in the poem, its historical references and social criticisms align it clearly within a general arena of leftist traditions. In this way, I would argue that Ginsberg's political philosophy was more pragmatic than rigidly ideological, or that it was "ideologically flexible" within the spectrum of left traditions—exhibiting a consistent belief in values

*Allen Ginsberg, "America," in *Collected Poems,* p. 147.

such as engaged citizenship, accountable institutions, peace, com-
passion, ecology, economic fairness, gay rights, civil rights, and
civil liberties, but not worrying about seeking a narrowly defined
political philosophy. After he had seen the ideological dogmatism
that led to severe repression in the Soviet Union and that under-
mined the efforts of America's Old Left—and that had created
friction between his own communist mother and social-
democratic father—it is not surprising that Allen should have re-
mained less rigid in these ideological matters.

The envisioned freeing of Carl Solomon from Rockland
takes place in the longest line of Part III, appropriately, since
long lines in "Howl" imply a desire to break free from bound-
aries: "where we wake up electrified out of the coma by our
own souls' airplanes roaring over the roof they've come to drop
angelic bombs the hospital illuminates itself imaginary walls col-
lapse O skinny legions run outside O starry-spangled shock of
mercy the eternal war is here O victory forget your underwear
we're free." Here, we should note that Ginsberg has transvalued
the biblical notion of apocalypse, creating, in the words of Tony
Trigilio, "an apocalypse without fatalism" and "apocalypse as a
mode of consciousness."* For Ginsberg in this section of
"Howl," apocalyptic release is viewed as earthly, beneficial, hu-
morous, and emanating from "our own souls" and interpersonal
solidarity, rather than from an external divine entity as in Reve-
lation and in opposition to the quite fatal apocalyptic threat of
growing nuclear arsenals.

While Allen's poetry has often been criticized by conserva-
tives or centrists for his progressive views (with aesthetic argu-
ments sometimes used to mask what are at bottom political
disagreements), a rare critique was leveled in the mid-1990s

*Trigilio, "Strange Prophecies Anew," p. 16.

from the left that seems instructive to address here. In "Why Johnny Can't Dissent," Thomas Frank—whose perceptive 2004 book, *What's the Matter with Kansas?*, looks at why so many working-class residents of middle America have lately been voting Republican—argued that countercultural challenges, as exemplified by Ginsberg, to America's corporate-dominated sensibilities were no longer liberatory. According to Frank, capitalism had changed, and corporate advertising by the mid-1990s was no longer attempting to induce personal conformity but was instead perfectly comfortable promoting products as helping consumers in a "Ginsbergian search for kicks upon kicks."[*] Even some of America's top corporate gurus had adopted Beat-influenced rhetoric: " 'Revolution,' of course, means for Peters the same thing it did to Burroughs and Ginsberg, Presley and the Stones in their heyday: breaking rules, pissing off the suits, shocking the bean-counters."[†] Frank concluded that by the late twentieth century a corporate co-optation of Ginsberg's message had occurred, and that this was possible only because Ginsberg wrote poetry in the first place that was insufficiently meaningful to resist.

But Frank's reductive reading ("breaking rules, pissing off the suits") of Ginsberg's poetry ignores the important notion of solidarity as most powerfully expressed in "Howl," Part III, and also fails to highlight the passionate critique in "Howl" of militarism and capitalist exploitation, as well as Allen's ensuing four-plus decades of writing and activist work on behalf of a wide range of human rights and ecological causes. Frank also prob-

---

[*]Thomas Frank, "Why Johnny Can't Dissent," in *Commodify Your Dissent: The Business of Culture in the New Gilded Age*, edited by Thomas Frank and Matt Weiland (New York: W. W. Norton, 1997), p. 34.
[†]Ibid., p. 38.

lematically assumes that if culture is absorbed, it is the fault of the artist for not being radical enough. But, as Terry Eagleton persuasively argues, it is naïve to think that "*art*, all by itself" can "resist incorporation." According to Eagleton, "If *they* win, continue to govern, then it is no doubt true that there is nothing which they cannot in principle defuse and contain. If *you* win, they will not be able to appropriate a thing because you will have appropriated them." When it comes to the effectiveness of oppositional art, Eagleton concludes that, ultimately, "the question of integration stands or falls with the destiny of a mass political movement."★ As long as large corporations hold sway, it is impossible to stop them from trying to co-opt countercultural energies, though we can certainly challenge those attempts by offering fuller pictures of our own (and, in this case, Allen's) social visions. In addition, under a Bush administration that has announced people ought to watch what they say and do, and rightward-moving mainstream media that have consistently criticized musicians and actors for speaking out against the Iraq war, it seems that the protest against conformity in "Howl" has found a renewed relevance in the twenty-first century.

Once Carl Solomon is imagined freed, Ginsberg celebrates. The first line of the poem's final section, "Footnote to Howl," depicts pure ecstasy, "Holy!" repeated fifteen times. As Part III had transvalued the apocalyptic qualities of Revelation so that sudden change was viewed as positive, and as emanating from within—and from interpersonal solidarity—rather than from an external divine force, the "Footnote to Howl" appropriates the biblical "Holy, holy, holy" and applies the description to hu-

★Eagleton, *Ideology of the Aesthetic*, p. 372, author's italics.

manity and the living world rather than to an external god. Having, in the structure of the poem, broken free from psychic and institutional repression, Ginsberg is able to see the divine within all: to celebrate body and soul, phenomena mainstream society values ("Holy the solitudes of skyscrapers and pavements!") as well as those that it abhors or ignores ("Holy the jazzbands marijuana hipsters peace peyote pipes & drums!").

In a rhetorical flourish that is extraordinarily shrewd for those of us interested in the poem's political implications, Ginsberg inventively celebrates a utopian socialist gathering that has not yet taken place: "holy the fifth International." In the *Annotated "Howl"* footnotes, Allen observes that there were four workers' internationals and writes that the "Fifth International of workers, entrepreneurs, peasants and indigenous communities of the world has not yet assembled to propose survival norms in an era of imperial private and state monopoly capital's near-absolute and potentially suicidal power."★ In "Howl," a young poet wisely imagines the possibility of refashioning a left historical legacy— one that furthers human freedoms in the spirit of the original socialist project rather than restricting them as in the "actually existing socialism" of the Soviet bloc. The witnessing of society that began the poem with an initial "I saw" has been transfigured into a witnessing of, and an urging toward, a better future. For all of those who have descended into existential frustration, "Howl" witnesses/envisions a potential path out—through increased political consciousness, psychological exploration, spiritual enlightenment, artistic creation, and solidarity.

At the poem's close, Ginsberg also celebrates internationalism, praising foreign cities: "Holy Paris Holy Tangiers Holy Moscow Holy Istanbul!" His inclusion of Moscow takes more

★Ginsberg, *Howl: Original Draft Facsimile*, p. 146.

than a tacit jab at 1950s U.S. Cold War ideology. In the mid-1950s U.S. left, there was considerable debate about how to frame discussions about the Soviet Union. In *If I Had a Hammer*, Maurice Isserman describes a falling-out that took place between C. Wright Mills and the journal *Dissent* when Mills argued with Irving Howe that Howe's continuing insistence that the U.S. left always be explicitly anticommunist was becoming "obsolete."[*] A similar debate took place in 1962, when the young organizers of SDS refused to accept Michael Harrington's entreaties to include a clear statement condemning communism in their Port Huron Statement—instead, SDS criticized America's restrictive Cold War mentality, with its absurd level of military spending, and observed that "anticommunism" has often been used by conservatives as a rationale for opposing "liberalism, internationalism, welfarism, the active civil rights and labor movements."[†] (One might sensibly make the same observations about the Bush administration's so-called war on terror today.) Like Mills, Allen always recognized the severely repressive aspects of Stalinism and never tried to rationalize them away, but—because he saw the mirror problems in the West of poverty, militarism, and McCarthyism, and because he valued socialist ideals—he refused to be conned into accepting the dominant Cold War mentality of the day, one more way in which the ideas in "Howl" prefigured those of the New Left.

Contrary to the destructiveness or pessimism that some of Ginsberg's early critics saw in the poem, "Howl" ends with one of the most unabashedly optimistic and faith-filled lines of twentieth-century American poetry. If one has the courage, energy, and persistence to uncover the sheets of denial that can surround

[*]Isserman, *If I Had a Hammer,* p. 117.
[†]Port Huron Statement, p. 9.

both the social and the psychological status quo, one can see the "supernatural extra brilliant intelligent kindness of the soul!"

In the second term of the disastrous administration of George W. Bush, we are living in an era somewhat like the one Allen Ginsberg described in "Wichita Vortex Sutra," when "almost all our language has been taxed by war."★ In the midst of an unwarranted and devastating military conflict in Iraq, regressive economic policies, the backsliding of civil liberties, and increasing environmental dangers like global warming, Allen's radical legacy remains as important as ever. Fortunately, it is still the case that young people who read Allen's work quite often come away with a strengthened belief that it is possible to create a far better world: one with considerably less poverty and war, with much cleaner air and water, and with a stronger commitment to civil liberties, civic participation, and democratically accountable social institutions.

Fifty years after "Howl" was written, the poem continues to inspire writers and activists around the world with its passionate commitment to get to the root of what ails us and its visionary insistence (via both form and content) on the viability of a more humane future. For many young poets, and some established ones as well, "Howl" provides a generous toolbox of literary techniques and strategies for turning social ideas and observations into memorable poetry. Like some previous twentieth-century long poems, such as Muriel Rukeyser's "Book of the Dead," Langston Hughes's "Montage of a Dream Deferred," William Carlos Williams's "Spring and All," or Pablo Neruda's "Canto General," "Howl" demonstrates that one does not have

★Ginsberg, "Wichita Vortex Sutra," in *Collected Poems*, p. 406.

to choose a single poetry path or style (like realism or surrealism, narrative or antinarrative, elevated diction or American speech); one can feel free to embrace multiple interests and mix them in original, personal, and surprising ways.* In terms of political poetry, the way "Howl" helped to revive poetry's oral tradition remains significant, as the resurgence of poetry readings in the last fifteen years has created new public spaces for people to explore, express, and debate their views on politics and current events.

Allen's signal poem also offers contemporary poets a challenge: how to capture today's new social problems, and envision or sketch new potential resolutions, with something close to the vitality and prescience of "Howl." Abbie Hoffman, with whom I had the pleasure to work a bit in the late 1980s student movement, used to say that trying to create social change without a counterculture is like trying to ski without snow. If we conceptualize culture and politics as differentiated categories that interrelate in various ways in different contexts, then the question for a political poet is how to write poems of literary value while pushing against the poetry-politics boundaries so that one's literary efforts might help at least in some small way to enlighten consciousness, illuminate public issues, stir public dreams and desires, improve ideological climate, aid political movements, or otherwise help alter the social landscape. Denise Levertov addressed the question of poetry's potential to help transform society in this way: "I don't think one can accurately measure the historical effectiveness of a poem; but one does know, of course, that books influence individuals; and individuals, although they

---

*Here's the Chilean poet Nicanor Parra, on this theme: "Young poets / Write any way you want to / In whatever style you please / Too much blood has gone under the bridge / To go on believing—I believe— / That only one road is right." In "Letters from the Poet Who Sleeps in a Chair," *Emergency Poems* (New York: New Directions, 1972), p. 23.

are part of large economic and social processes, influence history."*

If one is to make a political-poetic mark and inspire people around the globe for five decades and counting to work toward a more humane future, it helps to have written inspired verse. And in Allen Ginsberg's "Howl," we find strengths seldom equaled in American poetry: a dazzling and comprehensive poetic imagination, a unique mixture of humor and historical insight, an inventive prophetic voice and singular ear, a sophisticated extension of wide-ranging poetic traditions, and energetic yearnings for healthier human possibilities.

*Levertov, "On the Edge of Darkness," p. 169.

MARGE PIERCY

THE BEST BONES FOR SOUP

HAVE MEAT ON THEM

———

When I was in high school, I began to write poetry often and intensely. It was one of the few tools available to me for making sense of the world I inhabited in center city Detroit, and for sorting out the cognitive dissonance between the way things were supposed to be and the way I experienced them. My poetry was raw and rough, but it had an authenticity that I learned to abandon at the university. What was admired and taught was extremely studied rimed poetry usually in forms like villanelles, sonnets, and other forms more suited to Romance languages than to English. I wrote the crabbed intricate pieces I forced myself into, like the girdles women were expected to wear then. I was told repeatedly I could not write about what I cared about. Political poetry was uncouth and not real poetry—I had written reams of it in high school. So was everything to do with the body as it existed in reality and my experiences as a woman or a Jew. Everything was to be tidy, male, "universal." The most admired pieces seemed to be sonnets about paintings viewed in the Uffizi while abroad on Guggenheims.

When I first heard Allen Ginsberg read—I was working as a

secretary in Chicago and trying to publish my apprentice work—
he reopened the world to me. He wrote out of his sexuality, not
the way it was supposed to be, but as he experienced it in his
own body and mind. He wrote politically. He wrote with emo-
tion. He wrote as a Jew and as a leftie. I walked out of that read-
ing truly liberated to begin to write my own poetry, not an
imitation of his, but not an imitation of what was admired in
English departments, either. He showed me above all that I could
be honest in my work.

I carried "Howl" with me to Ann Arbor when I went back
to visit friends still in graduate school; they thought I had taken
leave of my senses. I had not. I had taken leave of the senses
forced upon me as appropriate and proper. I was freed to hon-
esty, to make what I could out of my own politics, my own pain
and joy, my working-class background, my sexuality, my Jewish-
ness, my woman's life. I was free to work my way toward my
own poetic voice, finally—the voice I had begun with but aban-
doned because I was told I could not write of those things in
poetry.

Poetry seems to close down periodically to something safe
and barely felt. Then comes a poet who thrusts the door open
with a great shocking bang. Allen Ginsberg did that for so many
of us.

What Ginsberg forced us to understand in "Howl" . . . is that nothing is safe from poetry.   —Paul Zweig, 1980

"Howl" was written by a young man hungry for love and hungry for God. More than that, they were written by a man whose hunger had been satiated, if only for a moment. Ginsberg had written poetry as a college student, but his real moment of conversion to that art came after he left school. In the summer of 1948, lying on his bed in an apartment in Harlem, Mr. Ginsberg heard what he took to be the voice of William Blake speak a series of poems to him . . . "This was the moment I was born for, this initiation," Allen wrote, . . . "this consciousness of being . . . alive myself onto the creator. As the son of the creator—who loved me, I realized." Eight years lie between his Blake epiphany and "Howl," years in which he was a student in a school of his own invention. From Williams he learned to transcribe "the American idiom"; from Whitman he learned to orchestrate the long line; from Cézanne's paintings he discovered the surprise of juxtaposition. But he did not abandon his vision. When the author of "Howl" speaks of "angelheaded hipsters burning for the ancient heavenly connection," he means it. "Angel," "heaven," these are not metaphors, they are meant to denote, just as "wheelbarrow" is meant to denote. "Howl" is a theodicy, spoken in prophetic voice of one who believes that angels help the poets write and that evil powers feed on the nation's tender hearts.   —Lewis Hyde, *The New York Times Book Review*, 1984

I saw the best minds of my generation destroyed by madness that said more to me than any of the stuff I'd been raised on.

—Bob Dylan, quoted in liner notes by
Cameron Crowe for *Biograph*, 1985

"Howl" left us standing in wonder, cheering and wondering, but knowing at the deepest level that a barrier had been broken, that a human voice and body had been hurled against a harsh wall of America and its supporting armies and academies and institutions and ownership systems and power support bases forever.

—Michael McClure, in *Howl: Original Draft Facsimile*, 1986

I truly appreciated "Howl" when I was a young man. I had the good luck to have enjoyed from my young days a close friendship with Jan Zabrana, the chief translator of Ginsberg and other Beat writers, so I had access to "Howl" even if it was not, could not be, published in my country. I have to admit that in those years—through the fifties and sixties—I found the Beat authors' way of writing, and their original way of thinking, very close to my heart. I believe I understood their views and their protest. I could share much of it. There was among many in my country a sensitive awareness of the Beat movement. I first met Allen at the renowned May Day festival at which he was elected King. Then I had the luck to see him in Viola, a poet's café, and I believe it must have been at that moment when the notorious theft of his notebook took place. Later, after 1989, when I had become President, I had the opportunity to see Allen a few times. I have always held the poet, and especially his poem "Howl," in the greatest esteem. I have cherished, and benefited from, the poem's intellectual power and scope of vision.

—Vaclav Havel, in *Howl: Original Draft Facsimile*, 1986

Ginsberg's "Howl," the single poem most representative of the break with Eliot, may owe as much, thematically, to "The Waste Land" as it does to the bardic Whitman or to the opening of the era of anything goes.   —Cynthia Ozick, "T. S. Eliot at 101,"
The New Yorker, November 20, 1989

There's something [in "Howl"] I can accept unconditionally.
                        —Denise Levertov, *The Letters of Denise Levertov
and William Carlos Williams*, 1998

The subject matter revealed the heroic dreamer in me & the biblical rhythms exuberated ancestral blood. I would drink, get high, and read "Howl" to my friends; telling them people really lived lives as exciting as the poem. What a triumph of human spirit, what fun to shout these verses!   —Andy Clausen, 2005

Forty years have passed since I first read "Howl" and felt emboldened to give my all to Poetry without fear no matter what, and it still rings true and rings revolutionary. It proves the power and beauty and grace of Poetry indomitably and invincibly. Like "Song of Myself," "Howl" stands as one of the most breakthrough poems in American and World Literature—one of the milestones in the positive evolution of human consciousness. It's the howl of our mammal soul caught in the steel-jaw trap of the military/industrial juggernaut. It still thrills with the epiphany "Everyday is in Eternity!" It still challenges America and every nation to not send their youths to the top of the pyramid to have their hearts torn out. It still annunciates to the present and future the affirmation of its last line: "Holy the supernatural extra brilliant intelligent kindness of the soul!"   —Antler, 2005

That night after the Berkeley poetry reading, Peter Orlovsky and I argued the length of Dwight Way while he walked me back to my co-op about whether "Howl" was as important a poem as *Leaves of Grass*. I insisted it wasn't, but what did I know fifty years ago as a budding English major at Cal? Only a few years later, in graduate school at Columbia, *Howl* and *Kaddish* and Kerouac's *The Dharma Bums* were the books that influenced me to spend my life as a Beat bibliographer, biographer, and scholar. You could say that I needed to go to graduate school before I finally learned that Peter was right.

—Ann Charters, 2005

Allen and Gary [Snyder] had hitched up from San Francisco to see me in Seattle, where I was teaching. I remember Allen was wearing a strikingly colorful shirt, with baggy pants, and had unusually long hair—what would later become one of the images of the beats. Allen was carrying a manuscript and, after just a few moments, he thrust it in my hand. "I want you to read the greatest poem of the century," Allen said. It was the first two sections of "Howl." And I read it, and Gary's "Rip Rap" as well, sitting in my kitchen, while they sat talking in the living room. I realized "Howl" was a remarkable poem, a new kind of poem. That night I arranged a reading at the University of Seattle for Allen and Gary to read from their work. There were about fifty people in the audience and they were shocked upon hearing "Howl." They had never heard anything like that, especially the academicians. There simply was nothing else like it.

—Stanley Kunitz, 2005

LUC SANTE

THE BALLOT OF ETERNITY

Was "Howl" the last poem to hit the world with the impact of news and grip it with the tenacity of a pop song? I can't think of another in the decades since. When I first read it, I was thirteen or fourteen and the poem was more than a decade old, although as far as I knew it might have been published that morning. I had no idea what most of it meant, but that didn't stop me from entering its rhythm. I recognized that rhythm, or I thought I did. Its long breath and hypnotic iterations were eerily evocative of the litanies in the Latin ritual of the Catholic church, which were probably the first music I ever heard. "Howl" immediately took me over, and stayed in my ear like a Top Ten hit. I undertook to memorize it, or at least its first part, which was the highest tribute I could pay as well as a way of owning it. I learned it well enough that I declaimed it whenever I felt myself sufficiently alone, in my room or in the woods. Later in adolescence, when I worked after school in a factory, I could bellow it at the top of my lungs, unheard over the din of the injection-molding machines.

What was the poem about? For me, then, the title accounted for most of it. It stood for I Want to Be Free and We

Are Multitudes and The Stars My Destination and incidentally
Get Your Hands Off Me. The elegiac aspects I could understand
in a general way—teenagers love to gaze back ruefully at the
ashes of a ruined past—but the specifics were beyond my com-
prehension. What could I know about extremes of desire and
exhaustion and need and rage and love and revolt? I pretended I
knew, of course. The rage to live I had in spades. I thought I al-
ready contained every possible emotion, needing only the par-
ticular settings in which to apply them. Poetic madness was
something I thought I could feel in my body. The scenes of the
poem were only just out of reach. They all sounded good, indis-
criminately: poverty and tatters and hollow-eyed and high all
equally alluring. The poem was a travel brochure for the color-
ful world I would settle in as soon as I could get away from my
parents, a world in which everything was large-scale, dazzling,
dramatic, dangerous, played for keeps. Its possible harshness
sounded many times better than any happiness I knew.

Allen himself was an icon whose image was everywhere.
There was the poster of him wearing the sandwich board read-
ing "Pot Is Fun," and the other one of him in his Uncle Sam
hat, and the picture of him chanting in a park surrounded by
hippies in beads and feathers. He was as modern as any figure of
the 1960s, and at the same time he was mythic, biblical, a sage
from the ancient world—you could imagine him parading along
the timeline of history, through Alexandria and Damascus and
Jerusalem in his beard and robe, and even his eyeglasses, which
were simply a part of his face. He was an ideal father figure,
comforting and reliable and permissive and inspirational. He was
maternal, too, in the same sense as William Carlos Williams's
image of Abraham Lincoln as the mother of the nation ("The
least private would find a woman to caress him, a woman in an
old shawl—with a great bearded face and a towering black hat
above it, to give unearthly reality"). He was in the news regu-

larly then, and every appearance confirmed his standing as the President of Youth. Being crowned King of May in Prague before being ejected by the authorities, pacifying the Hells Angels by chanting to them and persuading them to join in, talking countless saps like you or me down from bad acid trips—he was literally Christ-like: wandering the world healing the lame and the halt, distributing loaves and fishes, being alternately hailed and jeered.

It was thrilling to read him taking on the police, the government, the war in his later poems, which were prophetic and bristling with hard facts. "Howl" was of another order, though. As great as something like "Wichita Vortex Sutra" might be, it didn't rock the way "Howl" did. "Howl" was a transfusion of energy, a hurricane signed up for the cause. It wasn't mere ammunition, but the force itself. Reading "Howl" aloud or reciting it, you could feel the poem giving you supernatural powers, the ability to punch through brick walls and walk across cities from rooftop to rooftop. It had those long, unflagging lines, which emptied and then refilled your lungs, and to a teenager it contained every single one of the most powerful words in the language: "madness," "dynamo," "supernatural," "illuminated," "radiant," "hallucinating," "obscene," "terror"—and that's just a sampling from the first eight lines. At some point in high school a classmate played me a record that belonged to his parents, a recording made in San Francisco soon after the famous Six Gallery reading of 1956. The blue laws of the era required Allen to cut out the bad words, and he complied by substituting "censored" for them, as in "who let themselves be censored in the censored by saintly motorcyclists, and screamed with joy." The effect was hilarious and somehow subversive, as if the word "censored" contained more variegated shades of sin than all of the original words put together.

It was the first time I ever heard Allen's voice, that very

particular combination: the postwar street-hustler, bop-prosody cadences you can hear in recordings of Kerouac and in those tapes of nearly indecipherable monologic yammer by Neal Cassady in his last days, filtered through the accent—produced in large part by a vibrating larynx—that to me still sounds exotic coming from Allen, although I've since heard it issuing from other throats and can identify it as one strain of metropolitan-area middle-class Jewish. When I went off to college in New York City, I began attending frequent readings by Allen, reveling in that voice, although I never heard him read "Howl." He read new poems; he chanted, accompanying himself on harmonium; eventually he sang, sometimes backed by a full band, but I remained frustrated in my wish to hear "Howl." The only time I ever heard it live was during a collective reading at St. Mark's Church on a New Year's Day in the 1970s, when some guy, either a postmodernist engaging in iconoclastic appropriation or just a fan doing a tribute on the order of a Led Zeppelin cover band, marched to the podium and began calling it out, weakly. He made it through maybe three lines before Allen himself appeared and told him to shut up. (All the while, up in the gallery, another fan reaching for an Allen-like mantra kept intoning "Remember your brothers and sisters in prison," which only managed to produce mosquito-buzz irritation.) I didn't realize at that time how when you get to a certain point with your greatest hits, you may never want to see or hear them again.

While still in high school I read Jane Kramer's *Allen Ginsberg in America* and was greatly moved by her accounts of his openness, his benevolence, his mission as shepherd of my generation. Teenagers could just show up at his apartment and he would talk to them! I resolved to go there myself one day, although my arrogance and shyness prevented me from ever doing so. Then, a decade later, when I was badly in need of a new apartment, my

Strand Bookstore colleague Will Bennett (may he rest in peace) told me about four rooms soon to be vacated in his building on Twelfth Street. I visited, and Will served me drugs and put on some music, his turntable connected to a Marshall amp jacked up to the proverbial eleven. Whatever the record was, it sounded like a Boeing 747 giving birth. I marveled at this tolerant building, where such extremes could be absorbed without complaint. Then there was a knock on the door, and there stood Allen, who had come down two flights to request, gently but firmly, that the volume be lowered. I marveled further. Imagine getting a noise complaint from Allen Ginsberg!

I wound up living in the building for eleven years. When Allen was in town, I saw him nearly every day: on the stairs, in the street, eating breakfast at the Ukrainian coffee shop on First Avenue. A large percentage of the tenants were poets who had been drawn there by him, and a large percentage of the hallway traffic was Allen-related as well: the people who worked in his office or played in his band, and Gregory Corso, Herbert Huncke, Harry Smith, various passing celebrities. I had a considerable chip on my shoulder by then, as an unpublished writer who didn't particularly cotton to any of the prevailing schools and whose putative talents went unnoticed by all. My exchanges with Allen tended to be brief. I was in awe and also guarded and maybe a little resentful. I did waste a considerable amount of his time at the wedding of some mutual friends, bending his ear about how I thought Lautréamont was the greatest poet of all time. He suffered me, if not especially gladly. By that time I thought I had his number, maybe that of all the Beats, because I had read the Situationists, who in the first issue of their journal, in 1958, had written: "The rotten egg smell exuded by the idea of God envelops the mystical cretins of the American 'Beat Generation.'" Like the Sits, I had been raised in a Catholic

LUC SANTE

culture, so I was not about to fall for any incense or chanting or
beads, which I knew full well to be lollipops handed out by the
police in order to mask the sight of their truncheons.

Despite this, I remained in awe of Allen. However I might
have felt about the mystical claptrap, I could not deny "Howl"
(or, for that matter, "Kaddish"). "Howl" probably meant more
to me then than ever before, because finally I could reconcile it
with my own experience. "Poverty" and "tatters" and "hollow-
eyed" and "high" were more than poetic figures by then. I could
compile my own list of the best minds of my generation de-
stroyed by madness.* The decade during which I lived two
flights down from Allen was particularly notable for its body
count in suicides and overdoses, and those cadavers really had
contained some of the best minds I knew. As in the poem, not
all of those destroyed met their deaths, of course. Some did in-
deed vanish into nowhere Zen New Jersey, and some fizzled or
suffered malignant hangnails or converted to money. But I also
realized that if "Howl" is a catalog of flameouts and collapses, it
is ecstatic in its lamentation. And that is the basic measure of its
strength: it is a list of fuckups and leprous epiphanies as re-
doubtable as Homer's catalog of ships, but rather than stopping
at that, it seizes the opportunity to realize all the botched dreams
it enumerates. It envisions every broken vision, supplies the
skeleton key that reveals the genius of every torrent of babble,
reconstitutes every page of scribble that looks like gibberish the
next morning. It takes up the ragged flag of an entire generation
of confused questers groping for something they can't begin to
name, and in the process of recounting the story manages to in-

*And I had acquired my own context in which to view the smug disdain of the Co-
lumbia English Department—which in my time still contained faculty relics left over
from Allen's day, with attitudes intact—whose view was that the best minds of his gen-
eration, far from being destroyed, were leading Chaucer seminars all across the country.

carnate the nameless thing sought. It is an illumination. It blows *"the suffering of America's naked mind for love into an eli eli lamma lamma sabacthani saxophone cry that shivers the cities down to the last radio."*

And now Allen is dead, for me like a parent whose presence you take for granted while he is alive and ache for after he's gone. Right now we need him more than we ever did.

ROBERT POLITO

HOLY THE FIFTH INTERNATIONAL

_____

I.

The *tone* of "Howl" remains among its slipperiest distinctions and always was, I'd argue, intrinsic to the poem's majesty. Few beginnings simultaneously speak and misspeak what will follow with such vehemence or candor: "I saw the best minds of my generation destroyed by madness, starving hysterical naked." Strophe after strophe Ginsberg details, enhances, and reiterates that decisive "destroyed by madness" into a catalog of destructions. The devastation spirals along his chain of common, dead-end verbs—"who sank . . . who vanished . . . who wandered . . . who disappeared . . . who broke down crying . . . who howled"—and his fierce, aphoristic reversals: "battered bleak of brain all drained of brilliance . . . & their heads shall be crowned with laurel in oblivion . . . nothing but a hopeful little bit of hallucination."★

Yet what about the countertugs in that tone—the swagger

★All quotations from "Howl" are from Allen Ginsberg, *Howl and Other Poems* (San Francisco: City Lights Books, 59th printing, August 2003).

crisscrossing the poem right from the start in his hushed boast
"the best minds of my generation"? Often as you read *"Howl,"*
you can't decide whether Ginsberg wishes us to mourn his
friends' terrible, shocking ends or envy their glorious rides.
That streak of exuberance, even celebration, perhaps arises from
his recurrent slanting of anguish and madness into mystic emi-
nence—"who bared their brains to Heaven under the El and
saw Mohammedan angels staggering on tenement roofs illumi-
nated . . . who loned it through the streets of Idaho seeking
visionary indian angels who were visionary indian angels . . .
waking nightmares, alcohol and cock and endless balls, / incom-
parable blind streets . . . illuminating all the motionless world of
Time between." Amid the litany of adjectives at the onset—
"starving hysterical naked"—where "hysterical" now appears,
Ginsberg originally wrote "mystical."

However desolate and doomed their fates, Ginsberg's rav-
aged *who-who-who*s radiate energy, play, and pleasure, their lives
vivid, intense: "who chained themselves to subways for the end-
less ride from Battery to holy Bronx on benzedrine . . . who
talked continuously seventy hours from park to bar to Bellevue
to museum to the Brooklyn Bridge." Alongside the spiritual
bravado comes sexual bragging:

who copulated ecstatic and insatiate with a bottle of beer a sweetheart a
*   package of cigarettes a candle and fell off the bed, and continued*
*   along the floor and down the hall and ended fainting on the wall*
*   with a vision of ultimate cunt and come eluding the last gyzym of*
*   consciousness,*
who sweetened the snatches of a million girls trembling in the sunset,
*   and were red eyed in the morning but prepared to sweeten the*
*   snatch of the sunrise, flashing buttocks under barns and naked in*
*   the lake,*

*who went out whoring through Colorado in myriad stolen night-
cars, N.C., secret hero of these poems, cocksman and Adonis of
Denver.*

The second and third sections of "Howl" position the individ-
ual destructions inside the Cold War, the various suits, squares,
and bulls who judge, incarcerate, or ruin Ginsberg's friends also
converging into Moloch, the Old Testament god whose wor-
ship included the sacrifice of children by burning. The invoca-
tion of the Cold War is incisive, and caustic: "Ten years' animal
screams and suicides!" "an armed madhouse," "the fascist na-
tional Golgotha."

"Howl" is grim but funny, the joy and the human toll all
bound together, and still you are never certain whether Gins-
berg intends to steer his poem toward—or away from—despair,
apocalypse. The dark, mad core within the ecstasy? Or the re-
verse, the wisdom in the madness?

"HOWL" AND ROBERT LOWELL

During the spring of 1957, Robert Lowell plunged into a read-
ing tour that brought him to San Francisco. He was already
forty, and as he recounted:

> I had been giving readings on the West Coast, often
> reading six days a week and sometimes twice on a single
> day. I was in San Francisco, the era and setting of Allen
> Ginsberg and all about, very modest poets were waking
> up prophets. I became sorely aware of how few poems I
> had written, and that these few had been finished at the
> latest three or four years earlier. Their style seemed dis-

tant, symbol-ridden, and willfully difficult. I began to paraphrase my Latin quotations, and to add extra syllables to a line to make it clearer and more colloquial. I felt my old poems hid what they were really about, and many times offered a stiff, humorless, and even impenetrable surface. I am no convert to the "beats." I know well, too, that the best poems are not necessarily poems that read aloud. Many of the greatest poems can only be read to one's self, for inspiration is no substitute for humor, shock, narrative, and a hypnotic voice, the four musts for oral performance. Still, my poems seemed like prehistoric monsters dragged down into the bog and death by their ponderous armor. I was reciting what I no longer felt.*

I was reciting what I no longer felt. Lowell returned to Marlborough Street and started to write, as he said, "in a new style." By fall he had finished at least eleven poems that would define his breakthrough book, *Life Studies,* including "Skunk Hour," "Memories of West Street and Lepke," "To Speak of the Woe That Is in Marriage," and "My Last Afternoon with Uncle Devereux Winslow." In *Lost Puritan,* his biography of Lowell, Paul Mariani prints an early draft of "Man and Wife," likely the first of the new poems, shot through with small echoes of "Howl":

On [a] warm spring night . . . we can hear the outcry,
If our windows are open wide,
I can hear the South End,
The razor's edge
Of Boston's negro culture. They as we
Refine past culture's possibility,

*From "On 'Skunk Hour,'" in Robert Lowell, *Collected Prose,* edited by Robert Giroux (New York: Farrar, Straus and Giroux, 1987).

Fear homicide,
Grow horny with alcohol, take the pledge.★

The version Lowell would eventually publish excises "negro culture" but kicks off with lines that might be tagged a Back Bay rewrite of "Howl"'s opening: "Tamed by *Miltown*, we lie on Mother's bed; / the rising sun in war paint dyes us red."

Lowell condescended to Ginsberg. You hear it in the essay "On Skunk Hour," which I just quoted, but particularly in his letters. After Ginsberg visited him with Gregory Corso and Peter Orlovsky in the spring of 1959, Lowell wrote Elizabeth Bishop, "They are phony in [a] way because they have made a lot of publicity out of very little talent. But in another way, they are pathetic and doomed. How can you make a go for long by reciting so-so verse to half-jeering swarms of college students. However, they are trying, I guess to write poetry. They are fairly easy to listen to." And to Ginsberg himself, Lowell dismissed Kerouac as "uninspired Joyce," Burroughs as "very real but partially of psychopathic interest," and argued, "I think letters ought to be written the way you think poetry ought be. So let this be breezy, brief, incomplete, but spontaneous and not dishonestly holding back."†

Yet Lowell can't just let go of Ginsberg. He too knew his way around locked wards, and I suspect he found the strain in "Howl" that privileges madness sentimental and reckless. But as Lowell in these letters to Ginsberg starts to second-guess his

★The lines from the early draft of "Man and Woman" appear in Paul Mariani, *Lost Puritan: A Life of Robert Lowell* (New York: W. W. Norton, 1994). Note the poem that ultimately became "To Speak of the Woe That Is in Marriage" was originally part of "Man and Wife." This draft seems to mix lines and ideas that ended up in both poems.
†Lowell's letter to Bishop is dated March 30, 1959, and his letters to Ginsberg are dated April 1 and April 10, 1959. From *The Letters of Robert Lowell*, edited by Saskia Hamilton (New York: Farrar, Straus and Giroux, 2005).

own "rough brusqueness," or sends him a long list of the American writers he admires, or wrangles with him over William Carlos Williams, you suddenly hear something else in the uncharacteristically smug resistance: the sound of a poet changing despite himself, something Lowell did for *Life Studies*, and then would do over and over and over again.

II.

When I say "Ginsberg's friends," I wish to imply that "Howl" aims to create a community, a society, a new nation. Fellow travelers surface in the poem—obviously Carl Solomon and Allen Ginsberg, but also Peter Orlovsky, Lucien Carr, Jack Kerouac, Herbert Huncke, William Burroughs, and Neal Cassady, whose first or last names all appear in "Footnote to Howl." (On the 1956 recording of his reading at the Town Hall Theatre, Berkeley, he adds "Holy Gregory.")★ The community of "Howl" is a fellowship of those who recognize, who have been battered by, and who are struggling to cast off Moloch—"Moloch whom I abandon!" Ginsberg writes, "abandon" signaling implication as well as dismissal.

This community stretches, of course, beyond Ginsberg's little Beat cabal. Successive strophes circle back to the past:

who sang out of their windows in despair, fell out of the subway window,
    jumped in the filthy Passaic, leaped on negroes, cried all over the
    street, danced on broken wineglasses barefoot, smashed phonograph
    records of nostalgic European 1930s German jazz, finished the

---

★Included on *Holy Soul Jelly Roll! Poems and Songs 1949–1993* (Los Angeles: Rhino Records, 1994).

whiskey and threw up groaning into the bloody toilet, moans in
their ears and the blast of colossal steamwhistles,
who barreled down the highways of the past journeying to each other's
hotrod-Golgotha jail-solitude watch or Birmingham jazz incarnation,

then arc into the present:

who drove crosscountry seventytwo hours to find out if I had a vision or
you had a vision or he had a vision to find out Eternity.

The new human community "Howl" advances mainly in-
heres in the future. Ginsberg launches his pending social order
first as parody, when he imagines "twenty-five-thousand mad
comrades"—in Rockland—"all together singing the final stan-
zas of the Internationale." But he concludes "Footnote to Howl"
by apostrophizing an entire Fifth International: "holy the fourth
dimension holy the fifth International." His comment on this
passage in *Howl: Original Draft Facsimile* is revelatory: "Fifth In-
ternational of workers, entrepreneurs, peasants and indigenous
communities of world has not yet assembled to propose survival
norms in era of imperial private and state monopoly capital's
near-absolute and potentially suicidal power."★

For all Ginsberg's candor, though, the community here is
insistently coded—coded as in cryptography, or espionage. He
names—or all but names—a few friends in his "Footnote," but
each, like "N.C., secret hero of these poems," is also secreted
away in the body of the text. Beat legend renders shorthand ref-

★The full title of this book is *Howl: Original Draft Facsimile, Transcript & Variant Versions,*
Fully Annotated by Author, with Contemporaneous Correspondence, Account of First Public
Reading, Legal Skirmishes, Precursor Texts & Bibliography, and it is edited by Barry Miles
(New York: Harper & Row, 1986). All prose statements by Allen Ginsberg in my essay
come from this remarkable book.

erences to Neal Cassady, William Burroughs ("Tangerian bone-grindings"), Herbert Huncke ("who walked all night with their shoes full of blood"), and Ginsberg's Columbia years ("who were expelled from the academies for crazy & publishing obscene odes on the windows of the skull") as blatant as a dumb show; 1956 readers and listeners surely believed such lines symbolism, jive, or impenetrable.

The poet's annotations for *Howl: Original Draft Facsimile* ante up this secret community exponentially, as though every strophe hides a hermetic profile. Philip Lamantia, we learn, told Kerouac, who then told Ginsberg, that he once floated into another state of awareness while reading the Koran—hence "Mohammedan angels." Louis Simpson on the edges of a breakdown tossed a friend's watch out his apartment window, an episode "Howl" revamped as "who threw their watches off the roof to cast their ballot for Eternity outside of Time, & alarm clocks fell on their heads every day for the next decade." Someone Ginsberg glosses only as "Ruth G——" apparently is the woman "who talked continuously seventy hours . . . whole intellects disgorged in total recall for seven days and nights with brilliant eyes, meat for the Synagogue cast on the pavement." He flashes on his own college job mopping floors at the Forty-second Street Bickford's—"who sank all night in submarine light of Bickford's floated out"—or the mornings he stopped by St. Patrick's after working all night as a copyboy for Associated Press: "who fell on their knees in hopeless cathedrals praying for each other's salvation and light and breasts, until the soul illuminated its hair for a second."

The "brilliant Spaniard"? Ginsberg reprints a 1952 journal entry about him. He even gives the address of "Paradise Alley"—501 East Eleventh Street, if you're looking to rent. Alongside encrypted autobiography, he exposes his all-but-buried allusions:

"Saintly motorcyclists" responds to Brando's *The Wild One*; "last gyzym of consciousness" approximates the title of an old *Hudson Review* essay on Yeats.

"This actually happened," as Ginsberg almost pauses to marvel in a strophe about a failed suicide who jumped off the Brooklyn Bridge and survived. But there's nothing reductive and demystifying about his notes, or the notion that even his most woofin' phrases emerge as literal—or coded literal.

As for the future? "In publishing 'Howl,' I was curious to leave behind after my generation a time bomb that would continue exploding in U.S. consciousness."

That's yet another way to recast the opening line.

"HOWL" AND BOB DYLAN

Ginsberg's fingerprints are all over early Bob Dylan. You hear "Howl" in Dylan's lyrics maybe as early as "Lay Down Your Weary Tune" (1963) but definitely by "Chimes of Freedom" (1964) and "Mr. Tambourine Man" (1964), and the exalted verbal ricochet of so many songs is mostly inconceivable without "Howl"—from "Gates of Eden" (1964), "It's Alright, Ma (I'm Only Bleeding)" (1964), through "Like a Rolling Stone" (1965), "Tombstone Blues" (1965), "Ballad of a Thin Man" (1965), and "Desolation Row" (1965), on to "Visions of Johanna" (1966) and "Sad-Eyed Lady of the Lowlands" (1966). Greil Marcus speculates that "'Like a Rolling Stone' probably owes more to Allen Ginsberg's 1955 'Howl' than to any song." As Dylan himself recalled his time in Minneapolis circa 1960 for the liner notes to the retrospective *Biograph*: "I came out of the wilderness and just naturally fell in with the beat scene, the Bohemian, BeBop crowd, it was all pretty much connected . . . Suzie Rotolo, a girlfriend of mine in New York, later turned me on to all the French poets but for then it was Jack Kerouac, Ginsberg, Corso and Ferlinghetti—*Gasoline, Coney Island of the Mind . . .* oh man, it was wild—*I saw the best minds of my generation destroyed by madness* that said more to me than any of the stuff I'd been raised on."*

Ginsberg joined the Rolling Thunder Review in the fall of 1975, and the night after he died, in 1997, Dylan, on tour in Canada, performed "Desolation Row" during a show in Moncton, New Brunswick: "That was for Allen," he told his audience.

Still, for all the notable crosscurrents here, there are some surprising confluences. The masterful repetitions and the falling rhythms in "The Lonesome Death of Hattie Carroll" (1963):

Hattie Carroll was a maid of the kitchen.
She was fifty-one years old and gave birth to ten children
Who carried the dishes and took out the garbage
And never sat once at the head of the table
And didn't even talk to the people at the table
Who just cleaned up all the food from the table
And emptied the ashtrays on a whole other level.†

Might they loop back to this strophe from "Howl," itself according to Ginsberg derived from a Kerouac death blues:

who journeyed to Denver, who died in Denver, who came back to Den-
ver & waited in vain, who watched over Denver & brooded & loned
in Denver and finally went away to find out the Time, & now
Denver is lonesome for her heroes.

*From Greil Marcus, *Like a Rolling Stone: Bob Dylan at the Crossroads* (New York: PublicAffairs, 2005), and from the liner notes by Cameron Crowe for *Biograph* (New York: Columbia Records, 1985). Song dates are dates of composition, when available, not necessarily the dates of the official recording or release.
†First appeared on *The Times They Are A-Changin'* (New York: Columbia Records, 1964).

A later Dylan recollection of "Howl" is still more curious. On his 1989 album, *Oh Mercy*, he recorded the song "Shooting Star." Three spare, elegant verses track a pair of friends who perhaps fulfilled, perhaps disappointed each other's expectations, but the bridge veers away, turbulent and jarring:

Listen to the engine, listen to the bell
As the last fire truck from hell
Goes rolling by, all good people are praying.
It's the last temptation
The last account
The last time you might hear the sermon on the mount,
The last radio is playing.★

Dylan's lines circle a brutal passage in "Howl" in which Ginsberg speculates on Carl Solomon fucking his mother:

with mother finally ******, and the last fantastic book flung out of the tenement window, and the last door closed at 4 A.M. and the last telephone slammed at the wall in reply and the last furnished room emptied down to the last piece of mental furniture, a yellow paper rose twisted on a wire hanger in the closet, and even that imaginary, nothing but a hopeful little bit of hallucination—

The phrase "the last radio" occurs later in "Howl," when Ginsberg quotes not from the Sermon on the Mount but from Christ's dying words on the cross. A version of Dylan's album title also can be discovered in the poem—"O starry-spangled shock of mercy."

Is Ginsberg, then, the friend about whom Dylan wonders in a kind of final reckoning:

★On *Oh Mercy* (New York: Columbia/Sony, 1989).

Seen a shooting star tonight
And I thought of me.
If I was still the same
If I ever became what you wanted me to be
Did I miss the mark or
Over-step the line
That only you could see?

I've always thought the "just like a woman / just like a little girl" contrast in Dylan's "Just Like a Woman" (1966) is trivial as long as the subject of the song is a woman but, well, more interesting, if he's a man. Marianne Faithfull remarks in her autobiography, *Faithfull*, that "one of the funniest things in talking to Allen Ginsberg—and a cautionary lesson for us all—is that Allen thinks that nearly all Dylan's songs are about *him*. Well I never say anything. I just hold my peace. 'Yes, I'm sure that one is, Allen.' It's very sweet, isn't it? And there is one that really is about Allen. 'Just Like a Woman.'"★

III.

"The appeal in 'Howl,'" Ginsberg also insisted, "is to the secret or hermetic tradition of art 'justifying' or 'making up for' defeat in worldly life." Although he acknowledges Cassady in the poem as his "secret hero," a case certainly could be sustained that the true secret hero is his mother, Naomi. "Holy my mother in the insane asylum!" he wrote in "Footnote to Howl," just after the registry of his friends, and Naomi Ginsberg was

★"Just like a Woman" first appeared on *Blonde on Blonde* (New York: Columbia, 1966). Marianne Faithfull, *Faithfull: An Autobiography* with David Dalton (New York: Little, Brown, 1994).

dying in Pilgrim State Hospital, out on Long Island, as her son composed "Howl" in San Francisco and Berkeley. "I'm with you in Rockland," he chants to Carl Solomon, "where you imitate the shade of my mother."

Once spotted, Naomi is everywhere, as in one of those old prints in which the trick is to see how many times you can find the same face. She's behind Ginsberg's evocation of the Lower East Side: "who wept at the romance of the streets with their pushcarts full of onions and bad music."

There's her closet, amazingly, in that strophe on Solomon and his mother: "a yellow paper rose twisted on a wire hanger in the closet, and even that imaginary." Here's her food: "who cooked rotten animals lung heart feet tail borsht & tortillas dreaming of the pure vegetable kingdom."

Naomi hovers over the lines on "accusing the radio of hypnotism," and Ginsberg affirmed that he lifted his childhood memories of visiting her in Greystone State Hospital for the descriptions of Rockland, inside which neither he nor Solomon had yet been at the time of the poem.

Included among the documentation in *Howl: Original Draft Facsimile* is a fascinating almost-apology to Solomon for the notoriety "Howl" unloaded on his friend's otherwise civilian existence. "I used Mr. Solomon's return to the asylum," Ginsberg admits, "as occasion of a masque on my feelings toward my mother, in itself an ambiguous situation since I had signed the papers giving permission for her lobotomy a few years before. Thereby hangs another tale."

That tale presumably is "Kaddish." But for "Howl," Naomi inhabits "the world lost," as Ginsberg resonantly ticketed his theme, one that mixes "comradeship through thick and thin with Carl Solomon," "primordial filial loyalty to my mother," and the transformative powers of art. "It is in the poem," he pledged, "that we reconstruct the world lost."

"Howl" keeps returning to transfiguration through art—
Ginsberg's apparition of Solomon traveling cross-country to
him in Berkeley, where he is finishing the poem:

I'm with you in Rockland
  in my dreams you walk dripping from a sea-journey on the highway
  across America in tears to the door of my cottage in the Western
  night.

Or the willed, strident incantations in the "Footnote to Howl":

The typewriter is holy the poem is holy the voice is holy the hearers are
  holy the ecstasy is holy!

His art—specific formal aspects, as well as his ambitions—
agitates the dazzling final strophes of the first section:

and who therefore ran through the icy streets obsessed with a sudden
  flash of the alchemy of the use of the ellipse the catalog the meter &
  the vibrating plane,
who dreamt and made incarnate gaps in Time & Space through images
  juxtaposed, and trapped the archangel of the soul between 2 visual
  images and joined the elemental verbs and set the noun and dash of
  consciousness together jumping with sensation of Pater Omnipotens
  Aeterna Deus
to recreate the syntax and measure of poor human prose and stand before
  you speechless and intelligent and shaking with shame, rejected yet
  confessing out the soul to conform to the rhythm of thought in his
  naked and endless head,
the madman bum and angel beat in Time, unknown, yet putting down
  here what might be left to say in time come after death,
and rose reincarnate in the ghostly clothes of jazz in the goldhorn
  shadow of the band and blew the suffering of America's naked mind

for love into an eli eli lamma lamma sabacthani saxophone cry that
shivered the cities down to the last radio
with the absolute heart of the poem of life butchered out of their own
bodies good to eat a thousand years.

Ginsberg slides here from a technical poetics of juxtaposition, lists, and aesthetic planes to a visionary poetics of embodiment. His trustworthiness, if we trust him, arises from the long, painful inventory of human destructions we have been reading, and his earlier acknowledgment that visions sometimes wind up "stanzas of gibberish." This is a song of the end of a world, "the last radio," as he says in the words Dylan borrowed for *his* song, and of the bloody ("butchered out of their own bodies") birth of a new one. Against the "cannibal dynamo" of Moloch he offers the food of his art—food "good to eat a thousand years."

"HOWL" AND FRANK BIDART

Frank Bidart called the book that collected all of his poems through 1990 *In the Western Night*, after the last line of "Howl." This is also the title of an elegiac sequence of four fractured love poems, set in Berkeley, included in the volume. Bidart echoed Ginsberg's dating at the conclusion of "Howl"—"San Francisco, 1955–56"—and signed "In the Western Night" "Berkeley, California; 1983."★

"Two Men," the third lyric of "In the Western Night," glances at Ginsberg's line about food "good to eat a thousand

★From Frank Bidart, *In the Western Night: Collected Poems, 1965–90* by (New York: Farrar, Straus and Giroux, 1990).

years," but to invert the notion, and tilt it into a self-accusing taunt. Of the intractable lover "who does not know himself," "who / does not know his affections that his actions / speak," "who will SAY ANYTHING," Bidart writes:

> THIS MAN IS STONE . . . NOT BREAD.
> STONE. NOT CAKE. NOT CHEESE. NOT BREAD . . .
> The man who tries to feed his hunger
> by gnawing on stone is a FOOL, his hunger is
> fed in ways that he knows cannot satisfy it.

The final lyric, "Epilogue: A Stanza from Horace," similarly reverses "Howl"—Bidart retains Ginsberg's dreams, and the sea journey ("the waters"), but instead of traveling to him across America to Berkeley, his beloved is "fleeing":

> At night in dreams I hold you
>   and now I pursue you
> fleeing through the grass of the Campus Martius,
> you, through the waters (you are cruel) fleeing.

Still darker senses of "in the Western night" hover over "The First Hour of the Night," a long poem that registers and dramatizes blind alleys, contradictions, and impasses in the history of knowledge. The phrase as employed by Ginsberg can almost sound romantic, albeit carrying hints of the closing of the American continent and the dimming of a generation. For Bidart the words intimate nothing less than the dissolution of the West.

Bidart reprised Ginsberg's "good to eat a thousand years" for another long poem, "The Third Hour of the Night," in his most recent book, Star Dust. The line from "Howl" falls among other lines that also revisit earlier Bidart poems:

Then I ask him how to become food

In silence he repeats that others have
other fates, but that I must fashion out of the corruptible

body a new body good to eat a thousand years

Then I tell the eater's face that within me is no
sustenance, on my famished

plate centuries have been served me and still I am famished

He smirks, and in silence repeats that all life exists
at the expense of other life

You must fashion out of the corruptible
body a new body good to eat a thousand years

Because you have eaten and eat as eat you must
ignorant of cause or source or end★

    Star Dust is a book about making—about making art—some poems, like "The Third Hour of the Night," corrosive and sinister, others celebratory. Bidart again summons Ginsberg's line to flip it over, but this time the inversion is trickier. Here "good to eat a thousand years" returns as a nightmare replica of Moloch's "cannibal dynamo." Yet as a persistent source of Bidart's poetic art, "Howl" of course *is* food. We are back to "Howl"'s sly, impossible tone, and Bidart, much as Lowell or Dylan, writes his way into the Fifth International.

★From Frank Bidart, *Star Dust* (New York: Farrar, Straus and Giroux, 2005).

CAROL MUSKE-DUKES

"HOWL" IN AND OUT OF PRISON

———

When I brought "Howl" to a workshop at the Women's House of Detention on Rikers Island (for several years, beginning in 1972), I don't think anyone in the class had read it. When they did read it, they understood it as an "outlaw" manifesto, the kind of renegade poem that was capable of offending "upright" citizens, perhaps some high school teachers—certainly moralists of any stripe. They loved its wildness and its candor. They riffed brilliantly (writing their own imitations) on this line:

who crashed through their minds in jail, waiting for impossible criminals
with golden heads and the charm of reality in their hearts who sang
sweet blues to Alcatraz.

These women, most of whom were jailed for "victimless" crimes, like prostitution, shoplifting (boosting), or drugs, understood this hymn to "impossible criminals." Guilty or not guilty, they got what he was saying. They had the "charm of reality" in their hearts. Some had "crashed through their minds"—waiting for a trial date, not charged yet, just waiting in detention status,

CAROL MUSKE-DUKES

interminably. Many had had their children taken away, made wards of the state. They were desperate crazy writers—and "Howl" is a desperate crazy poem that made absolute sense to them.

I began to understand that there was a different way of apprehending poetry—closer to the way my mother (who'd memorized Whitman, Tennyson, Milton, and Dickinson in her prairie high school classes in North Dakota in the 1930s) loved poetry. My mother recited, by heart, poem after poem—but in her own anarchical fashion. She galloped over breath stops, shaking up the meter, but still gave the superb passion of the lines all she had: "Sunset and evening star, / And one clear call for me!"— sometimes splicing in comments to her children: "Let me not to the marriage of true minds—Put that down right now!—Admit impediment." Poetry was a kind of salvation to my mother— the sheer emotion and the beauty of the words came together unforgettably in her heart and in her wild private rhetoric.

Words also meant something private and public to the women in prison. "Howl" fit perfectly this model of inward and outward word-as-defiance. Words meant something to their souls. Writing itself was a way of keeping body and soul together, a way of keeping sane. Writing poetry was not therapy—we rejected this idea—and the inmate-students worked hard to better the poems as verbal objects through revision and discussion. But, like that of "Howl," their process was closer to Keats's idea of "soul-making." This pedagogical process—"who crashed through their minds in jail"—seemed perhaps concerned less with Beauty and more with Truth, as Keats would have had it—but perhaps not. I felt, often, in reading their work—raw, furious, unkempt—that a new kind of beauty was being born for them. And for me.

"Howl" broke out of a prison of conformity and social repression in the fifties—shook up and scandalized the polite society of letters. "They saw it all! the wild eyes! the holy yells! They

244

bade farewell! They jumped off the roof!" I don't think that the women writers in prison had a privileged glimpse of the imaginative transformation and jubilation of "Howl" necessarily— they labored over their sometimes awful poems and worked carefully at learning to write. But they understood the energy of transformation and transgression as an Escape from the Cage. They took their cue stylistically and substantively from the power and relentlessness, the refusal to be intimidated, for which "Howl" is justly famous. These women who were locked up for stealing Kotex—or for blowing away their pimps—"jumped off the roof" of conventional rhetoric when they read "Howl." And then they flew into "Breakthroughs! over the river!"—they were writing poems, writing "Epiphanies! Despairs!" "Howl" was teaching them how to howl back at a cruel indifferent moon—and imagine walking free on the earth once again.

FRANK BIDART

A CROSS IN THE VOID

———

Four words or phrases: *who; Moloch; I'm with you in Rock-land; holy*. In the first section of "Howl," the repeated word that introduces each strophe (with a few striking exceptions) is *who*; in the second, *Moloch*; in the third, *I'm with you in Rockland*; in the fourth (labeled a "Footnote") *holy*. From *who* (each *who* prefaces an action or desire, *who did this, who wanted that*, a litany of actions usually ill performed, a litany of the tragedies and pratfalls that greet every reach for transcendence); to *Moloch* (cause of the tragedies and pratfalls, the power that presides over human fate is not simply history or economics, but a god planted in our souls early, the ancient god who, at war with our "natural ecstasy," devours its own children); to *I'm with you in Rockland* (the assertion of defiant human connection in the face of isolation and failure); all this finally underlain by *holy* (the insistence that all life has transcendent value, even the most despised, e.g., the "asshole"). From action and desire to cause, from cause to the connection and transcendent value that defy cause.

•

Within this structure, "Howl" celebrates those who find the
world's limits intolerable, celebrates those who are forever unap-
peased however comic or self-annihilating their posture, how-
ever tragic their fate. The third strophe of the poem announces
what they want:

*angelheaded hipsters burning for the ancient heavenly
    connection to the starry dynamo in the machin-
    ery of night, . . .*

This is not one of forty aims pursued in the poem: it is *the* aim.
"The machinery of night" is of course whatever mechanism
keeps the stars moving in orderly progression; the mystic's an-
cient desire is connection to the power that animates the stars.
(The end of *The Divine Comedy* is a version of the same desire.)
Because the world is fallen, Ginsberg's heroes can try to realize
this desire only through sex (surely, for most of us, sex is the re-
current promise that ecstatic transcendence is possible), through
drugs or delirium or madness. To reach transcendence they
"purgatoried their torsos night after night / with dreams, with
drugs, with waking nightmares, alcohol and cock and endless
balls." They are students of the mystical tradition: the texts they
study are by Plotinus (the father of neoplatonic mysticism, who
asserts that the soul can move step by step from matter to the
source, the ground of matter); by Edgar Allan Poe; by a Chris-
tian mystic and poet the Church jailed during his lifetime:

*who studied Plotinus Poe St. John of the Cross telep-
    athy and bop kabbalah because the cosmos in-
    stinctively vibrated at their feet in Kansas,
who loned it through the streets of Idaho seeking vi-
    sionary indian angels who were visionary indian
    angels, . . .*

No one in "Howl" is just a druggie or simply obsessed with sex. No one is paying a mortgage or raising kids or sweating out getting tenure. Reaching for connection to the starry dynamo in the machinery of night results in comic dislocation or worse:

> *who cowered in unshaven rooms in underwear, burn-*
> *ing their money in wastebaskets and listening*
> *to the Terror through the wall, . . .*
> *who threw their watches off the roof to cast their ballot*
> *for Eternity outside of Time, & alarm clocks*
> *fell on their heads every day for the next decade,*
> *who cut their wrists three times successively unsuccess-*
> *fully, gave up and were forced to open antique*
> *stores where they thought they were growing*
> *old and cried, . . .*

Hallucination, comedy, and delusion pursue Ginsberg's heroes:

> *who thought they were only mad when Baltimore*
> *gleamed in supernatural ecstasy, . . .*
> *who scribbled all night rocking and rolling over lofty*
> *incantations which in the yellow morning were*
> *stanzas of gibberish, . . .*

•

"Howl" isn't just a brilliant improvisation without a center, a fast sprint through extravagant or startling or culturally iconic images. What I've been trying to suggest is that it's animated by a world view, a passionately held vision of the failures inherent in serious human life. The writing, often, is exhilarating; which is of course the reason the poem has endured. The central paradox the poem bites into—that those who "purgatory their torsos" as they reach for transcendence must be celebrated, though they are often deluded or comic or self-erasing—is embodied by language that is astonishingly inventive. Within a single strophe the shifts from earnestness to pratfall are so mercurial they seem inextricably linked:

a lost battalion of platonic conversationalists jumping
    down the stoops off fire escapes off windowsills
    off Empire State out of the moon, . . .
who reappeared on the West Coast investigating the
    F.B.I. in beards and shorts with big pacifist
    eyes sexy in their dark skin passing out incom-
    prehensible leaflets, . . .

Each strophe is a roller-coaster ride whose end might be comedy or tragedy or some middle state, the pathos of a life without catharsis that yearned for catharsis. In lines about the sexual adventures of "N.C., secret hero of these poems," the writing captures the wacky bravado dreamt of by every male adolescent:

who sweetened the snatches of a million girls trembling
    in the sunset, and were red eyed in the morning
    but prepared to sweeten the snatch of the sun-
    rise, . . .

The mockery and envy and affection in such writing are balanced elsewhere by fierce gravity. The greatest example of such gravity is the end of Part I, the passage that begins "ah, Carl, while you are not safe I am not safe." The wildness in these strophes reminds me of what has been called "heroic bloodshed" in John Woo's Hong Kong movies; I find myself green with envy. The passage begins almost antiseptically, academically: Ginsberg is imagining an artist

who dreamt and made incarnate gaps in Time & Space
  through images juxtaposed, and trapped the
  archangel of the soul between 2 visual images
  and joined the elemental verbs and set the noun
  and dash of consciousness together jumping
  with sensation of Pater Omnipotens Aeterna
  Deus . . .

This alludes to Pound's theory of the ideogram: when a writer juxtaposes two visual images—if he has chosen his two images cunningly—the result is not a third image, but an idea. Eisenstein employed the same principle in his theory of film montage. Ginsberg's variation is less mechanical than Pound's or Eisenstein's: the gap opened up in Space and Time by juxtaposing two images allows the writer to "trap the archangel of the soul." When the page succeeds in trapping the soul, writing becomes the "noun and dash" of consciousness itself; the crack in everything God made is healed; you have the sensation of God's power and presence. The aim is finally to embody in art the true nature of the mind:

to recreate the syntax and measure of poor human
  prose and stand before you speechless and intel-
  ligent and shaking with shame, rejected yet con-
  fessing out the soul to conform to the rhythm
  of thought in his naked and endless head, . . .

Prose strophes aim to show us what "poor human prose" ordinarily cannot, "speechless" yet able (by becoming naked and endless as thought itself) to give soul presence. It is a brave ideal, the secret of the poem's naked and endless linked prose strophes. The passage continues:

the madman bum and angel beat in Time, unknown, yet
*   putting down here what might be left to say*
*   in time come after death,*
and rose reincarnate in the ghostly clothes of jazz in
*   the goldhorn shadow of the band and blew the*
*   suffering of America's naked mind for love into*
*   an eli eli lamma lamma sabacthani saxophone*
*   cry that shivered the cities down to*
*   the last radio . . .*

To "blow the suffering of America's naked mind for love" is ultimately a sacrificial act—in Eliot's term, "costing not less than everything." Ginsberg in his notes tells us that he was thinking of, among others, Charlie Parker. But even without a note we know the "madman bum and angel" is not simply a single historical figure: in this hair-raising passage, what "rose reincarnate in the ghostly clothes of jazz" redeems ordinary life not by offering reassurance of life after death, but by producing a music that expresses what Jesus expressed still on the cross: *My God, my God, why have you forsaken me* (eli eli lamma lamma sabacthani)? This cry "shivers the cities"

with the absolute heart of the poem of life butchered
*   out of their own bodies good to eat a thousand*
*   years.*

Good art is nourishment, bad art isn't. T. E. Hulme attacking Romanticism condescends to those for whom art is "spilled religion," but art is the food left to those whom religion has failed.

•

Nothing later matches the sustained grave rhetoric of the end of Part I. The rest of the poem doesn't try. Instead it gives us accusation, exhortation, farce, pathos; as well as the more-than-pathos fleeting grandeur of "fifty more shocks [electroshock therapy] will never return your soul to its body again from its pilgrimage to a cross in the void." The final lines before the "Footnote" have a *sotto voce* just-emerged-from-the-struggles-of-the-sea purity that is like nothing else in the poem:

> in my dreams you walk dripping from a sea-
> journey on the highway across America in tears
> to the door of my cottage in the Western night

The body of this long poem, which has been so full of wrench-ing assertions, quietly ends poised at a threshold.

•

Like Whitman, the Ginsberg of "Howl" doesn't believe in Original Sin. By this I mean he believes that evil proceeds from something planted in our souls not native to our souls ("Moloch who entered my soul early! . . . Moloch who frightened me out of my natural ecstasy!"). The final line of the "Footnote" asserts "the supernatural extra brilliant intelligent kindness of the soul!" Ginsberg would not say with Auden, "You shall love your crooked neighbor / With your crooked heart." The suffering that is the fate of the heroes of "Howl" proceeds from the spirit's inability to manifest, in matter, the purity that is its na-ture. The worm the spirit discovers here is not inherent in spirit itself. Within spirit itself there is no unresolvable dilemma, no dilemma inherent in the demands placed upon it by its own na-ture or the nature of being. In other poems, like the great "Dream Record: June 8, 1955," something like this knowledge is hinted at; but it's suppressed or ignored in "Howl." The vast skepticism about the self that Bishop or Lowell writes out of, Ginsberg seems not to share.

The divisions that dominated the literary camps of my youth—placing, roughly, Ginsberg and O'Hara on one side and Bishop and Lowell on the other—never seemed to me the divisions that mattered. In each "camp" there were a handful of writers who had written well, and many more whose work was plausible but boring. Whatever the value of Ginsberg's oft-repeated "first thought best thought" (I think its value is zero), it doesn't describe the way he wrote "Howl." The poem was much revised, which is made clear in Barry Miles's edition of the manuscripts, published in 1986. (This invaluable edition includes Ginsberg's notes.) Perhaps "first thought best thought" became part of his practice after the second volume, *Kaddish*, several years later; to my eye, in each subsequent volume, painfully, there are fewer and fewer good poems. In the sixties his immense fame turned him into a guru; he seemed no longer to believe that what was crucial was making art. (These are the simplifications of someone who did not know him well.)

One reads that in the last half of the nineteenth century there was a vast gulf between the Brahmsians and the Wagnerians, the camp of Classicism and the camp of innovation. The split always seemed to me incomprehensible—Brahms and Wagner were each great in very different ways, and there was no need to choose between them. Eliot in "Little Gidding" sees this more profoundly than anybody:

If I think, again, of this place,
And of people, not wholly commendable,
Of no immediate kin or kindness,
But some of peculiar genius,
All touched by a common genius,
United in the strife that divided them . . .
Why should we celebrate
These dead men more than the dying? . . .

These men, and those who opposed them
And those whom they opposed
Accept the constitution of silence
And are folded in a single party.

In this light, Ginsberg and Lowell and Bishop belong to a "single party." All were undoubtedly "touched by a common genius"; all desperately tried to make fictions that embodied their deepest insights. The passions that divided Ginsberg from a significant part of what naturally should have been his audience soon will look quaint.

ROBERT PINSKY

NO PICNIC

––––

The world's least postmodern poem. Pain, rage, terror, panic heartfelt and body-felt without protective irony or afterthought or sneaking reservations. The horror fortissimo, unqualified:

What sphinx of cement and aluminum bashed open their skulls and ate up their brains and imagination?

And the ecstasy, too, heartfelt and unhedged:

who dreamt and made incarnate gaps in Time & Space through images juxtaposed, and trapped the archangel of the soul between 2 visual images and joined the elemental verbs and set the noun and dash of consciousness together jumping with sensation of Pater Omnipotens Aeterna Deus.

A poem profoundly the opposite of the current, early twenty-first-century fashion for the oblique. Majestic in its crazed vulnerability, able to be funny while it is absolutely earnest:

who created great suicidal dramas on the apartment cliff-banks of the
Hudson under the wartime blue floodlight of the moon & their heads
shall be crowned with laurel in oblivion.

A poem based explicitly, as William Carlos Williams says in his
introduction, on the experience of horror and defeat.

Horror and defeat. And yet when I first read it as a teenager,
what thrilled me was the leash-breaking manner, the deliberate
unthrottled throwing around of parts of speech and images and
phrases, a musical parade of words celebrating their berserk
Mardi Gras of freedom:

who were expelled from the academies for crazy & publishing obscene
odes on the windows of the skull.

I was a teenager. *Expelled for crazy* felt like the party I was
desperate to discover. If I were a little more wide-awake, or
smarter, I would have heard the howl of the feeling and the
howl of the mind as well as the howl of the writing. Williams
says, "Everyone in this life is defeated, but a man, if he be a
man, is not defeated."

The poem was not a party, not a picnic. He was explicit
enough!—

who threw their watches off the roof to cast their ballot for Eternity out-
side of Time, & alarm clocks fell on their heads every day for the
next decade,
who cut their wrists three times successively unsuccessfully, gave up and
were forced to open antique stores where they thought they were
growing old and cried.

The excitement of the speed, the rush of spontaneity, the
quickness of moves like "successively unsuccessfully," the on-

fire directness of attack, all dramatize the subject matter, the panic and aspiration of the half-destroyed, agonized spirit, pitted against and enveloped by the repressive, parental money-monster of the actual, social world:

Moloch whose love is endless oil and stone! Moloch whose soul is electricity and banks! Moloch whose poverty is the specter of genius! Moloch whose fate is a cloud of sexless hydrogen! Moloch whose name is the Mind!
Moloch in whom I sit lonely! Moloch in whom I dream Angels! Crazy in Moloch! Cocksucker in Moloch! Lacklove and manless in Moloch!
Moloch who entered my soul early! Moloch in whom I am a consciousness without a body! Moloch who frightened me out of my natural ecstasy! Moloch whom I abandon! Wake up in Moloch! Light streaming out of the sky!

What poem could be more contrary to the current modes of language doubting itself? Rereading now the work of art that inspired me with its freedom, directness, and ebullience when I was a teenager, I marvel more than ever at how dire it is, how wholeheartedly tormented, meaning every word, with no implied quotation marks. A howl: that is, utterly the opposite of doubt about the efficacy of language. The sex, for example, is not "camp" or coy, it too is unironic, tormented, and ecstatic and actual:

who hiccuped endlessly trying to giggle but wound up with a sob behind a partition in a Turkish Bath when the blond & naked angel came to pierce them with a sword.

There's nothing superior or disengaged—in an important way, even, nothing alienated—about the relation to our country, imagined as a fellow patient, sick in mind and body, comforting and discomfiting, sharing a bed in a mental hospital:

I'm with you in Rockland,
   where we hug and kiss the United States under our bedsheets the
   United States that coughs all night and won't let us sleep.

I think that back then I welcomed the poem partly as a counter-force to the literary fashion of that day, the nearly religious emphasis on "metaphor" and "image" and "objective correlative," Eliot's phrase associated with his notion that the apparent subject of the poem is like a piece of meat the poet-burglar uses to distract the watchdog conscious intelligence of the reader. Ginsberg seemed to break down the partitions of that formula: the bait and the household goods, the beast and the thief and the householder all part of the same parade, the meat as much a part of it as the safe, the bite as much as the howl.

That snarling, ever-hungry dog changes over time. "The Waste Land," like "Howl" a great poem that helped conduct me into poetry, feels today more personal than it once did: still, I guess, a work where Eliot broods about the shadowy archetypal roots and malaises of civilization—but more of a personal lyric, more about the wounds and cravings of the poet. Bodily and spiritual cravings: the incantational "Shantih" of Eliot's resolution, at the top of its voice, resembles the incantational "Holy!" of Ginsberg's "Footnote to Howl." The soon-to-be-Christian anglophile royalist seeming to resemble more than he used to the Jewish Buddhist supercommunist. And the supercommunist truly meaning the word "Holy," used in his manner that is comical but not ironical:

The world is holy! The soul is holy! The skin is holy! The nose is holy!
   The tongue and cock and asshole holy! . . .

NO PICNIC

Holy New York Holy San Francisco Holy Peoria & Seattle Holy Paris
Holy Tangiers Holy Moscow Holy Istanbul!

For decades now I have smiled at how in my ear "Holy Peoria" and "Holy Istanbul" sound like "Holy Cow" and "Holy Moly."

If "Howl" were published for the first time tomorrow, it would be sensational and challenging: a critique maybe not only of a world where Moloch now claims Jesus as his best friend but also, implicitly, of our postmodern cool.

ANNE WALDMAN

PREMISES OF CONSCIOUSNESS

I. PRIVATE HOWL

everyday is in eternity!—A.G., "Howl"

The lineaments and landscape of "Howl" when it hit the universe in the mid to late 1950s were familiar. I came to it age fourteen. And I came to it again and again those early "coming of age" years. Having grown up on Mac-Dougal Street, Greenwich Village, Manhattan, New York, daughter of bohemians, itinerant piano-playing father turned educator by the grace of the G.I. Bill, mother who had spent time with her then father-in-law the poet Anghelos Sikelianos a decade, Pete Seeger organizing hootenannies down the block, folkies in protest in Washington Square Park (my older brother being one of them), Thelonious Monk I visited once with Steve Lacy (who was married to my former sister-in-law) not far away, struggling with heroin, school friends in all kinds of disarray (sex problems, drug problems, mental problems, pregnancy problems), the poem was an exhilarating and heartbreaking reflection of aspects and spirits of comrades of a "naked" "raw" "artistic" "sensitive" personal life. I lived in my own howlesque subculture.

If you were odd, at all eccentric, you were Beat. My friends with knapsacks of "Christ Climbed Down" and rolling papers, kids on junk, high school girlfriend in a ward getting shock treatments. My own godfather closet gay, alcoholic, bedridden.

Andrea Dworkin, radical feminist, was already suffering an embedded stint in the Women's House of Detention when we were in high school. My friend Martin Hersey (son of the novelist John Hersey) had copies of "Howl" and *Naked Lunch* in his raggedy guitar case. These were hip readerly reference points. My boyfriend was incarcerated in the Wingdale mental hospital; I would visit him, horrified at the institutionalized neglect, the "mad" bereft of dignity. I wrote tentative poetry:

I am a bird over the Harlem Valley
at Wingdale.

I knew "tenement roofs." I knew "chained themselves to subways for the endless ride from Battery to holy Bronx."

(New York, New York, it's a wonderful town!
The people ride around in a hole in the ground
The Bronx is up and the Battery's down)

This was before "flower power," the rise of hippiedom, "Be In" glee; it was getting close to the civil rights push, I had friends traveling to Tent City in Mississippi in 1962. But before feminist and gay and lesbian movements, and psychedelics. Before AIDS, although maybe a prophecy of AIDS. Before the American War in Vietnam. Pre–French Structuralism. Before Lacan, Foucault, Derrida. Before the voyeurism of the culture industry.

But "Howl"'s experience was also of the generation before mine. Closer to my father's consciousness—being a male person dropout, jazz musician for a time, smoker of weed. Going to Columbia in the late forties, suffering a kind of postwar trauma. This was the turf of the American psyche before the Vietnam War—still caught in the gray post–World War II doldrums, a time constructed of false material promise. Oh, those shiny new gadgets that would make life easier and enhance family living, what illusion! How to escape? Respond? And how the Cold War was to continue the dichotomy of this dangerous illusion.

"Howl" was decidedly written from a psychologically synergistic point of view that seemed highly referenced to the East Coast—specifically the New York City nexus. This made it immediately palpable. The underbelly evoked was "New York"—wild, phantom New York, which is where Allen Ginsberg came to experience his streets at dawn, which became every street at dawn. In spite of reference to Denver and California and Kansas and Idaho, and despite being composed in California, "Howl" carried the brilliant taint and power of New York. It's on a cellular level, this identity with this particular city. I felt that. I felt I was in on the sites of the poem. It was akin to my own experience, strange as that may sound for a very young female person.

The map of "Howl" was both microcosmic and macrocosmic. Of the particular, I had childhood friends we visited in Newark, summers to the Zen New Jersey Atlantic City shore, we celebrated birthdays in restaurants in Chinatown, Big Wilt Small's in Harlem was exotic, one engaged in romantic trysts on the Staten Island ferry, Empire State Building was where you ushered out-of-towners, Third Avenue Elevated Railway "iron dreams" was iconic, rivers of the Bowery, yes, they were surely running under our feet. I observed Gregory Corso on this very MacDougal Street where I still sit writing. My father invited Allen Ginsberg to read at Pace University in 1959, a success. New York friends were getting busted, shipped off to expensive mental hospitals—some exclusive, like Riggs, others houses of bedlam like Wingdale . . . and so on. Allen Ginsberg jump-cuts all over the map, but the reference point, the Ur-point, the point of origin is New York. This was the city that contained "multitudes," where any experience or combination thereof was possible. Where the races mingled, homosexual and lesbian persons had active spheres, where we had Commie friends and maybe my father was once a member of that party, I was never quite sure . . .

And "Howl"—perhaps most important for someone set on a path of poetry—was a monumental oral construct, more challenging and direct in its consciousness than "The Waste Land." You could hear its verticality projecting upward/outward in the horizontal lines of "Moloch," in the "Holy" litany. The long breath lines outdid Whitman's and created amazing, filmlike flickering noir montages of thrust and activity:

who wandered around and around at midnight in the railroad yard wondering where to go, and went, leaving no broken hearts,
who lit cigarettes in boxcars boxcars boxcars racketing through snow toward lonesome farms in grandfather night

or

who sang out of their windows in despair, fell out of the subway window, jumped in the filthy Passaic, leaped on negroes, cried all over the street, danced on broken wineglasses barefoot smashed phonograph records of nostalgic European 1930s German jazz finished the whiskey and threw up groaning into the bloody toilet, moans in their ears and the blast of colossal steamwhistles.

It was a cri de coeur, an alarm, a vision. Its structure matched its energy, which seemed the voices of many, not one. It was a rhizomic collage, just like life, a pastiche of the experiences of many others, encompassing flashes of Blake's "minute particulars." It was recognizing the first Buddhist Noble Truth of Suffering, which I was beginning to hear about in my comparative religion class at Friends Seminary, a realization that could trigger empathy with the universe. How did one do this in a poem?

I could sense, viscerally, the possibilities this poem created for a contemporary poet—the permission it gave to an expansive poetics of our time. Surrealist, cut-up, dream, documentation, aleatory strategies all played in here. Whitman caught an America of a different time. A different war. "Howl" was something both of the invisible America, an America not discussed, not analyzed, fringe, "fellaheen," as Jack Kerouac would say, and of the America that was facing the bottomless-pit reality of the atomic bomb, which had already been dropped and might well explode again. Meanwhile, the culture was imploding around us.

And there was my own obligatory rite of passage, traveling with my brother and a friend to California, site of the composition of "Howl," and hitchhiking back from Mexico all the way to Manhattan. So 1965 I was in San Francisco, age twenty, and although I had seen Allen close up, I missed his reading at the Berkeley Poetry Conference because my first LSD trip kept me from getting across the Bay Bridge. I could intuit his pulse, however. "Howl" was already on the premises of my consciousness. We met later that week.

II. "THE BREAKTHROUGH THING"/ "UNWORLDLY LOVE"

I keep thinking I would like to be able to write another "Howl." You know like taking the problems of the eighties, like ecology and the Moral Majority, and all that. But you know you can't do that deliberately, it has to come accidentally almost.
—*A. G., 1989*

Allen in a lecture at Naropa University on July Fourth, 1989, entitled "Revolutionary Poetics" spoke thus:

The breakthrough thing. I experienced that with "Howl"—a breakthrough, not of universal consciousness or the social consciousness, but a discovery of my own consciousness, and then a proclamation of that. I'm trying to lay it out on the page: what is it I really desire. Instead of what I'm told I should know, or desire.

  . . .

    Can you name what you desire? I took one key— from one line in Williams: "Unworldly love, that has no hope of the world, and cannot change the world to its delight."

  . . .

    So what eternal spring of feeling do you have in you, that you feel sure of, or that you feel unsure of, but returns over and over again, in dreams, and in waking moments of longing? What object of love, or what desire, or what delight, returns over and over despite the appearances, despite discouragement, and despite all rational calculation—even trying to repress it, it still comes through. What freshness of feeling, and what freshness of perception, comes through anyway, even despite blocking it, even despite, either the condition of not noticing it, or thinking you better not do it (you better go straight, you better get a job)—what comes through anyway? What unworldly love, that has no hope of the world, and cannot change its world to its delight, persists, and breaks through always, if only in dreams? because in dreams you get these great baths of eroticism or liberation or recognition. You know, your mother recognizes you, Kissinger recognizes you.

This sense Allen has of the "discovery" of his own consciousness with the making of "Howl" is what has kept the poem regeneratrive, resilient. In fact, it is the activation of the quickened consciousness through the poem itself that is the key to its imprint in the world-poem-psyche. "Poetry is news that stays news" (Ezra Pound). "Howl" will continue to be a kind of rune for readers of the future. It carries "transmission," in the Buddhist sense, which moves beyond literal historical time. It exudes a sense of immediacy, of discovery, of generosity. And what makes the poem seem more and more, over time, like a sacred text, a sutra, a ritual, is that as it is read silently or aloud, "Howl" is reactivated. The magnanimity of its reach never closes. Its anaphoric "who," its lists of minute particulars, reverberates through time. It is a time machine; it is also a time bomb. "Howl" carries warning, prophecy. The desire or "eternal spring of feeling"— its aspiration—is what drives its persistent relevance.

III. MOLOCH

The visionary Moloch section, written while under the influence of peyote, seems chillingly prescient. The Canaanite fire god demanded that parents sacrifice their children in a propitiatory ritual of auto-da-fé. We see the death toll of young soldiers in Iraq and Afghanistan rising, the untold deaths of countless innocent citizens of those countries, and the ritual sacrifice made by teenage suicide bombers set to act by calculated ideologies. We send children to slaughter the world over, into the maw of the bloodthirsty beast.

Ginsberg references William Blake's Urizen in a footnote to Part II of "Howl":

the Jehovic hyper-rationalistic judgmental lawgiver Urizen, creator of Spiritual disorder and political chaos. His abstract calipers limit the infinite universe to his egoic horizon, a projection of unmindful selfhood, the result of aggressively naive mental measurements which substitute hypocrite or modish generalizations for experience of event, and oppress physical body, feelings and imagination.

This seems our human condition under the mind-set of Urizen, who comes to symbolize all the tyrants of imagination and freedom. Post 9/11, certain phrases seem especially apt to our state of affairs in an Empire State driven by the vices of late capitalism—excessive greed, hypocrisy, and an ideology that thrives on a hallucination of a perpetual "enemy." A dark state of mind that doesn't nourish its many denizens—plant, animal, mineral—that prefers the "vast stone of war."

Boys sobbing in armies! Old men weeping in the parks!

Moloch the incomprehensible prison! Moloch the crossbone soulless jailhouse and Congress of sorrows! Moloch whose buildings are judgment! Moloch the vast stone of war! Moloch the stunned governments!

Moloch whose love is endless oil and stone! Moloch whose soul is electricity and banks!

They saw it all! the wild eyes! the holy yells! They bade farewell! They jumped off the roof! to solitude! waving! carrying flowers! Down to the river! into the street!

The image of human beings jumping off the World Trade Towers arises in an ironic twist of time—searing—in the mind's memory-eye.

IV. OUTRIDER

And how did this poem epitomize what I've termed the "outrider" tradition since 1974, when Allen Ginsberg and I founded the Jack Kerouac School of Disembodied Poetics at Naropa University? The Outrider holds a premise of imaginative consciousness. The Outrider rides the edge—parallel to the mainstream, is the shadow to the mainstream, is the consciousness or soul of the mainstream whether the mainstream recognizes its existence or not. It cannot be co-opted, it cannot be bought. Or rides through the chaos, maintaining a stance of "negative capability," but also does not give up that projective drive, or its original identity, which demands that it intervene on the culture. This is not about being an Outsider. The Outrider might be an outlaw but not an outsider. Rather, the Outrider is a kind of shaman, the true spiritual "insider." The shaman travels to zones of light and shadow. The shaman travels to edges of madness and death, and comes back to tell and enact the vivid stories.

Far out.
Way out.
Outed.
Come out.
Outspoken.
Outrage.
Outburst.
Outcry.
Outlast.
On the "outs."
One that rides.
To ride herd on.
To ride high.

How "out" might you go from the strictures of standard verse culture? From the thinking or the amnesia or the "denial" of the status quo?

Consider how Walt Whitman changed poetry from a very fixed and classical form to an open form anyone might participate in. Consider the ramifications in the political world, the social world, a world of defined gender and race and class. Consider the open field.

How might you ride your vehicle of poetry? How might you descend or ascend the map of your own imagination? How might you mirror the chaos you live in through a liberated and electrifying language?

Allen Ginsberg fought his whole life for the right of free speech, for the unfettered articulated power of the imagination. Even as he died, readings or recordings of "Howl" could not—and still can't—be broadcast on daytime radio in the United States of America. The struggle continues on many fronts. And one struggle is against the "institutionalization" of poetry, creative writing, of the imagination.

Allen had his own generation's terms and identifications. I felt—coming after—the need to define the ongoing hybrids of the New American Poetry lineage further, to include more women, and a more polysemous relationship to language and its "intentionality," and to define the pedagogy of such a lineage so that it might flourish and continue, building on an ever-expansive poetics the concerns of the Black Arts movement, Black Mountain School, New York School, San Francisco Renaissance, as well as—perhaps most important—the spirit of the Beat movement as it engages with, is able to inhabit a larger public and oral space, as "Howl" has been able to. This poem has touched and changed and charged many lives. Hearing Allen Ginsberg read it live was an event in eternity.

"Howl" is still activated and re-created in many conscious-nesses. "Howl" plugs you in to the socket.

Holy 21st Century

Holy! Holy! Holy! Holy! Holy! Holy! Holy! Holy! Holy! Holy! Holy!
Holy!
Is the composite world holy? Holy phonemes holy neurons!
Holy the 5 senses! Holy the aggregates of being!
Holy impermanence! Holy the interconnectedness of all beings!
Karma of atrocities holy and un-holy!
Is 21st-century endless continuation of 20th-century war holy?
Environmental degradation continuation of 20th-century environmental
degradation holy?
Every Woman's a holy dakini! Matriot acts holy!
Holy! Holy! Holy! Holy! Holy! Holy! Holy! Holy! Holy! Holy! Holy!
Holy!
Body parts blown over the charnel ground holy! Eyes ears nose hands
mouth holy!
Manipulated Bible holy? Koran holy? Anarchist tracts holy? Fatwas
holy?
Geneva Conventions holy? Holy Contract with America, come on, citi-
zens, is that holy?
Star Wars' "Rods from God" holy? Daisy cutters holy?
Thermobaric version of the Hellfire Missile that can turn corners and
blast into caves holy?
Allen Ginsberg's "Mysterious rivers of tears under the sheets" holy!
Holy Kerouac's "tender reward"!
Holy Baghdad! Holy Dharamsala! Holy Columbine!
Holy Kabul! Holy Israel/Palestine! Holy Bosnia! Holy Rwanda!
Holy Manahatta Isle! Holy Trade Center! Holy East Timor!
Holy Justice! Holy Forgiveness! Holy Truth! Holy Accountability!

Bagram holy? Guantánamo holy? Abu Ghraib un-holy!
All hooded torture un-holy! All bodily sadistic harm un-holy!
All the hate un-holy! Big lies unholy! All the rape un-holy!
Holy rap! Holy hip-hop! Holy klezmer! Holy Afro-pop!
Holy jazz! Holy gamelan! Holy Arvo Pärt!
Holy pneumatic drills boring into the depths of Brooklyn!
Holy old slave graves!
False the military recruitment centers
knocking on tenement doors get a fresh martyr for Moloch!
Holy Robert Creeley! Holy Lucia Berlin! Holy Jackson Mac Low!
Holy Stan Brakhage! Holy Carl Rakosi! Holy Philip Lamantia!
Holy Steve Lacy, blowing his saxophone in heaven!
Cloning holy? Stem cells holy?
Amphetamine holy? Un-holy the polarized universe!
Holy the unfettered Universe!
Holy Negative Capability! Holy No Ideas But In Things
Holy Projective Verse! Holy Modal Structures!
Banish grief & greed o compassionate green-skinned savioress of the
    Mind
HOLY OM TARA HOLY TUTTH TARA HOLY TURE
    SOHA!

SOURCES

The Annotated Howl, edited by Barry Miles (New York: Harper & Row, 1986).

Allen Ginsberg, "Revolutionary Poetics," in *Civil Disobediences: Poetics & Politics in Action,* edited by Anne Waldman (Minneapolis: Coffee House Press, 2004). Used by permission of the editor.

"Holy 21st Century," copyright © 2005 by Anne Waldman. Used by permission of the author.

CHRONOLOGY

1926   Irwin Allen Ginsberg is born on June 3 in Newark, New Jersey, to Louis and Naomi Ginsberg, their second son. Louis is a published poet, high school teacher, and Jewish democratic socialist; Naomi is a Communist.

1930s   Ginsberg is exposed to poetry by his father, who routinely recites Dickinson, Shelley, Keats, Poe, and Milton.

1932   Naomi Ginsberg is hospitalized for a mental breakdown, the first in what will be a lifetime of mental illness and visits to the hospital.

1937   Eleven-year-old Ginsberg starts capturing his thoughts in his first journal; Naomi Ginsberg attempts suicide.

1938   Ginsberg graduates from grammar school and begins attending Paterson's Central High, becoming president of the Debating Society.

1941   Ginsberg discovers Walt Whitman through his teacher Frances Durbin; Ginsberg's brother, Eugene, assumes a military post in Great Britain; Ginsberg enlists as an-errand boy for a local labor leader, his entrée into politics.

1942   Ginsberg enters Columbia University with the intention of becoming a labor lawyer.

1943   In December, Ginsberg meets Lucien Carr, who introduces him to David Kammerer and William Burroughs.

1944   In June, Ginsberg meets Jack Kerouac; Carr stabs his close friend Kammerer to death, Burroughs and Kerouac are arrested as material witnesses; Carr is sentenced to 1 to 20 years and released in 1946.

1945   Ginsberg is suspended from Columbia for scrawling in the dust of his dorm room, "Fuck the Jews" and "Butler [the university president] has no balls"; in August, Ginsberg joins the Merchant Marines and during his tour of duty experiments for first time with marijuana.

1946   Ginsberg returns to Columbia; he and Kerouac meet Neal Cassady.

1947   Ginsberg travels to meet Cassady in Denver and Burroughs in Texas, the first of many cross-country trips; Naomi Ginsberg has a lobotomy.

1948   Ginsberg experiences illuminative audition of William Blake's voice simultaneous with Eternity-vision in his Spanish Harlem apartment.

1949   Ginsberg is arrested (for storing stolen goods of roommates) and agrees to enter New York State Psychiatric Institute as part of his release; there he meets Carl Solomon; Louis Ginsberg remarries; the word "Beat" enters the lexicon via Jack Kerouac.

1950   Ginsberg meets William Carlos Williams and Gregory Corso.

1951   At Ginsberg's urging, Solomon, who is working at Ace Books, offers Kerouac a $250 advance for his book *On the Road*; Ginsberg visits Burroughs in Mexico.

1953   Ginsberg returns to Mexico for six months, begins writing "Siesta in Xbalba" and "The Green Automobile."

1954   Ginsberg moves to San Francisco, meets the painter Robert La Vigne and Peter Orlovsky, who will become Ginsberg's lover and life partner.

1955   In August, Ginsberg writes the first and last sections of "Howl"; Ginsberg meets Gary Snyder and Philip Whalen; in October, Ginsberg reads part of "Howl" for the first time. Philip Lamantia, Michael McClure, Philip Whalen, and Gary Snyder also read; Ginsberg moves from San Francisco to Berkeley, writes "Sunflower Sutra" and "Supermarket in California."

1956   Ginsberg reads "Howl" in its entirety at a poetry reading in Berkeley; Naomi Ginsberg dies of a brain hemorrhage; in October, *Howl and Other Poems* is published as part of the Pocket Poet Series at City Lights Books.

1957   Publisher Lawrence Ferlinghetti of City Lights Books is arrested for the distribution of the "obscene and indecent writings of *Howl and Other Poems*"; "Howl" is later deemed not obscene by Judge Clayton Horn; Ginsberg and Orlovsky visit Morocco.

1958   Ginsberg returns to New York and reads to a sellout crowd at Columbia University's McMillin Theatre; he reads "Kaddish" for the first time.

1959   Ginsberg signs on as a subject for an LSD study at Stanford University.

1960   Ginsberg travels to Chile and Boliva with Ferlinghetti; Ginsberg meets the Harvard psychiatrist Timothy Leary, tries magic mushrooms for the first time with Leary's guidance.

1961   Ginsberg travels to Paris with Orlovsky; in April, *Kaddish and Other Poems* is published by City Lights Books, number 14 of the Pocket Poet Series; Ginsberg travels to Tangiers, Istanbul, and Greece.

1962   Ginsberg travels to Israel, East Africa, and India for fifteen months in search of "spiritual guidance."

1963   *Reality Sandwiches* is published by City Lights Books.

1965   Ginsberg attends a literary conference in Cuba; many there are arrested; Ginsberg travels to Moscow and meets Yevgeny Yevtushenko and Andrey Voznesensky; Ginsberg is crowned King of May Day celebration in Prague; his journals are confiscated and he is expelled from the country; Ginsberg joins Bob Dylan onstage in London, meets the Beatles; an FBI file on Ginsberg is active for "reported engagement with drug smuggling."

1966   Ginsberg establishes the Committee on Poetry, a not-for-profit organization to support artists and play a role in politics; Ginsberg testifies before the U.S. Senate and argues against making LSD possession illegal.

1967   Ginsberg meets Ezra Pound in Italy; Ginsberg is arrested for the first time for antiwar activities.

1968   Neal Cassady is found dead in Mexico; Ginsberg purchases a farm in Cherry Valley, N.Y., for retreat; Ginsberg attends the Democratic National Convention in Chicago and leads protests; *Planet News* is published by City Lights Books.

1969   Ginsberg records Blake's songs; Kerouac dies.

1970   Ginsberg meets the Tibetan lama Chögyam Trungpa Rinpoche.

1971   Ginsberg visits India and West Bengal.

1972   *The Gates of Wrath: Rhymed Poems, 1948–51* is published by Four Seasons.

1973   Ginsberg's stage adaptation of "Kaddish" is mounted at Chelsea Theater in Brooklyn; Ginsberg attends the Republican National Convention and is arrested for disruption; *The Fall of America* is published by City Lights Books; Ginsberg is elected to the National Institute of Arts and Letters.

1974 With support from Trungpa Rinpoche, Ginsberg cofounds the Jack Kerouac School of Disembodied Poetics with Anne Waldman in Boulder, Colo.; Ginsberg receives the National Book Award for *The Fall of America*; *Iron Horse* is published by Coach House Press.

1976 Ginsberg ends his tour with Bob Dylan's Rolling Thunder Review; Louis Ginsberg dies at age 80.

1978 *Mind Breaths: Poems, 1971–76* is published by City Lights Books.

1979 Ginsberg tours Europe.

1981 Ginsberg performs and records with the Clash; Ginsberg moves to Boulder for several years.

1982 *Plutonian Ode: Poems, 1977–1980* is published by City Lights Books.

1983 Ginsberg's double album, *First Blues*, is released by John Hammond.

1984 Ginsberg visits China with Toni Morrison, William Gass, and Gary Snyder as part of an American Academy of Arts and Letters delegation; *Collected Poems: 1947–1980* is published by Harper & Row; City Lights maintains rights to publish individual editions.

1985 Ginsberg begins teaching at Brooklyn College as Distinguished Professor of English.

1986 *White Shroud: Poems, 1980–1985* and the annotated "Howl" are published by Harper & Row; Chögyam Trungpa Rinpoche dies at age 47.

1989 Ginsberg collaborates with Philip Glass to move "Wichita Vortex Sutra" to the stage and opera; Ginsberg meets the Tibetan lama Gelek Rinpoche.

1990   Ginsberg's first collection of photographs is published by TwelveTrees Press.

1994   *Holy Soul Jelly Roll!* four CDs featuring the best recordings of Ginsberg's career, is released; Ginsberg sells his archives to Stanford University, purchases a loft in Manhattan; *Cosmopolitan Greetings, Poems, 1986–1992* is published by Harper & Row.

1997   On April 5, Allen Ginsberg succumbs to liver cancer and dies surrounded by family and friends in his East Village loft.

ABOUT THE CONTRIBUTORS

GORDON BALL edited *Allen Verbatim*, a finalist for the Pulitzer Prize, as well as two volumes of Allen Ginsberg's journals. An award-winning filmmaker, he is the author of *'66 Frames* and has completed a memoir, *East Hill Farm: Seasons with Allen Ginsberg*. A photographer of Ginsberg and his colleagues for over three decades, he teaches at the Virginia Military Institute.

AMIRI BARAKA was named New Jersey Poet Laureate by the New Jersey Commission on Humanities, 2002–2004, and Newark Schools' Poet Laureate by the Newark Board of Education. He is the author of numerous books of poetry, prose, and plays, including his most recent book of poetry, *Un Poco Low Coup* (I Reed Publishers). Since 1990 he and his wife, Amina Baraka, have operated the arts space Kimako's Blues People in Newark.

FRANK BIDART is the author of six books of poetry, including *In the Western Night: Collected Poems: 1965–90* (FSG, 1990) and, most recently, *Star Dust* (FSG, 2005). A finalist for the Pulitzer Prize in poetry, he has received numerous awards, including the Wallace Stevens Award. He lives in Cambridge and teaches at Wellesley College.

SVEN BIRKERTS is the author of five books of essays and a memoir, *My Sky Blue Trades*. His essays and reviews appear frequently in *The New York Times*, *Harper's*, *The Oxford American*, and other journals. A member of the core faculty of the Bennington Writing Seminars, he also edits the journal *Agni* at Boston University. He was recently appointed Briggs-Copeland Lecturer at Harvard University.

KURT BROWN is the author of the poetry books *Return of the Prodigals*, *More Things in Heaven and Earth*, and *Fables from the Ark*, which won the 2003 Custom Words Prize, and the forthcoming *Future Ship*. He is the editor of many anthologies, including *The True Subject*, *Writing It Down for James*, *Drive, They Said: Poems About Americans and Their Cars*, *Verse & Universe: Poems About Science and Mathematics*, and the tribute anthology for the late William Matthews, *Blues for Bill*. Founding director of the Aspen Writers' Conference, he teaches at Sarah Lawrence College.

JOHN CAGE extended the boundaries of music through his work with percussion orchestra, his invention of the prepared piano, music on magnetic tape, and other pioneering initiatives. He authored innumerable compositions in many genres and published several books. His many honors include election to the American Academy of Arts and Letters. He was the musical adviser for the Merce Cunningham Dance Company. He died in New York in 1992.

ANDREI CODRESCU is a regular commentator on National Public Radio and winner of the Peabody Award for his film *Road Scholar*. He is the author of numerous books of poetry, prose, and translations, including most recently the novel *Wakefield* (Algonquin, 2004). His other books include *The Blood Countess, Ay, Cuba!: A Socio-Erotic Journey, Hail Babylon!: NPR's Road Scholar Goes in Search of the American City*, and *The Hole in the Flag: A Romanian Exile's Story of Return and Revolution*. He is the MacCurdy Distinguished Professor of English and Comparative Literature at Louisiana State University in Baton Rouge, where he edits *Exquisite Corpse: A Journal of Letters and Life*.

BILLY COLLINS's latest collection is *The Trouble with Poetry: And Other Poems* (Random House, 2005). He is the editor of two collections of contemporary poetry, *Poetry 180* and *180 More*. He was the Poet Laureate of the United States and is serving as the New York State Poet Laureate.

MARK DOTY's seventh book of poems is *School of the Arts* (HarperCollins, 2005). He is also the author of three books of nonfiction prose and the recipient of the National Book Critics Circle Award, the Los Angeles Times Book Prize, a Whiting Writers Award, and, in the United Kingdom, the T. S. Eliot Prize. He teaches in the graduate writing program at the University of Houston and lives in New York City.

DAVID GATES, senior editor at *Newsweek*, is the author of the novels *Jernigan* (a Pulitzer Prize finalist) and *Preston Falls*, as well as the short story collection, *The Wonders of the Invisible World*.

VIVIAN GORNICK is the author of eight books, including the memoir *Fierce Attachments* and the essay collections *Approaching Eye Level* and *The End of the Novel of Love*.

ELIOT KATZ is the author of three books of poetry, including *Unlocking the Exits* (Coffee House Press). He is the coeditor of

Poems for the Nation, a collection of political poems compiled with Allen Ginsberg and Andy Clausen. He is completing a nonfiction book *Radical Eyes: Political Poetics and the Work of Allen Ginsberg*. He serves as poetry editor of the online politics quarterly *Logos* and lives in New York City.

JANE KRAMER is the European correspondent for *The New Yorker* and the author of nine books, including *The Last Cowboy*, *Unsettling Europe*, *Europeans*, and *The Politics of Memory*. Her honors include a National Book Award and an Emmy Award. She is the first American and first woman to receive the Prix Européen de l'Essai, Europe's most distinguished award for nonfiction, and in 2004 she was named Chevalier de la Légion d'Honneur.

PHILLIP LOPATE's many books include *Waterfront: A Journey Around Manhattan*, *The Art of the Personal Essay*, *Getting Personal*, *Writing New York: A Literary Anthology*, and *Bachelorhood: Tales of the Metropolis*. His forthcoming books include *American Movie Critics: From the Silents Until Now*.

RICK MOODY's most recent books are *The Black Veil*, a genealogical narrative, and *The Diviners*, a novel.

CAROL MUSKE-DUKES is the author of seven books of poems, three novels, and two collections of essays. Her recent book of poems *Sparrow* was a finalist for the National Book Award. She writes a column, "Poet's Corner," for the *Los Angeles Times Book Review* and is the founder and director of the Ph.D. Program in Creative Writing and Literature at the University of Southern California, where she is Professor of English. She lives in New York and Los Angeles.

EILEEN MYLES has published two volumes of fiction, *Cool for You* and *Chelsea Girls*, and many books of poetry, including

Skies, School of Fish, and *Not Me.* She's currently teaching at University of California, San Diego, and has written a libretto for the opera *Hell,* and is completing a new novel, *The Inferno.*

ALICIA OSTRIKER has published eleven volumes of poetry, most recently *No Heaven.* Her most recent volume of criticism is *Dancing at the Devil's Party: Essays on Poetry, Politics and the Erotic,* from which her essay in this book is taken. Twice nominated for the National Book Award in poetry, she teaches in the low-residency MFA program at New England College.

MARJORIE PERLOFF is the author of numerous books on modern and postmodern poetry and poetics, including *The Poetics of Indeterminacy, The Futurist Moment,* and, most recently, *Differentials,* which received the Warren-Brooks Award for literary criticism. She is also author of the memoir *The Vienna Paradox.* She is Professor Emerita of English at Stanford University, where she helped to bring Ginsberg's archives.

MARGE PIERCY is the author of sixteen collections of poetry, including *What Are Big Girls Made Of?, The Art of Blessing the Day: Poems with a Jewish Theme,* and, recently, *Colors Passing Through Us.* Her seventeenth novel, *Sex Wars,* was published in December 2005 by HarperCollins. Her memoir, *Sleeping with Cats,* is in paperback from HarperPerennial. A CD of her political poetry, *Louder: We Can't Hear You (Yet!),* is out from Leapfrog Press. Her work has been translated into fifteen languages.

ROBERT PINSKY's most recent books are *The Life of David,* in prose; *First Things to Hand,* a chapbook of poems; and *An Invitation to Poetry,* an anthology with an enclosed DVD featuring video segments from *The Favorite Poem Project.* His "Poet's Choice" columns appear weekly in *The Washington Post Book World.*

ROBERT POLITO edited *Kenneth Fearing's Selected Poems* (Library of America). His other books include the poetry collection *Doubles* (University of Chicago Press), *A Reader's Guide to James Merrill's The Changing Light at Sandover* (University of Michigan Press), and *Savage Art: A Biography of Jim Thompson* (Knopf/ Vintage), for which he received the National Book Critics Circle Award in biography. He also edited for the Library of America *Crime Novels: American Noir of the 1930s and 1940s*, and *Crime Novels: American Noir of the 1950s*, and the Everyman editions of Dashiell Hammett and James M. Cain. He directs the Graduate Writing Program at the New School in New York City.

BOB ROSENTHAL worked as Allen Ginsberg's secretary for twenty years until Ginsberg's death in 1997 and is currently the trustee of the Allen Ginsberg Trust. His poetry collections include *Cleaning Up New York, Morning Poems, Rude Awakenings, Eleven Psalms*, and most recently *Viburnum*. A playwright and adjunct professor of English at New York Technical College, he is currently writing an account of his work with Allen Ginsberg.

LUC SANTE's books include *Low Life, Evidence*, and *The Factory of Facts*. He has received a Whiting Award, a Guggenheim Fellowship, and an Award in Literature from the American Academy of Arts and Letters, as well as a Grammy for album notes. He is a fellow of the American Academy of Arts and Sciences and a visiting professor of writing and the history of photography at Bard College.

ANNE WALDMAN is the author of more than forty books, including most recently *In the Room of Never Grieve: New and Selected Poems, 1985–2003* with CD, *Dark Arcana: Afterimage or Glow*, with photographs by Patti Smith, and *Structure of the World Compared to a Bubble*. Her many awards include the Shelley Memorial Award for poetry. She is the cofounder (with Allen Ginsberg) of the Jack Kerouac School of Disembodied Poetics and teaches in the New England College low-residency MFA program.

ACKNOWLEDGMENTS

Many people helped in the making of this book. Chief among them was Bob Rosenthal, poet and secretary to Allen Ginsberg from 1976 until the time of his death in 1997. As the trustee of the Allen Ginsberg Trust,★ he responded generously to every request for information and documents. His advice and thoughtfulness was critical in shaping the content and context of the book. He has been Ginsberg's chief supporter, advocate, and administrator, and is responsible, more than anyone else, for preserving the legacy of Allen Ginsberg.

Peter Hale, writer and director of the Allen Ginsberg Trust, was also very generous and helpful in contributing supportive information and advice. When I was developing the table of contents, poet and critic Eliot Katz was instrumental in suggesting possible contributors. Bibliographer and biographer Bill Morgan and writer Gordon Ball also provided important scholarly data.

★The Allen Ginsberg Trust was established to "manage Ginsberg's tangible and non-tangible assets in a manner consistent with Allen's world-view, sensibilities and artistic and literary values . . ." For more information on the Trust's many activities, view their Web site at http://www.allenginsberg.org/trust.asp.

Alex Smithline, literary agent at Harold Ober Associates, helped shape the original proposal. I was very fortunate to have Denise Oswald, senior editor at Farrar, Straus and Giroux, provide invaluable editorial direction throughout every phase of the book. Jonathan Galassi, president and publisher at Farrar, Straus and Giroux, expressed early and strong support for the book. My gratitude to Sara Jane Stoner for her excellent and daily attention to various matters of production. Sarah Russo and Cary Goldstein provided most valuable promotional assistance at Farrar, Straus and Giroux as well.

Thanks to Jean W. Ashton and Jennifer B. Lee of the Rare Books and Manuscript Library at Columbia University for their help in locating and securing permission to publish, for the first time, the 1956 mimeographed version of "Howl." Thanks also to Bill O'Hanlon, of the Special Collections at the Stanford University Libraries, for his help in securing the early 1956 photograph of Allen Ginsberg reading from his work. For editing a 1986 collection of writings on Allen Ginsberg's entire career, I am indebted to the writer and critic Lewis Hyde.

This book is dedicated to the 6 Poets who read at the Six Gallery Reading in San Francisco in 1955, where Ginsberg read from "Howl" for the first time. Yet the book could also have been dedicated to its many contributors, all of whom were very eager to reflect upon "Howl" and its impact.

"Howl" called forth the need for community. Steven Bauer, Sophie Cabot Black, Lucie Brock-Broido, Carol Muske-Dukes, Tony Hoagland, Marie Howe, Stanley Kunitz, Sheila Murphy, Elyse Paschen, Liam Rector, Victoria Redel, Liz Rosenberg, and Tree Swenson were among many in my community who provided unswerving faith, support, and guidance in helping complete this book. My deepest gratitude. Love also to Jamie, Jennah, Jordan, Martin, and Nina.

PERMISSION ACKNOWLEDGMENTS

Grateful acknowledgment is made for permission to reprint the following previously published and unpublished material:

"Writing Through Howl" by John Cage, reprinted by permission of The John Cage Trust.

Lyrics from "The Lonesome Death of Hattie Carroll" by Bob Dylan, copyright © 1964 by Warner Bros. Inc., copyright renewed © 1992 by Special Rider Music. All rights reserved. International copyright secured. Reprinted by permission.

Lyrics from "Sad-Eyed Lady of the Lowlands" by Bob Dylan, copyright © 1966 by Dwarf Music. All rights reserved. International copyright secured. Reprinted by permission.

Lyrics from "Shooting Star" by Bob Dylan, copyright © 1989 by Special Rider Music. All rights reserved. International copyright secured. Reprinted by permission.

"I've Lived With and Enjoyed 'Howl'" by Allen Ginsberg, from *Howl: Original Draft Facsimile, Transcript and Variant Versions, Fully Annotated by Author . . .*, edited by Barry Miles (1986), reprinted by permission of The Allen Ginsberg Trust.

Audio recording in the hardcover edition reproduced by permission of The Allen Ginsberg Trust.

Mimeograph version of "Howl" reproduced by permission of the Rare Books and Manuscripts Library at Columbia University and The Allen Ginsberg Trust.

Frontispiece photograph of Allen Ginsberg reprinted by permission of the Special Collections at Stanford University.

"The Poet as Jew: 'Howl' Revisited" by Alicia Ostriker, from *Dancing at the Devil's Party: Essays on Poetry, Politics, and the Erotic* (2000), reprinted by permission of the University of Michigan Press.

"The Western World" by Louis Simpson, from *The Owner of the House: New Collected Poems 1940–2001* (BOA Editions, 2003), reprinted by permission of BOA Editions, Ltd., www.boaeditions.org.

Excerpt from "Rain" by William Carlos Williams from *Collected Poems, Volume I: 1909–1939* (1938), reprinted by permission of New Directions Publishing Corp. and Carcanet Press Ltd.